Poverty Relief in a Mixed Economy

Karin Heitzmann

Poverty Relief in a Mixed Economy

Theory of and Evidence for the (Changing) Role of Public and Nonprofit Actors in Coping with Income Poverty

PETER LANG
Frankfurt am Main · Berlin · Bern · Bruxelles · New York · Oxford · Wien

Bibliographic Information published by the Deutsche Nationalbibliothek
The Deutsche Nationalbibliothek lists this publication in the Deutsche Nationalbibliografie; detailed bibliographic data is available in the internet at http://dnb.d-nb.de.

Cover design:
Olaf Glöckler, Atelier Platen, Friedberg

Printed with the support of the Federal Ministry
of Science and Research in Vienna.

ISBN 978-3-631-55916-1

www.peterlang.de

Acknowledgements

A study is hardly ever the result of the effort of one author alone. The financial support of the Austrian National Bank (through the Dr.-Heinz-Kienzl Research Price) and the Wirtschaftsuniversität Wien (WU), which made it possible to dedicate some time exclusively to the project, is gratefully acknowledged. I would also like to thank all of my colleagues and friends who reviewed earlier versions of this book. Particularly, I would like to thank Elisabeth Hammer, Angelika Schmidt, Birgit Trukeschitz and Prof. August Österle for their valuable comments and support that helped to omit errors and improve the book. Prof. Ulrike Schneider accompanied me throughout the (long) process of completing this study with invariably precious and thought-provoking remarks. My family, Oliver and Emil Ellinger, and my coach, Theresia Remoundos, made me keep going whenever my motivation was low. Thanks are also due to Roswitha Fraller who made the English of a non-native readable. The errors and idiosyncrasies of the analysis included in this study are, of course, my own responsibility.

I would like to dedicate this book to two of my academic teachers. With his empathic manner of lecturing economics and social policy, Prof. Christoph Badelt managed to enthuse me and many of my fellow students at the WU for these subjects. Following graduation at the WU, I had the privilege to attend the Masters' programme on European Social Policy Analysis in the UK and Ireland, which was managed by Prof. Graham J. Room. Having evaluated the European anti-poverty programmes for many years, he introduced me to the topics of poverty and poverty alleviation. Then, as a young post-graduate student, I was lucky to get a research job at the Institute for Social Policy at the WU, which was headed by Prof. Badelt. The first project I was involved with was on the Austrian nonprofit sector. Once Prof. Badelt and Prof. Room had aroused my interest in the issues of nonprofit organizations and poverty alleviation, these have lost nothing of their fascination for me.

Karin Heitzmann

Contents

List of tables and figures

Introduction

This study examines, both conceptually and empirically, (i) the welfare mix in the activity field of poverty relief, and (ii) specific shifts of this mix, i.e. changes towards 'privatization' and/or 'marketization'. Thus, two concepts are at the core of this assessment: the 'welfare mix' (as well as changes thereof) and 'poverty relief'. The notion of 'welfare mix' (as well as related concepts such as the 'mixed economy of welfare' or the 'plural economy', which I use synonymously in this book) is widely discussed both in the literature and in political debates. However, it often remains vague what it comprises and its interpretations vary. This also applies to specific shifts of the mix, including 'privatization' and 'marketization'. One aim of this study is therefore to disentangle the meanings of and connect the concepts of 'welfare mix', 'privatization' and 'marketization' with each other. For this purpose, I developed a conceptual framework that captures the fuzzy concepts and allows operationalizing them for an empirical investigation.

The second notion this study focuses on is that of 'poverty relief' or, used synonymously here, 'poverty alleviation'. The main rationale for concentrating on this activity field is the lack of empirical data on this core area of social policy concerning both (i) the prevalent welfare mix as well as (ii) changes towards 'privatization' and 'marketization'[1]. A further objective of this study is thus to examine empirically both the characteristics of the contemporary mixed economy of poverty relief as well as recent shifts that qualify as 'privatization' and/or 'marketization' in this activity field. Not least, this allows examining in how far the framework developed is able to assist in such an empirical assessment.

---

[1] Studies on the 'mixed economy', on 'privatization' or 'marketization' have focused on a variety of social policy areas, such as social care (Wistow *et al.* 1994, Ascoli and Ranci 2002c), care for the elderly (Evers and Svetlik 1993), pensions (Holzmann and Heitzmann 2002: 514f, Weller 2006), health care (Newman and Kuhlmann 2007), and many other social services (O'Higgins 1989, Smith and Lipsky 1993).

The empirical part of the study focuses on Austria. In this country, mainly two types of organizational actors, namely public agencies and nonprofits, provide poverty alleviation. Thus, I examine the roles and contributions of these two types of providers only[2].

This introduction proceeds as follows: Section 1 illustrates the empirical relevance of the topic, thereby introducing the concepts that are at the core of this study. Section 2 clarifies the theoretical and empirical research questions. Section 3 finally explains the research approach adopted and outlines the plan of this book.

1. Background

Per capita welfare state expenditures have risen in real terms in almost all European welfare states from the 1980s onwards (e.g. Castles 2004: 24ff, Eurostat 2008). This expansion is to some extent the result of new needs and the related introduction of welfare state programmes (e.g. care for the elderly, see Österle 2001: 89ff). Moreover, changing demographic (e.g. increased life expectancy) and socio-economic structures (e.g. altered family formations, enhanced labour market problems) have led to an increasing demand for statutory social security[3]. Despite these developments, several pressures call for a reduction of public expenditures (e.g. Bonoli *et al.* 2000: 2). For example, there is concern that rising fiscal costs might threaten the very sustainability of welfare states. High social security contributions are viewed as significant obstacles for competitive economies, and thus for economic growth. Moreover, neo-liberal attitudes towards the 'proper' role of the state in society, which are prominent in many contemporary European governments, are characterized by a general suspicion against 'too generous' state welfare.

Owing to these developments and attitudes, welfare states throughout Europe have been subject to reform, restructuring and/or retrenchment in recent decades. Many routes have been chosen to reorganize the provision of welfare. One of these strategies includes the **'privatization of social security'** (Burton 1987, Gurin 1989, Kamerman and Kahn 1989, Feldstein 1998, Kotlikoff *et al.* 1998, Kotlikoff 2000, Fullerton and Geruso

---

[2] On the role of informal actors and for-profit companies in poverty relief, see Section I.2.2.

[3] The terms 'welfare' and 'social security' are used interchangeably in this book.

2006, Weller 2006). Put into a nutshell, privatization implies both a decrease of public provision of welfare and – usually – a parallel increase of private provision. In many cases of privatization, the state does not refrain completely from welfare provision, but maintains some role as regulator or financier of social security. Examples of this form of 'partial privatization' include contracting arrangements in the provision of many social services or the statutory regulation of private health or pension insurances (Smith and Lipsky 1993, Deakin 1996). Especially the trend to regard nonprofits or, used synonymously here, third-sector organizations (such as associations, charities, private welfare societies, religious congregations, etc.) as a better alternative to statutory provision of welfare and to encourage their engagement seems universal (e.g. Pearson and Martin 2005: 9).

Many scholars agree that due to their inherent incentive structure, private actors tend to manage provision more efficiently than the state (e.g. Fershtman 1990, Shleifer 1998). In contrast to for-profit companies, however, nonprofits follow a profit-distribution constraint (see Section I.2.2.4). Although they may generate profits, these must remain within the organization and benefit its mission. Therefore, third-sector organizations are not likely to maximize profits (e.g. Rose-Ackerman 1996, Brown and Slivinski 2006) and 'commercialize' welfare services to the detriment of their clients (e.g. Salamon 1993, Badelt and Österle 2001a: 107). Consequently, politicians from both the left and the right prefer nonprofits to for-profit organizations as welfare providers. This is especially the case regarding instruments which are difficult to measure in terms of quality (such as many social services, see, for example, Blank 2000), or which target particularly vulnerable groups in society (such as the income poor or the socially excluded). In many of these delicate policy areas, nonprofits already maintain a prominent role. In Austria, for example, more than three quarters of all employees in the social services (*Sozialwesen*) are employed by third-sector organizations. The share of employees in homes for the elderly amounts to almost 30 per cent. With regard to other institutions (such as homes for the disabled), it adds up to more than 50 per cent (Schneider *et al.* 2007: 72ff). These contributions notwithstanding, various scholars and politicians believe that further expanding the role of nonprofits (as well as for-profits) in social security might enable governments to "*square the welfare circle*" (Bonoli *et al.* 2000: 2). Governments could meet the growing demand for social security by enhancing the contributions of both nonprofits and for-profit organizations, with the former providing commodities with a lower degree of marketability and the latter offering goods and services with a higher degree of marketability[4].

A second reform strategy (which is closely related to the first one) concerns the increasing importance of market ethics and market principles in the provision of social security. This is sometimes referred to as **'commercialization' or 'marketization' of welfare**. This trend is visible at various levels. First, the entitlement to many welfare benefits has been linked more closely to some kind of obligations or behavioural criteria (also called 'social engineering', see also Section II.1.2.3): Through the use of sanctions and incentives welfare beneficiaries are compensated for engaging in socially approved behaviours such as consuming health prevention or going to work (Gilbert 2001: 216f). Especially with regard to the latter, i.e. the willingness to remain in, or (re-)integrate into the labour market, some scholars argue that 'welfare' benefits have become 'workfare' benefits in many countries (e.g. Lødemel and Trickey 2001, Koch *et al.* 2005).

Second, market ethics have become relevant in the management of both public organizations and nonprofits. Examples of a market-oriented management include the introduction of new public management in public agencies (e.g. Zimmer 1997, Zimmer and Nährlich 1997, Sarker 2005), or the revaluation of 'professionalization' or 'managerialism' in nonprofits (Anheier 2005: 377f, Badelt *et al.* 2007a: 629f, Meyer 2007). The main rationale for introducing market principles in non-market organizations is the conviction, widespread in politics, that the state and its partners in provision could reduce costs by more closely imitating at least some of the principles of the for-profit sector, such as competitiveness, etc. (Ascoli and Ranci 2002a: 226f). Given that organizations from different societal sectors are increasingly managed in similar ways, it becomes difficult to distinguish clearly between public organizations, non-

---

[4] James and Rose-Ackerman (1986: 61), for example, suggest that "*for-profits exist in most areas where fees can be charged sufficient to cover costs. They are less prevalent in areas where demand is very limited, where exclusion cannot be practiced, where provision to the needy (those unable to pay) is the goal or where the government, for some other reason, has decided to provide the service at minimal private cost*".

profits and for-profits. This trend, which is sometimes called 'hybridization' (Evers 2005), not least implies that "*the traditional concept of sector has lost much of its theoretical and analytic power.*" (Kramer 2004: 220).

The adoption of market principles has, third, also changed the mode of cooperation between public and private organizations. For example, when purchasing welfare goods and programmes from private organizations, the state often relies on competitive processes (such as bidding) to choose contracting partners. After the choice for a contracting partner has been made, the stipulations of the contract – which in itself leads to a formalization of the relationship between the cooperating partners – include (usually quantifiable) indicators (e.g. quota regulations etc.) based on which (performance-related) payments are made (e.g. Zauner *et al.* 2006, Schneider and Trukeschitz 2007b). Consequently, organizations become (i) more prone to adopt market-principles themselves and – yet again – (ii) more alike.

The reform paths presented so far concern (i) changes across different types of welfare actors (e.g. privatization), (ii) changes within specific types of welfare actors (concerning, for example, the governance of welfare actors), and (iii) changes with regard to welfare benefits (through the introduction of workfare benefits) In other words: the specific mix of welfare actors and of welfare instruments has changed. Different expressions are used in the literature to describe this 'mix' in welfare provision. These include the 'mixed economy of welfare' (e.g. Powell 2007), the 'plural economy' (e.g. Evers and Olk 1996) or the 'welfare mix' (e.g. Evers 1993, Ascoli and Ranci 2002c). Quite often, however, these terms are used without being clearly defined – which may indeed lead to misunderstandings. Lewis (2004: 169), for example, has pointed out that the "*approach to 'welfare mixes' differs considerably between different networks of academics and commentators.*" Apart from differences in the understanding of these concepts across countries underlined by Lewis, there is also an interpretative variation across scientific disciplines. For example, textbooks of economics and public finance usually define 'mixed economies of welfare' as economies in which actors from different sectors contribute to welfare provision. Scientists with a background in sociology or political science, on the other hand, focus on the norms and rationales that govern welfare actors (and their actions) when referring to a 'welfare mix' or a 'plural economy' (e.g. Evers and Laville 2004: 14).

Evers, moreover, suggests that the literature has applied concepts, such as the 'welfare mix', in two ways:

> *"On the one hand, the concept has been used for the description of the empirical and historical diversity of welfare systems which de facto were always "mixed", and for an analysis of the different types of mixes which can be found there. (...) On the other hand, more recently the concept has been used as a reference point for specific social policy suggestions (...)." (Evers 1993: 4).*

Despite differences in the interpretation of these concepts across countries and disciplines, the 'welfare mix' is an empirical fact evidenced by a variety of research studies (e.g. Evers and Wintersberger 1988, Pinker 1992, Wistow *et al.* 1994, Evers and Olk 1996, Johnson 1999, Ascoli and Ranci 2002c, Powell 2007).

It is also an empirical fact that the welfare mix is subject to change. Developments such as 'privatization' and/or 'marketization' indicate either processes of change or (expected or realized) outcomes of change. However, what have been their **points of departure**?

Several concepts have been forwarded to describe the provision of welfare *before* movements towards privatization or marketization took place. Regarding 'privatization', no one seriously argues that prior to privatization processes there was only statutory provision of welfare. Rather, private actors have always contributed to social security provision (Katz and Sachße 1996: 10). This relates not only to the large contributions of the informal sector (and thus, for example, the provision of care services by family members) but also to those of formal private actors. For-profit firms have engaged in the provision of hospitals, homes for the elderly, or in the provision of health or pension insurances in many countries for a long time. In addition to for-profits and the large informal sector, non-profits have participated in European welfare markets for quite a while – albeit with substantial differences across countries (for a general overview, see Salamon *et al.* 2003). Third-sector organizations play a crucial role in providing social services in conservative (e.g. Germany, France) and liberal welfare states (e.g. USA, UK), while their contribution in social-democratic states (e.g. Sweden) is smaller (Salamon and Anheier 1998: 241ff). Thus, concerning privatization, the point of departure has been a mix of public and private welfare actors. While the balance of this mix changes due to privatization processes, the result is – at least in terms of partial privatizations – yet another mix of public and private contributions in the provision of welfare.

Market principles such as maximizing profits, increasing cost-efficiency and competitiveness or introducing performance-related salaries for employees and managers are dominant values in managing for-profit firms. As mentioned above, the hypothesis of a 'marketization' of social security provision suggests that (some of) these principles become increasingly relevant in the management of public organizations and nonprofits. However, which principles do these newly introduced market ethics substitute? The literature suggests that (traditional) rationales governing activities of public actors are power, hierarchy, bureaucracy, redistribution or paternalism (e.g. Stiglitz 2000: 156ff). Dominant (and traditional) values in the management of nonprofits are much more complex. Especially in a European debate, nonprofits are often located between the public, the for-profit and the informal sector (e.g. Evers and Laville 2004, Zauner 2007), which is why they are also called intermediary organizations (e.g. Bauer 1993). One line of arguments suggests that nonprofits, as they attempt to combine the dominant values of all other sectors, are governed by a multitude of different norms (Evers 1993: 13ff). Another line of arguments holds that the dominant values differ between third-sector organizations, depending on their proximity to other organizational sectors (Neumayr *et al.* 2007, Neumayr and Schneider 2008). Nonprofits that are more closely related to the state than to the informal or the for-profit sector are governed by values similar to those of public organizations (such as bureaucracy). Nonprofits close to the informal sector tend to adopt principles relevant to informal actors (such as solidarity or love), while third-sector organizations close to the for-profit sector are most likely to adopt market ethics (Zauner 2007: 146ff).

As mentioned earlier, the implementation of market ethics has influenced not only the management of public and nonprofit actors, but also their modes of cooperation. This refers both to the choice of a contracting partner by the state and the stipulations of the contract. Competition through bidding, performance-related funding arrangements and business-like relationships between contracting partners (based on, for example, control and accounting) are dominant values in contemporary contracting (Ascoli and Ranci 2002a: 230ff). And what about the past? Protection against competition, long-term or ever-repeating contracts, lump-sum subsidies and informal relationships based on trust rather than control have characterized contracting in the past in many countries, including Austria (Heitzmann 2004c: 209ff). As mentioned, a potential outcome of 'marketization' is an increasing hybridization of welfare actors belonging to different societal sectors, which implies that prior to marketization processes it must have been less likely to confuse public, nonprofit and for-profit organizations or their specific modes of provision. In other words: the boundaries between these types of actors (and their provision) must have been blurred less than they are at present.

Table 1 summarizes the different facets of the two reform strategies discussed so far, i.e. 'privatization' and 'marketization'.

Shifts of the welfare mix thus affect providers of welfare, their contracting arrangements and their modes of provision. These changes might have quite some implications for efficiency outcomes if private actors outperform public actors. However, changes of the welfare mix might also affect the recipients or users of welfare products and thus change equity outcomes. This leads to the question: How effective is a welfare system after the mixed economy has changed?

Ringen (1988) suggests that a good indicator for the effectiveness of a welfare system is the extent to which poverty prevails in a country:

> *"The trend in poverty is the litmus test of the social quality of the mixed economy system. If poverty remains rampant in spite of the economic growth, the market does not do its job; if it remains rampant in spite of expanding public transfers, the welfare state does not do its job". (Ringen 1988: 352)*

Badelt and Österle (2001b: 222) also argue that the mere existence of poverty is an expression of the limited success of prevalent welfare systems – which would indeed provide a justification for reform. Available data suggest that the average percentage of the population at risk of poverty in the EU-15 remained relatively stable within the last decade: It amounted to 17 per cent in 1995 and to 16 per cent in 2005 (Eurostat 2008).

Thus, the extent of poverty has not changed much in Western Europe between 1995 and 2005. However, have changes of the welfare mix, particularly privatization and/or marketization, taken place at all in the **ac-**

tivity field of poverty alleviation? Is there any evidence that public agencies and nonprofits providing poverty alleviation have undergone processes of privatization or marketization? And if there is evidence of this kind – have poverty rates changed despite or because of these shifts?

Interestingly, there is not much information available on either the current balance of the welfare mix concerning this activity field or on recent shifts thereof. Studies on poverty alleviation tend to concentrate on the mix of instruments targeted to the poor (Alcock 1997, Schiller 2001). For example, there has been increased conditionality with regard to social security benefits for the poor (which has been described as a shift from welfare to workfare benefits previously). Only few studies focused on welfare actors in poverty relief, the most well researched being the contributions of statutory organizations in this respect (e.g. Stitt 1994, Alcock 1997: 210ff, Becker 1997, Schiller 2001). Available data suggest that the relative efforts of the state in providing poverty relief differ between welfare states. For example, the UK spent 16 per cent of all social protection expenditures in 2005 on means-tested benefits which directly target the poor. In Sweden, this proportion amounted to only 3 per cent, in Austria to 7 per cent (Eurostat 2008: 23ff). In contrast to the welfare state, both the current role and contributions of nonprofits in poverty relief were hardly ever at the centre of research studies – in 1990 only two of eight countries taking part in the renowned Johns Hopkins Comparative Nonprofit Sector Project reported data on nonprofits engaged in activities such as granting income support or maintenance or providing material assistance[5] (Salamon and Anheier 1996). In Italy, only 0.1 per cent of all paid employees in the third sector (measured in full-time equivalents) were engaged in this type of organizations. In the UK, the proportion amounted to 0.2 per cent (Salamon *et al.* 1995: 11ff). These data suggest that in these two countries nonprofit engagement on behalf of poverty relief was very small, underreported, or relied primarily on unpaid workers.

---

[5] The data published for 1995 (Salamon *et al.* 1999: 477ff) and 2000 (Salamon *et al.* 2003) only include information on social services in general, without differentiating these data into subgroups.

Table 1: Selected reform strategies in the provision of social security

Privatization	Main issues	Main trend	Examples
(i) partial privatization	• Who does what in welfare provision?	Shift between organizations from: public (and private) provision towards: less public / more private provision	Contracting-out Deregulation Increase of private funding sources
(ii) total privatization	• Who does what in welfare provision?	Shift between organizations from: public (and private) provision towards: pure private provision	Termination of public programmes
Marketization	**Main issues**	**Main trend**	**Examples**
(i) …concerning the design of welfare benefits	• Which targeting criteria do welfare actors apply?	'Social engineering', e.g.: from: welfare benefits towards: workfare benefits (sanctions and incentives)	Benefit receipt subject to willingness to enter paid employment
(ii) …concerning the management/governance of welfare providers	• How is the organization managed? How is this reflected in welfare provision? • What are dominant values for the activity? How is this reflected in welfare provision?	Change of values, norms and rationales, by which welfare actors are governed (towards market ethics and principles employed by for-profit organizations); these changes lead to adoptions in the modes of provision <u>Public organizations:</u> from: bureaucracy etc. towards: new public management <u>Nonprofit organizations:</u> from: amateurishness etc. towards: professionalization, managerialism etc. *Potential outcome: Hybridization*	New public management

(iii) …concerning the contractual relationship between welfare providers	• How are partners chosen? • How are contracts stipulated? • How does the relationship between contracting partners look like?	Shift in the mode of cooperation between actors (towards market ethics and principles employed by for-profit organizations) from: choice of contractor through decision of public actor; subsidies; informal relationships towards: choice of contractor through competition; performance-related payments; formal ('professional') relationships *Potential outcome: Hybridization*	Bidding Performance-related payments

Source: own illustration

Whereas studies on poverty alleviation largely neglect the mix of welfare actors, studies on the mixed economy usually do not focus on goods and services targeted to the heterogeneous group of people on low income (see footnote 1). Rather, they concentrate on specific population groups (e.g. the sick, the handicapped, the elderly, lone parents, the unemployed, migrants, etc.), or on specific goods and services (e.g. health care, health insurance, pension insurance, long-term care, etc.), which are available to the poor and the non-poor.

As may have become clear from this short review, there is a considerable lack of information regarding the mixed economy of poverty relief, especially concerning the role of nonprofits in this field. Moreover, there is a lack of information concerning the issue of whether the mixed economy of poverty relief has been subject to change in recent years and whether these changes qualify as privatization and/or as marketization. Some explanations for these information gaps have already been forwarded. First, studies on poverty relief usually take into account only the contributions of public organizations or – even though much more seldom – of nonprofits without discussing the mixed economy or the welfare mix. Second, studies on the mixed economy have so far largely neglected the activity field of poverty relief. Third, given that there are different interpretations of concepts such as the 'mixed economy', it is often difficult to ascertain whether shifts of this mix qualify as 'privatization' and/or as 'marketization'. Fourth, the concept of poverty relief in itself is uncommon in social policy research. Many studies focus exclusively on the 'demand-side' of poverty relief, i.e. on the poor, while others include an analysis of instruments to combat poverty. These usually include measures to prevent poverty, to mitigate against negative consequences if poverty should hit, to reduce exposure to poverty risks and to relieve poverty (Holzmann *et al.* 2003). Dealing with the latter aspect is uncommon, though (exceptions include, for example, Gilbert 2001), at least in a European perspective. Fifth, evidence for two countries suggests that the share of nonprofits in poverty relief is very small – at least when measured in terms of paid labour input. This might have accounted for the small amount of research in this field. In many instances, however, poverty alleviation is only one of several activities of nonprofits. Thus, there is reason to believe that the actual contributions of these types of actors to poverty relief have been underestimated, the more as in the aforementioned Johns Hopkins project they were classified according to their *main* activity. Sixth, the extent of income poverty did not change much between 1995 and 2005 in the EU-15. This suggests that (i) the welfare mix did not change in this period or (ii) that shifts – if they had taken place – hardly affected the outcome, i.e. the share of the population at-risk-of-poverty, or (iii) that shifts – if they had taken place – neutralized the outcome that would have been realized without the shifts.

2. Research questions

Against the background illustrated in the previous section, and particularly the information gaps detected, this study is guided by the following research questions:

- How can we capture the concepts 'welfare mix', 'privatization' and 'marketization'? How are these concepts linked together?

- In how far does a conceptual framework that organizes and links the concepts 'welfare mix', 'privatization' and 'marketization' help to illustrate both (i) the characteristics of the current welfare mix in poverty relief as well as (ii) recent shifts thereof that might qualify as 'privatization' and/or 'marketization' in an empirical investigation?

Finding answers to the **first research question** requires assessing the concepts 'welfare mix', 'privatization' and 'marketization', and elaborating a conceptual framework that links these concepts sensibly together. Therefore, I separate the concept of the 'welfare mix' into two different types, namely 'Type I welfare mix' and 'Type II welfare mix'. 'Privatization' involves specific changes of 'Type I welfare mix', whereas 'marketization' refers to specific shifts of 'Type II welfare mix'. The characteristics of all of these four concepts may be captured through a thorough analysis of yet another concept – 'provision' –, which thus also needs to be disentangled. With the assistance of three distinct elements of provision, the conceptual framework then helps to examine both (i) the contemporary welfare mix in poverty relief as well as (ii) recent shifts thereof.

The establishment of the conceptual framework is a prerequisite to answer the **second research question**, for which empirical information on the welfare mix and changes thereof in the activity field of poverty relief is needed. On a conceptual basis, this involves, first, examining the model of 'poverty relief'. Therefore, both parts of the concept, i.e. 'poverty' and 'relief', will be discussed from a theoretical perspective, and poverty alleviation will be delineated from other forms of combating poverty.

The empirical part of this study focuses on Austria[6], as this country – compared to other conservative welfare states, e.g. Germany, France or the Netherlands – has been less often the subject of social policy research. Policies aimed at 'privatizing' or 'commercializing' the welfare state (or, for that matter, other activity fields of society, e.g. state-owned industries) have not been as prominent as, for example, in the UK or the USA (e.g. Megginson and Netter 2001). Consequently, reform programmes were implemented much later than in many other countries (e.g. Krejci 1996: 7ff, Nowotny 1996: 11ff). In order to answer the second research question it is necessary (i) to map the current balance of the mixed economy of poverty relief in Austria and (ii) to examine whether developments that have led up to the current balance qualify as 'privatization' and/or 'marketization of poverty alleviation. Based on the (results of the) empirical investigation, it will then be possible to evaluate the capability of the conceptual framework elaborated in assisting the investigation.

3. Research strategy and plan of the book

The author is a social policy analyst with a background in economics. This study is guided, however, by the research questions and objectives of, and not by the (necessarily limited) pool of theories and methods available within economics. It has therefore adopted a multidisciplinary and interdisciplinary approach to allow for openness towards concepts and theories from neighbouring disciplines (e.g. political science and sociology).

---

[6] The Austrian welfare state is conservative and highly influenced by corporatism (Esping-Andersen 1990: 27, Heitzmann and Österle 2008). Social security relies primarily on gainful employment (accompanied by employment-related social insurance) and traditional family formations (assisted by universal cash transfers granted to families). Austria has a long history of statutory welfare provided from cradle to grave, but also a strong involvement of nonprofits in the delivery of social services (Bachstein 1997, Trukeschitz 2006: 187ff, Schneider *et al.* 2007).

Research strategy

Various information sources have been utilized to answer the first research question. A comprehensive literature review was conducted to collect and examine prevalent interpretations of the main concepts discussed in this book, including 'poverty relief', the 'welfare mix', 'privatization' and 'marketization'. Based on this literature assessment, a conceptual framework has been elaborated that differentiates between two types of a welfare mix and between 'privatization' and 'marketization'.

The main aim of the second research question is to test the appropriateness of the conceptual framework in completing an empirical investigation on the mixed economy of poverty relief and recent changes thereof. Therefore, it has first been necessary to operationalize the framework's crucial concepts. Second, and based on operationalization, data needs have been deducted and data sources containing relevant information have been identified. Only secondary data sources have been utilized for the empirical part of the study. Information has been derived from various databases (e.g. Eurostat 2008) and publications, including not only journals and books, but also many grey papers, such as unpublished government reports or documentation (in part derived from internet sources) of various organizations containing information on the contributions of public and nonprofit actors in poverty relief in Austria.

Plan of the book

The outline of this monograph is as follows. Apart from this introductory chapter, the book includes four more chapters. Chapters I and II contain the conceptual and theoretical framework of this study. Chapter III comprises the empirical information collected. The concluding chapter discusses policy implications of the findings and lists potential future research endeavours.

Following this introduction, **Chapter I** starts with clarifying one of the principal concepts used in this book, namely 'poverty relief'. It first disentangles the concept into its two parts, and presents working definitions for the terms 'poverty' and 'relief'. Then, it concentrates on (i) different types of measures of poverty relief and (ii) different types of providers, focusing on public and third-sector organizations. **Chapter II** first elaborates on the concept of the 'mixed economy'. It starts by separating interpretations of the notion of 'welfare mix' that concentrate on a mix of welfare actors (which is labelled 'Type I welfare mix') from interpretations that focus on a mix of welfare norms, values and rationales. The latter establishes how welfare actors provide welfare (the resulting mix in the modes of provision is termed 'Type II welfare mix'). The chapter continues to examine the concept of 'provision', as it is argued that a thorough analysis of this concept allows capturing the very characteristics of both Type I and Type II welfare mix. The concept of 'provision' is disentangled into three different components: production/delivery, finance and – introduced in this study – 'provider decisions'. All of these elements are discussed in relation to the dual concept of the 'welfare mix'. Chapter II then goes on to conceptualize 'privatization' and 'marketization'. The first concept is identified as a specific type of shifts of 'Type I welfare mix'. The latter refers to specific changes of 'Type II welfare mix'. Again it will be shown that the characteristics of 'privatization' and 'marketization' can be captured through the three elements of provision.

Drawing on these theoretical and conceptual underpinnings, **Chapter III** deals with the empirical evidence collected for this book. First, it operationalizes the main concepts elaborated in the first two chapters and identifies data needs and available information sources. Second, it illustrates the current balance of the welfare mix in poverty relief in Austria, utilizing a variety of secondary data on the provision of public and nonprofit organizations. Third, Chapter III examines recent changes of the welfare mix in Austria in order to ascertain whether they qualify as an increasing 'privatization' and/or 'marketization' of poverty alleviation. Finally, it discusses the conceptual framework's capability to assist in the empirical investigation.

The **Conclusions** summarize the main results of this study and discuss implications of the findings. This includes identifying potential future research endeavours deriving from this study.

Part A: Concepts and theories

I. 'Poverty relief'

It is vital at the beginning of each research project to clarify the terminology used, especially if interpretations vary across scientific disciplines, across the literature, across societies, and across time. This chapter aims to define and capture the concept of 'poverty relief', as this activity field is at the core of the empirical part of this study. To achieve this aim, the chapter proceeds in the following way: Section 1 starts by differentiating between several interpretations of 'poverty', seeking to identify the meaning of this concept for the purpose of this study. The section then continues to discuss the concept of 'relief'. For this purpose, it utilizes a conceptual framework elaborated by the World Bank that distinguishes between measures which are applied before a risk, such as poverty, occurs (*ex ante* management), and measures which are applied afterwards (*ex post* management). It locates the concept of 'relief' within this framework, and thus offers a preliminary working definition for the empirical research endeavour. Subsequent to these conceptual clarifications, Section 2 proceeds to examine instruments and providers of poverty relief. It first categorizes poverty relief instruments into cash transfers and in-kind transfers, and examines these types of measures in more depth. As will be shown later, information on the type of poverty relief products supplied is vital for an in-depth analysis of both the welfare mix and changes thereof. The second part of Section 2 examines four types of actors that are usually engaged in providing poverty alleviation. Two of them – public organizations and nonprofits – are at the core of the empirical analysis of this study and will therefore be presented in more detail. Section 3 finally summarizes the main findings of this chapter.

1. What constitutes 'poverty relief'?

Prior to defining 'poverty relief', it is vital to discuss what the notion of 'poverty' may comprise. In what follows, Section 1.1 first illustrates some of the connotations of this and related concepts. Based on this overview, a preliminary working definition of poverty will be forwarded for the purpose of this study. Section 1.2 then discusses what is meant by poverty 'relief'.

1.1 Capturing the concept of 'poverty'

A quick look through the literature suggests that there is no unanimity whatsoever on what constitutes poverty. One explanation for this disagreement is rooted in the fact that poverty is not only a scientific term: everybody has a certain understanding of what the term comprises (see, for example, Jacobs 1995). In fact, many are critical of using this term within the context of developed welfare states on the grounds that there are much more serious problems of poverty in less-developed countries. Yet poverty is a normative concept. As Orshansky (1969) puts it:

> *"Poverty, like beauty, lies in the eye of the beholder" (Orshansky 1969: 37)*

The various definitions of poverty thus ultimately derive from value judgments on what constitutes 'equity' or 'equality' within a society (see, for example, Sen 1992, Österle 2001: 55ff). Allowing for 'poor' people in developed welfare states implies that there is recognition of inequity. Providing measures to combat poverty suggests that a society does not tolerate inequity – at least with regard to those who are worst off. Whether this level of inequity is called 'poverty', 'deprivation' or 'social exclusion' might not only be a terminological subtleness. However, what is at the core of all these concepts is the issue of having little (or indeed too little).

The literature distinguishes between many different approaches regarding the concept of 'poverty' (for an overview, see, for example, Alcock 1997: 67ff, Coudouel *et al.* 2002, Lister 2004, Eiffe and Heitzmann 2006). In what follows, a short overview of selected interpretations of 'poverty' prevalent in the literature is presented which form the basis of the working definition applied for the purpose of this study.

1.1.1 Absolute and relative poverty

One classification of 'poverty' differentiates between absolute and relative approaches (e.g. Lister 2004: 20ff). A person experiences absolute poverty if his or her resources are below a minimum subsistence level necessary to survive. There is controversy on what this minimum should comprise (Schiller 2001: 17). Once an absolute poverty threshold is set, however, it is usually fixed over time (in terms of purchasing power), and applicable across countries. Many empirical studies have utilized the concept of absolute poverty, among them the famous research conducted by Rowntree on poverty in York in 1899 (Rowntree 1901/1971/2001, Harris 2000). Based on research of early nutritionists, his calculation of the poverty level took account of a minimum caloric intake. However, he also allowed for tea in his basket – which was not only a sign of a broader understanding of necessities needed to survive, but also an indication of the national idiosyncrasy of such 'minimums' (Atkinson 1998: 22). Defining poverty in absolute terms is not only a historical relic, though. The World Bank, for example, calculates an absolute poverty level based on minimum subsistence costs worldwide. Some OECD countries rely on absolute poverty definitions as well, most notably the USA (see, for example, Orshansky 1963, Orshansky 1965, 1969, Burtless and Smeeding 2001, Rosner 2003: 305).

Many other OECD countries define poverty in relative rather than absolute terms. For example, the European statistical office, Eurostat, defines people as being 'at-risk-of-poverty' if their equivalized disposable income is below a threshold, which is set at 60 per cent of the national median equivalized disposable income. Relative definitions of poverty thus closely relate to concepts of equality. A person will be defined as poor if his or her standard of living is significantly below some average standard in the reference population (Schiller 2001: 17). Consequently, and in contrast to setting absolute poverty lines, relative poverty thresholds change over time and differ between countries.

Both absolute and relative definitions of poverty have their flaws. None of them is completely objective. Defining an absolute poverty line requires deciding on what a person minimally requires. More or less subjective decisions on where to set the poverty threshold, which separates the poor from the non-poor, are also at the core of the relative approach. These issues have been the subject of many debates and fill many articles (e.g. Hagenaars and Van Praag 1985, Atkinson 1993, Gillie 1996).

1.1.2 Poverty and social exclusion

Arguably, the notion that appears most often in current debates on social disadvantage is that of social exclusion. Similar to the term poverty, 'social exclusion' is not only applied in a scientific context but also in political debates. Consequently, its meanings are blurred. Sometimes it is used synonymously to poverty. More often, however, it describes a problem distinct from poverty (see, for example, Rodgers 1995, Jordan 1996, Hills *et al.* 2002). A useful approach to differentiate poverty from social exclusion is presented by Berghman (1995: 16ff) who argues that the two concepts differ in terms of their comprehensiveness and dynamic character (see table 2).

Table 2: The concepts of poverty and social exclusion

	Process	
Comprehensiveness	**Static Outcome**	**Dynamic Process**
One-dimensional	Poverty	Impoverishment
Multidimensional	Deprivation	Social exclusion

Source: adapted from Berghman (1995: 21, Table 2.1)

Regarding its comprehensiveness, poverty is a one-dimensional disadvantage, whereas social exclusion is a multidimensional one. Thus, the former concept covers individuals who are disadvantaged in terms of one indicator only, which is usually income or expenditure, while the term social exclusion is applied only if several disadvantages, e.g. being unemployed, living in substandard housing, not being allowed to vote, etc., apply at the same time. However, a migrant person, for example, must not necessarily qualify as income poor, even though he or she is not allowed to vote (which may be termed political exclusion) and is excluded regarding other dimensions of participation as well. While there is thus some overlap between the concepts of poverty and social exclusion, they are in part also mutually exclusive (Badelt and Österle 2001b: 232ff).

Poverty and social exclusion differ not only in terms of comprehensiveness, but also in terms of their dynamic character. Berghman (1995: 20ff) argues that poverty is an outcome, while social exclusion is a dynamic process. Impoverishment leads to poverty. Social exclusion leads to deprivation. Poverty may thus be one of several outcomes of a process of social exclusion. It may also trigger social exclusion, which consequently pushes a person deeper into poverty[7].

[7] This characteristic of poverty as an outcome rather than a dynamic process must not be confused with the duration of poverty spells. In recent years, many studies on income poverty based on cross-sectional data have been supplemented by a dynamic analysis of poverty (e.g. Jenkins 2000). This type of investigation not only allows examining the process of impoverishment (and thus ways into and out of poverty), but also the length of poverty spells. This makes it possible to differentiate be-

Room (1999: 167ff) adds some further dimensions to distinguish the concept of poverty from the concept of social exclusion. He suggests that social exclusion shifts the focus from the resources of households (which are at the core of common poverty analyses) to those of the local community. Moreover, the focus of social exclusion is on relational rather than distributional dimensions of stratification and disadvantage (with the latter being the focus of poverty analyses). Finally, Room argues that social exclusion concentrates on catastrophic rupture rather than on a continuum of inequality.

Consequently, both Room as well as Berghman stress the differences between the concepts of poverty and social exclusion which are rooted in two distinct views on society (Jordan 1996, Room 1999: 169). Poverty derives from a liberal vision rooted in the Anglo-Saxon history, whereas the concept of social exclusion stems from the French tradition of social analysis[8].

1.1.3 Defining 'poverty' for the purpose of this study

In this study, I interpret poverty rather narrowly (i) as a one-dimensional, and a primarily finance-based form of disadvantage, and (ii) in relative rather than absolute terms. However, which indicator reflects poverty best? Researchers and political authorities responsible for poverty statistics answer this question in various ways. Generally, monetary and/or non-monetary indicators may be used to operationalize poverty. If poverty is measured in terms of monetary indicators, researchers have the choice between income, expenditure or consumption (see, for example, Atkinson 1998). While all of these indicators have advantages and disadvantages (see, for example, Coudouel *et al.* 2002), the main argument for one or the other is usually the availability and quality of existing data.

---

tween temporary and persistent forms of poverty (for Austria, see, for example, Heitzmann 2003: 43ff).

[8] Interestingly, 'social exclusion' has become a dominant notion at the level of the EU only recently. In the 1970s and 1980s, the European Commission embraced the language of 'poverty', evidenced by various research programmes on poverty (Room 1998). Only in the 1990s did the Commission start using the notion of 'social exclusion'; not least under the inspiration of its French President Delors (Room 1995: 5ff, 1999: 166).

Many of the contemporary studies on poverty, and most notably official statistics from Eurostat, use income as the primary indicator to measure poverty (e.g. Dennis and Guio 2003). This is mainly because income data are broadly available within and across member states of the European Union. However, several scholars argue that also from a methodological perspective, income is an appropriate indicator to reflect well-being in Western societies (e.g. Förster and d'Ecole 2005: 18f) – even though others disagree with this view (see, for example, Sen 1999: 88). At the core of this discourse is the question of what money can buy (and what it cannot buy). Despite these arguments, I use income as the main indicator to reflect poverty in this study. In order to stress the strong monetary focus of poverty, I use the term 'income poverty' henceforth.

Now that 'poverty' has been defined for the purpose of this study, the following section discusses what is meant by income poverty 'relief'.

1.2 Capturing the concept of 'relief'

A useful conceptual approach to categorize different measures of combating poverty is the social risk management framework elaborated by the World Bank (see, for example, Holzmann and Jørgensen 1999, Holzmann and Jørgensen 2000, Holzmann *et al.* 2003). This framework differentiates between measures taken before someone is affected by poverty, and measures taken after someone has become poor[9]. I locate the concept of 'relief' within this framework, thus defining this concept for the purpose of this study.

The social risk management framework assumes that individuals, households, communities or nations face risks from different sources. These risks include earthquakes, floods, illnesses, unemployment, old age, parenthood, war, poverty, etc. If risks materialize, they may negatively affect individuals, households, communities and/or regions. However, risks can be 'managed' in several ways (see table 3).

[9] It is thus similar to approaches that differentiate between prevention and alleviation in the provision of welfare (e.g. Badelt and Österle 2001a: 19f).

Table 3: Risk management strategies: aims and focal points

***Ex ante* risk management, i.e. actions taken before the risk materializes**	
Risk reduction	Prevents or reduces risk
Lowering risk exposure	Lowers exposure to risk
Risk mitigation	Provides compensation against the expected loss (e.g. social insurance)
***Ex post* risk management, i.e. actions taken after the risk has materialized**	
Risk coping	Copes with realized losses caused by shocks (e.g. social assistance)

Source: adapted from Heitzmann et al. (2002: 9, Box 3)

On a general level, actions can be taken before a risk materializes (*ex ante* risk management) or after it has occurred (*ex post* risk management). *Ex ante* risk management includes actions to eliminate or reduce the occurrence of risky events. For example, a high educational attainment or good vocational training reduces the risk of becoming unemployed. Moreover, regulations providing for a minimum employment income may be an effective shield against income poverty of employees. *Ex ante* measures can also be taken to prevent or reduce exposure to risks. An example is a farmer's decision to move away from a geographical area that is prone to flooding. A third option of *ex ante* risk management includes measures to compensate for risk-generated loss in case the risk materializes in the future. An example of this form of risk management is the purchase of insurance against the risks of sickness, unemployment or old age. *Ex post* risk management involves activities aimed at dealing with actual losses. This form of risk management thus attempts to cope with realized outcomes. Examples of *ex post* measures include applying for means-tested social assistance, selling assets, seeking loans from banks, searching for cheaper housing, etc.

Risks combined with the household responses lead to an outcome. An example of an outcome is poverty. If *ex ante* measures of risk management have not been successful, poverty may be the result. While the social risk management framework originally focused on discontinuous or singular shocks with regard to the materialization of risks – and thus on catastrophic ruptures –, it has been recognized since that a continuum of, for example, inequality might also lead to a harmful outcome, such as poverty or deprivation (Holzmann *et al.* 2003: 10f).

It is difficult to determine *a priori* which strategies of risk management are preferable over others (Heitzmann *et al.* 2002: 11). From an economic perspective, it is vital to compare the expected costs with the expected benefits of a specific mix of instruments. Moreover, it has to be considered that the risk management strategy chosen might increase or decrease the vulnerability of individuals or households over time. For example, households that decide to cope with an income loss by selling assets enhance their income in the short run. In the long run, however, this strategy might increase their future vulnerability. A different coping strategy such as public assistance, together with a forward-looking risk reduction strategy, may have less adverse effects on their vulnerability.

A working definition of 'relief' for the purpose of this study

Against the background of the social risk management framework, the concept of 'poverty relief' applied in this study comprises only those measures that attempt to cope with poverty. Thus, the analysis will be limited to instruments that can be classified as *ex post* strategies to combat income poverty (Heitzmann *et al.* 2002: 11). Hence, measures of 'poverty relief' exclude instruments targeted (i) to prevent poverty, (ii) to reduce the exposure to poverty or (iii) to mitigate against the expected outcome in case a person experiences poverty. Concentrating on coping measures also implies that this study is concerned with measures targeted to income poor people only. It excludes instruments targeted to the non-poor (e.g. universal benefits etc.) or the 'not-yet-poor' (e.g. social insurance). Sometimes it is difficult to draw a clear line between *ex ante* and *ex post* instruments to combat poverty, though. For example, means-tested benefits usually classify as *ex post* measures of poverty alleviation. However, instruments of social insurance may also include means-tested transfers. An empirical analysis must therefore carefully examine whether instruments qualify as *ex ante* or *ex post* measures.

So far, this chapter has presented working definitions of the concepts of 'poverty' and 'poverty relief'. These definitions will be operationalized and refined in the empirical part of this study (see Section III.1.1). The following section is concerned with identifying relevant measures and actors of poverty alleviation, as both of these aspects are relevant features of the welfare mix and shifts thereof.

2. Instruments and providers of poverty relief

Despite the limitation of this study to strategies of *ex post* risk management, a multitude of instruments is available to cope with income poverty. Section 2.1 discusses these measures in more depth, differentiating between cash and in-kind transfers. Section 2.2 then focuses on potential actors of poverty relief, i.e. the providers of instruments to relieve income poverty. Since at the core of this study are public and third-sector organizations, these are given specific consideration in this respect.

2.1 Measures of poverty relief

Which measures may a society apply in order to assist the income poor? To provide an answer to this question is the aim of this section. It categorizes potential instruments of poverty relief in terms of cash transfers and in-kind transfers, examines different forms of these measures, and exemplifies them with a view to the activity field of poverty relief. Furthermore – given that the focus of this study is on poverty alleviation – it discusses the impact of different measures on the income distribution in general and the income poor in particular.

Clearly, there is a close link between the very definition of poverty and measures targeted at coping with it. If poverty is interpreted as low income, as is the case in this study, cash transfers are a chief instrument to relieve this type of disadvantage. They are also the first category of measures this section focuses on.

2.1.1 Cash transfers

Perhaps the most effective instrument to alleviate income poverty is to enhance the disposable income of the income poor. This may be achieved by granting unbounded or bounded cash transfers. Cash transfers are deemed unbounded when there are no strings attached in terms of how the recipients spend the money they receive. Examples include means-tested welfare benefits such as income support, cash gifts from relatives or friends, cash transfers granted by third-sector organizations, or advance payments granted by employers. Specific types of unbounded cash transfers are tax allowances and tax credits: In many countries, people on low income either pay no taxes or low taxes. A reduction of the tax burden through a tax allowance, such as childcare allowance (*Kinderabsetzbetrag*) in Austria, decreases tax expenditures. As this does not result in extra cash for the recipients, these transfers are sometimes called 'implicit' (see, for example, Barr 2004: 156). Under specific circumstances, people on low income qualify for a tax credit. In contrast to a tax allowance, a tax credit can cause a person's tax bill to fall below zero. In such cases, tax credit becomes a negative income tax. This is an extra cash transfer (an 'explicit' transfer) usually delivered to the recipients by their tax offices. Examples include the working tax credit in the UK.

In contrast to unbounded cash transfers, bounded transfers are granted for specific purposes only. They are 'earmarked'. The recipients of these transfers, i.e. the 'users', are restricted in their choice on how to spend the transfer – the provider of the transfer thus decides what the recipient may consume. However, users are often free to choose among a bundle of goods or services or among different providers. To make sure that the bounded transfers are only spent for those purposes for which they have been approved, they are provided in different forms, such as vouchers (Bendick 1989: 109f), refunds or price subsidies. Bounded transfers thus allow recipients to consume specified bundles of goods of services either at no or at low costs. It is thus often difficult to differentiate clearly between bounded cash transfers and in-kind transfers (for the latter, see below).

As for welfare effects, economists largely agree that unbounded cash transfers are more favourable than bounded transfers (see, for example, Badelt and Österle 2001a: 78ff, Rosner 2003: 61ff, Barr 2004: 84ff) – not least because it is the recipients of these transfers who take the consumption decisions. For various reasons, however, bounded transfers are often preferred options to alleviate income poverty (e.g. Rosner 2003: 61ff). One argument in favour of bounded transfers is that restricting individuals' choice might protect them from irrational or unwanted behaviour. Thus, granting a bounded transfer, such as a housing benefit, to indebted people ensures that they spend the money on the rent rather than on other purposes. Clearly, the decision to grant bounded rather than unbounded transfers implies a paternalistic attitude on the part of the provider of the transfer.

Regarding distributional consequences, providing income poor people with more cash (regardless of whether it is bounded or unbounded) may enable them to exit income poverty. This is the case if the amount of the transfer exceeds the difference between the disposable income of the income poor person and the income poverty threshold[10]. However, cash transfers may lead to changes in the distribution of disposable income within a society – for example, if they are financed by the wealthier population and only accrue to the poor. This may change the poverty threshold. The net effect of redistribution could thus result in a situation in which the formerly income poor are income poor again, even though they dispose of a higher income than before.

Concerning gender implications, statutory benefits that qualify as poverty alleviation usually are granted on the basis of a means test, which guarantees eligibility only of the income poor (Schiller 2001: 194). Eligibility for poverty relief benefits is thus contingent on an assessment of available income and/or other assets. This distinguishes this kind of benefits from many other welfare measures such as universal or insurance benefits. Often, however, means-tested benefits are not based on the means of the poor individual but the household he or she lives in. Consequently, household members who contribute less to household income, i.e. usually women, are often denied means-tested benefits because household income is too high.

2.1.2 In-kind transfers

In 2005, about two thirds of total social expenditures in the EU-25 were cash benefits. The remaining third was made up of in-kind benefits (Eurostat 2008: 23). In-kind transfers are provided in the form of goods or personal social services. Similar to several cash transfers (e.g. tax allowances) they lead to a reduction of expenditures rather than an increase of income. Examples of goods provided as in-kind transfers include food from a soup kitchen, second-hand clothes, furniture, medicine, etc. Delivery of such in-kind transfers is often subject to the presentation of a voucher (e.g. food stamps) – which makes a clear delineation from unbounded cash transfers difficult, as has been mentioned earlier.

---

[10] This difference is called the poverty gap.

A specific type of in-kind transfers are personal social services (Johne 1993, Badelt 2001: 116ff, Trukeschitz 2006). These are characterized by the so-called *uno actu* principle (e.g. Badelt and Österle 2001a: 90), meaning that production and consumption of such services occur at the same time. They cannot be stored once they have been produced. Examples include health care, care for the elderly, childcare or the provision of shelter or debt counselling. In terms of actors, family members deliver the largest part of such services in most countries. In Austria, for example, informal carers (and indeed family members) deliver roughly 80 per cent of all care services for persons aged 60+ (Klimont *et al.* 2007: 28). Moreover, social workers, who may be employed both by statutory or nonprofit organizations, are important deliverers of social services (e.g. Dowling 1999, Jordan 2001: 529ff).

The provision of in-kind transfers improves the standard of living of the income poor, as they get goods or services without paying for them. However, in-kind transfers do not lift the income poor above the poverty line – if this line is defined in monetary terms, as is the case in this study. However, rather than spending a proportion of the low income on necessary goods and services such as medicine or health care, the income poor receive them for free. This enables them to use their scarce income for other purposes, e.g. vocational training, childcare services etc. These investments may allow them to exit income poverty in the longer run.

In-kind transfers have similar welfare effects as bounded monetary transfers (Rosner 2003: 61ff). Indeed, Smeeding et al. (1993: 229) argue – based on a study of the impact of, among others, health and health education benefits – that non-cash income reinforces the redistributive impact of conventional (cash) transfer mechanisms rather than acting to offset them in any major way.

Gender implications are different, though: Especially the delivery of personal social services through organizations is regarded as a necessary precondition for emancipating women from domestic duties: Providing them support in care-work may encourage them to take on paid employment. This in turn is an imperative requirement to achieve financial independence from their male partners (e.g. Lewis 1992), which reduces their vulnerability concerning future poverty risks.

To summarize the range of potential poverty relief instruments, table 4 structures these measures and presents some examples regarding the activity field of poverty alleviation.

Table 4: Instruments of poverty relief: types, effects and examples

Cash transfers	Effects	Examples
Unbounded cash transfers	Enhance income	Income support, advance payments, tax credit (if tax credit < tax bill)
	Reduce expenditures	Tax allowance, tax credit (if tax credit > tax bill)
Bounded cash transfers (→ some also qualify as in-kind transfers)	Enhance purchasing power	Vouchers (e.g. coupons for the supermarket)
	Reduce expenditures	Refunds for goods/services consumed (e.g. for medical expenses) Subsidized prices for goods and services (e.g. public transport, housing)
In-kind transfers	**Effects**	**Examples**
Goods	Reduce expenditures	Food, clothes, furniture, medicine, sleeping bags, etc.
Social services	Reduce expenditures	Health care, family care, counselling, etc.

Source: own illustration

Following the identification of poverty relief instruments, the next section shortly illustrates the range of potential providers of poverty relief instruments, including working definitions for the two organizational types that are at the core of the empirical study, namely public and nonprofit organizations.

2.2 Providers of poverty relief

The European programme to combat poverty and social exclusion regards the "*mobilization of all actors*" (European Commission 2002) as one of its principal aims. However, who actually can be an 'actor' in poverty relief, and particularly a 'provider'? The answer to the latter question ranges from the income poor themselves to the state, from private commercial companies to private charities, from international aid organizations to families and friends of the income poor. Most commonly, these actors are clustered into four societal sectors: the informal sector, the for-profit sector, the public sector and the nonprofit sector.

In what follows, 'public organizations' and 'third-sector organizations' are discussed in more depth, as they are the key providers of organized poverty relief in Western welfare states, including Austria. Therefore, Sections 2.2.3 and 2.2.4 (i) put forward working definitions for both types of providers, (ii) discuss the principal role of these actors within a society, and (iii) examine perceptions in terms of efficiency as well as equity outcomes of public and nonprofit provision. Prior to that, however, informal actors (Section 2.2.1) and for-profit organizations (Section 2.2.2) are shortly presented regarding their contributions to poverty relief.

2.2.1 Informal actors

The informal sector, which is also called household sector (e.g. Cécora 1991, Thomas 1992), contains actors that provide help informally, i.e. outside an organizational framework. It thus covers the income poor themselves, family members, neighbours or friends that assist in combating income poverty. For example, parents who financially support their unemployed child help relieve his or her income poverty. Individuals who pay for the care expenses of a relative assist in combating income poverty. Private transfers, e.g. in the form of loans, affect the position of the recipient in the income distribution of a country. In addition, in-kind transfers in form of food, clothing as well as social services provided to neighbours, friends, or relatives may qualify as measures to help the income poor.

2.2.2 For-profit organizations

For-profits are the main actors within a market economy. Their principal aim is to maximize profits. Actors belonging to this sector include private companies that distribute profits among their owners or shareholders. In contrast to informal groups, for-profits hardly engage in poverty relief as part of their core business (see also the quote in footnote 4). Initiatives such as Corporate Social Responsibility, however, sometimes include activities to relieve income poverty, e.g. through the funding of nonprofit programmes – even though the role of commercial companies in this area is still limited, as in Austria (Pomper 2007). Sometimes, the owners or managers of corporations establish their own nonprofit agencies to engage in social activities. Examples include various charity foundations such as the Bill & Melinda Gates foundation in the USA.

2.2.3 Public sector organizations

What differentiates public from private actors? The answer to this question very much depends on how concepts such as 'public' and 'private' are interpreted. Katz and Sachße (1996: 12) suggest that

> *"(t)he term 'public' refers to multiple dimensions of political and social experience. First, public means belonging to and/or financed and administered by the state, as in public education or public welfare. Second, it signifies accessibility and universal aid, as in public highway or a public service. Third, it refers to activities that take place in full view of others as contrasted to those conducted in the family or other closed setting, that is, in private. (...) Fourth, public refers to the whole rather than to a part; as in 'the' public or public opinion it means everyone."*

In this monograph, I use the notions of 'public' and 'private' in an economic sense, i.e. as broadly equivalent to the contrast between the state (that largely consists of democratic and bureaucratic institutions, see also Dahl and Lindblom 1953) and the market (for alternative interpretations of this dichotomy see, for example, Starr 1989: 17). And yet, even if this definition is employed, what exactly is the 'state'? Johnson (1999: 30) argues that

> *"(t)he state is an abstraction in that there is no single entity that can be said to constitute the state (...). It is, however, possible to identify the institutions of the state. The focus in this approach is on governmental institutions – those concerned with promulgating laws, rules, and regulations, and ensuring that they are enforced."*

Stiglitz (2000: 12ff) emphasizes two important characteristics of state institutions or – used synonymously here – 'public organizations' in democracies, which differentiate them from other actors in society (e.g. Nowotny 1999: 90ff). First, individuals who are responsible for running public institutions are appointed either directly through an electoral process or indirectly (i.e. they are appointed by someone who has been appointed directly, or yet again indirectly, through the electoral process). Second, public agencies have the power to use compulsion. They may take actions private actors may not perform. For example, they are in principle authorised to raise taxes, legislate, issue administrative regulations or decisions, etc. Within this study, I consider organizations as public if both of these two criteria apply. Based on this working definition, a vast amount of organizations may qualify as public entities at a local, a regional, a national or a supranational level. Public organizations include not only governmental departments or local authorities. More autonomous organizations, such as social insurance institutions, may belong to the public sector, as long as the persons running the organizations have been appointed directly or indirectly through an electoral process, and as long as they carry out sovereign tasks. The aggregate of all of these public actors (often termed as 'governmental actors' or 'government') makes up the public sector[11].

Which role do public organizations play in a society? Answers to this question vary largely, depending on the respondents' ideological background (for an overview of different theories of society, see, for example, Barr 2004: 42ff). The following paragraphs summarize some arguments on the role of public organizations in society, applying primarily economic ascriptions.

There is broad agreement amongst economists that market mechanisms alone are not able to fulfil all economic tasks properly. Musgrave *et al.* (1990) forwarded three economic rationales that justify government intervention: allocation, stabilization and distribution. These also represent the principal functions of public actors in a market economy. Allocation problems arise because of market failures, which are, for example, caused by collective goods, externalities or natural monopolies (e.g. Cullis and Jones 1998: 45ff). Public organizations having the power to compel taxes or issue administrative regulations are potential alternatives to private market provision. Moreover, they may intervene (e.g. through regulation or taxation) in the private market, thereby also correcting allocation failures. The responsibility of the public sector to ensure that the economy remains at full employment and prices remain stable is at the core of arguments that focus on stabilization problems in the economy. For the area of poverty relief, however, arguments that justify public intervention on the grounds of distributional problems are more important

[11] Despite this definition, it is sometimes difficult to classify an organization as a public actor. For example, does an organization that fulfils only one of the two criteria mentioned still qualify as a public organization? The answer to this question might yield different results in different states – given historical, cultural and ideological legacies and attitudes towards the state. For an application of the concept of the 'public organization' in the context of Austria, see Section III.1.1.2.

than allocation and stabilization. The distributional branch of the public sector is concerned with equity issues, and trade-offs between equity and efficiency, in the case that goods or income have not been distributed 'fair' among the members of a specific reference society. In the centre of this rationale to publicly intervene in a market economy are questions of reducing inequalities, and thus also of coping with income poverty.

However, many economists are convinced that private actors, and particularly for-profit actors, do a better job than the government – despite efficiency failures and despite equity concerns (e.g. Foldvary 1994). They argue that governments ultimately fail in their attempts to better the economy (e.g. Cullis and Jones 1998: 273ff, McNutt 2002). The reasons for government failure are manifold, reaching from limited information and limited control over private market responses or bureaucracy towards limitations imposed by political processes. Due to these government failures, many economists, such as proponents of the theory of property rights, call for the partial or complete privatization of public sector provision (e.g. Fershtman 1990, Shleifer 1998). While these arguments mainly refer to efficiency implications related to public sector activities, there are also concerns with regard to equity: Economic theory provides arguments that imply that a pure market economy creates rich and poor, which then – if rendered unfair – justifies redistribution through the state (Brodkin and Young 1989: 123). Economic scholars disagree on the distributional effects of governmental intervention, though. On the one hand, the normative public finance literature (e.g. Musgrave *et al.* 1990) assumes that government undertakes redistribution for the purpose of reducing inequality. Public choice theorists (e.g. Cullis and Jones 1998), on the other hand, demonstrate that governments are likely to implement programmes that generate private benefits to members of a 'controlling coalition' – at the expense of those outside this coalition. Since 'controlling coalitions' are usually dominated by the more affluent members of society, governmental redistribution is as likely to be regressive as progressive (Brodkin and Young 1989: 124). Thus, scholars following the theory of public choice apply the logic of microeconomics to politics, suggesting that self-interest in political decisions does not lead to benevolent results, given the existence of different kinds of 'free-riding' and 'rent-seeking' behaviour of voters, bureaucrats, politicians, and recipients of public funds. For example, bureaucrats are modelled as monopoly providers attempting to maximize budgets (e.g. McNutt 2002: 124ff). Based on these behaviour models, it is concluded that the public sector works inefficiently and does not achieve societal principles of equity.

2.2.4 Nonprofit organizations

Actors belonging to the so-called third sector have been defined in numerous ways (see, for example, Anheier and Salamon 1992, Schaden 1995, Morris 2000, Martens 2002). Interestingly, definitions vary across continents. For example, according to the structural-operational definition elaborated within the already mentioned Johns Hopkins Comparative Nonprofit Sector Project, an actor has to meet five criteria to qualify as a third-sector organization (Anheier and Salamon 1992). It (i) needs to be formally organized, (ii) has to be private, (iii) must be self-governing, (iv) must follow a non-distribution constraint, and (v) must work with volunteers or dispose over voluntary giving. Although this definition has been used in comparative studies on nonprofit sectors worldwide, some scholars argue that it derives from the US-led debate on nonprofits, which differs from the European discussion (see table 5).

Table 5: European and American perceptions on the 'nonprofit' sector

'European' definition of the nonprofit sector	'American' definition of the nonprofit sector
Emphasis on an analytical approach	Emphasis on a classificatory approach
Criterion of limits on private acquisition of profits: inclusion of cooperatives and mutual aid societies	Non-distribution constraint central, exclusion of cooperatives and mutual aid societies

Source: adapted from Evers and Laville (2004: 13)

For example, Evers and Laville (2004: 11) argue that a distinctive feature of the European approach towards the nonprofit sector is the attention given to the historical-dynamic perspective of its development. Moreover, they stress the importance of organizational types such as mutual societies or cooperatives, and thus of organizations which may distribute profits, albeit to a limited extent. Such actors, while they are excluded from the structural operational definition elaborated by Anheier and Salamon (1992), constitute an important feature of many European third sectors. Consequently, European contributions often substitute the term 'nonprofit' by other expressions such as 'third-sector organizations', 'voluntary organizations', 'community organizations' or the 'social economy' (e.g. Evers and Laville 2004: 23ff).

Perhaps the most important characteristic of nonprofits is their constraint to distribute (all of, or at least the largest proportion of) their profits. Third-sector organizations usually attempt to achieve aims other than profit maximization. These aims can often be derived from the 'mission' of the organization (Minkoff and Powell 2006, Horak *et al.* 2007: 179). Any profits generated must remain within the organization. This criterion clearly demarcates nonprofits from for-profit organizations. Thus, the working definition of third-sector organizations applied for the purpose of this study includes actors that are (i) private (i.e. not 'public' as defined above), (ii) organizations (i.e. excluding informal actors), (iii) and not allowed to distribute their profits (except for a very small part; this differentiates them from for-profit organizations).

Much of the discussion on 'providers' or 'producers' in economics is based on a perceived dichotomy of (i) the market and (ii) the state. Actors outside this dichotomy are omitted or are interpreted as 'demanders' or 'consumers' (e.g. informal actors). Consequently, many economists have been puzzled by the very existence of nonprofit organizations. Why do they exist? What is the role of this type of organizations in society? Economists have been baffled not only by the very existence of third-sector organizations but also by their steady growth in the twentieth century (Salamon 1995: 1f). This counteracted common arguments that public intervention – which has risen considerably as well – would crowd out private activity. Only in the 1970s did some economists – at first in the USA, and somewhat later also in Europe – start to explicitly target their research on nonprofits (e.g. Weisbrod 1977, Hansmann 1980, Kramer 1981, James and Rose-Ackerman 1986, Rose-Ackerman 1986, Anheier and Seibel 1990, Badelt 1996). Various economic theories have been forwarded since to explain the functions of third-sector organizations in society. These theories are sometimes competing and sometimes complementary (see, for example, Steinberg 2006). Some of them are shortly described in the following paragraphs to make understood the very functions of this type of welfare actor – and thus its potential role in poverty relief.

Both the theory of property rights (e.g. Fershtman 1990, Shleifer 1998) as well as the theory of public choice (e.g. Cullis and Jones 1998) ultimately argue for private provision of goods and services as a consequence of government failures. Yet the twin theories of market failure and government failure suggest that nonprofits be attributed a certain role (Steinberg 2006). If states and private for-profit organizations have peculiar weaknesses, nonprofits might be an alternative to fill the void. One of the oldest economic theories on third-sector organizations along these lines has been developed by Weisbrod (1977, 1986, 1988). He argues that nonprofits engage in the provision of those public goods[12] that neither for-profit nor public organizations provide in the quantity or the quality demanded. Due to the specific characteristics of a public good, for-profits do not have any incentive to provide them. The state fails to satisfy total demand for public goods, because it either limits the provision of goods and services to its median voter or fails to provide them in the quality demanded (James 1986). Nonprofits are an organizational alternative that might fill the niche left both by for-profit organizations and the public sector (Weisbrod 1977, James 1990: 21ff). Consequently, nonprofits tend to engage for specific groups (which is often referred to as 'client differentiation') and/or provide selected goods and services (also referred to as 'product differentiation', see, for example, Badelt 2007: 110), which are neglected by other actors.

Another theory on the role of nonprofits in society is based on the work of Hansmann (1987a: 29ff). Within his trustworthiness theory (or contract failure approach), he argues that nonprofits tackle the problem of asymmetric information. In many instances, providers or producers of a service have more information than the demanders. For the latter it is often impossible to control the quality of the services (e.g. health care, care for the elderly, childcare). For-profits have an incentive to exploit this advantage in order to enhance their profits. As nonprofits are not allowed to distribute profits, they are assumed to be more trustworthy than commercial enterprises. In general, Hansmann's theory is seen to complement Weisbrod's thoughts, as it also includes third-sector organizations that provide private goods. Key elements of Hansmann's theory are specifically relevant to explain the existence of donative nonprofits. It is argued that potential donors will donate their money to a third-sector or-

[12] Evidence has been provided for the relevance of the theory for private goods with positive externalities (e.g. Kingma 2003).

ganization – because of its non-distribution constraint – rather than an organization of another societal sector (Hansmann 1987a: 30).

A different explanation for the role of nonprofits in society derives from entrepreneurship theories (e.g. Rose-Ackerman 1997, Badelt 2003, Borzaga and Santuari 2003, Young 2003). These place the focus on the supply behaviour, pointing out that nonprofits are the result of a specific form of entrepreneurial behaviour. Different types of organizations attract different types of personalities. Motives of nonprofit entrepreneurs include the search for personal identity, the need for autonomy and independence, the belief in a cause or the desire to gain power or control, etc. This implies that one function of nonprofits is to enable entrepreneurs (and employees as well as volunteers more generally) with a specific motive structure to engage formally within an organization. For example, the main motivation of employees in third-sector organizations engaged in the provision of poverty relief may be the belief in a good cause or private charity. This attitude also influences which type of assistance these actors provide, which individuals they target and how they administer the provision of their transfers.

While these and several other theoretical approaches[13] explain why nonprofits exist, scholars disagree on the efficiency of nonprofit provision. On the one hand, behavioural models of nonprofit activity assume that nonprofits aim to maximize the quality and/or quantity of their provision (Hansmann 1987a: 37f). Budget maximization might be another goal as it enhances the importance of (or justifies a higher salary for) the managers of the organization. On the other hand, scholars argue that nonprofits are inherently subject to productive inefficiency. Those who control the organization are unable, due to the non-distribution constraint, to claim the net earnings obtained by reducing costs for themselves. Thus, they have little economic incentive to minimize costs (Steinberg 2006: 126). Moreover, studies (e.g. Steinwald and Neuhauser 1970, Hansmann 1987b) found that nonprofits tend to respond much more slowly to increases in demand than their for-profit counterparts. One explanation for this phenomenon is that, compared to for-profit firms, third-sector organizations are constrained in their access to capital. An alternative explanation of nonprofits' relatively poor supply response refers to prob-

[13] For an overview of economic theories on the third sector, see, for example, Steinberg (2006).

lems of entrepreneurship, and especially the non-distribution constraint and its disincentive effects (Hansmann 1987a: 39f).

Literature on the distributional effects of nonprofit provision is twofold (e.g. Brodkin and Young 1989: 123). On the one hand, nonprofits are expected to contribute to more equality due to both the nature of the missions they follow and the profit-distributing constraint. On the other hand, however, the isolated and particularistic provision of third-sector organizations points to the fact that redistribution might not lead to more equality as it is limited to specific population groups only (Steinberg 2006: 125). For example, the resource dependency model suggests that nonprofits will focus on those population groups for which they are most likely to obtain resources from either the state or private donors. Thus, groups which are deemed as 'undeserving' (e.g. drug addicts) are less likely to be served by nonprofits since the latter might not obtain enough financial support through private giving for these groups. This suggests problematic distributional effects of nonprofits in favour of 'deserving' population groups (e.g. poor children).

The following section summarizes the main findings of this chapter, before the study proceeds to discuss a further important concept – the 'mixed economy' and changes thereof.

3. Summary of this chapter

This chapter aimed to discuss and define the activity field that is at the core of the empirical part of this study, namely 'poverty relief', from a conceptual perspective. First, it illustrated some of the facets of the concept of 'poverty', applying a rather narrow definition of 'income poverty' for the purpose of this study. Despite the problems arising from such a constricted focus, income is a key indicator that co-determines the relative position of people in Western welfare societies. It is thus also a suitable approximation of deprivation in general. Second, the concept of 'relief' was delineated from other forms of combating poverty by applying the social risk management framework elaborated by the World Bank. The concept of poverty relief was located within this framework and was defined as comprising all measures targeted to the income poor.

Based on these definitions, Section 2 examined potential instruments and providers of poverty relief. First, it structured potential instruments of poverty relief into cash and in-kind transfers. The first type of instruments can be separated into bounded and unbounded transfers. In-kind transfers may be provided either in the form of goods or personal social services. All of these measures were described and shortly discussed in terms of their distributional implications. It was pointed out that bounded transfers and in-kind goods restrict the choice of users and shift (parts of) the consumption decision towards the providers. Regarding poverty relief actors, the chapter mainly focused on two types of organizations, namely public and third-sector providers, forwarding working definitions for both of them. Public organizations were defined according to two criteria: First, the person running the organization must have been appointed directly or indirectly through an electoral process. Second, the public actor must have the power to use compulsion. Nonprofits were defined according to three criteria: First, they must be organizations. Second, they must be private actors. Third, they are not allowed to distribute (most of their) profits. The main roles attributed to both types of organizations were shortly described. Moreover, a short overview of arguments concerning efficiency and equity outcomes of interventions by these types of providers was presented. It has been shown that scholars disagree on both of these issues and thus, ultimately, on the potential effectiveness of these two actors in a market economy.

So far, this study examined the concept of poverty relief in some depth. It has thus touched upon an objective (i.e. to relieve income poverty), on instruments to achieve this objective (i.e. cash or in-kind transfers), and on actors that apply these instruments (including public and nonprofit organizations). As in many other fields of welfare, a mix of public and private actors provides poverty relief. These actors are characterized by a variety of different norms, values and rationales, which determine the modes of provision chosen by them. The literature has widely examined such issues under terms such as 'welfare mix', 'mixed economy' or 'plural economy'. In what follows, Chapter II examines these concepts in more detail and discusses the implications of changes in the welfare mix.

II. The ‘mixed economy of welfare’ -- and shifts thereof

In the last decades, the provision of statutory welfare has come under economic and ideological pressure. Diagnoses of a ‘crisis of the welfare state’, and – linked to such assessment – the resulting need to ‘reform’, ‘retrench’ or ‘restructure’ statutory welfare has dominated much of the pertinent literature (e.g. Johnson 1990, Snower 1996, Atkinson 2000, Powell and Hewitt 2002, but also: Castles 2004). One result of these debates has been a shift of the primary focus of research from statutory welfare towards welfare provision in general, acknowledging that it is not only public organizations that provide social security – and never has been. Katz and Sachße suggest that “*(a)ll welfare regimes share one attribute: a complex mix of public/private provision throughout their histories*” (1996: 10). Yet, what exactly do concepts such as the ‘mixed economy of welfare’ comprise? Similar to the notion of ‘poverty’, different interpretations of this and related terms prevail in the literature. For example, the Wolfenden Commission (1978: 29) uses the notion of ‘pluralism’ to discuss the role of the third sector in welfare provision. Marwell and McInerney (2005: 7) suggest that ‘mixed-form markets’ are markets for goods and services in which for-profit, nonprofit and public providers coexist. Johnson (1999: 22) defines a ‘mixed economy of welfare’ as one in which actors from four societal sectors, including the informal sector, are involved in the provision of welfare. Evers (1993: 22f) suggests that the ‘welfare mix’ does not relate primarily to the concrete combination of welfare-providing agents (which he terms ‘welfare pluralism’) but to the synergetic effects of their interaction. His interpretation of a ‘welfare mix’ thus stresses the dynamics of a plural society. These few examples already suggest that the content of notions such as the ‘welfare mix’, ‘welfare pluralism’ or the ‘mixed economy of welfare’ differs across the literature. This also holds for changes of this mix, including ‘privatization’ and ‘marketization’.

The main theoretical objective of this study is to establish a conceptual framework that both (i) disentangles the concepts ‘welfare mix’, ‘privatization’ and ‘marketization’, and (ii) links them together in a sensible way. To achieve this aim, this chapter proceeds as follows: Section 1 clusters different definitions of ‘welfare mix’ prevalent in the literature into two broad categories. One focuses on a mix of welfare providers. For a welfare system to be mixed, providers of at least two and up to four societal sectors, including the public and the nonprofit sector, engage in the welfare market – either side by side or jointly through a division of labour in the provision of welfare. The second interpretation of 'welfare mix' is based on differences of welfare providers in terms of the norms, values, and rationales by which they are governed. I argue that these differences are mirrored (i) in the specific modes of provision which these actors employ, and/or – in case of joint provision – (ii) in the modes of cooperation between the contracting partners. Based on this dual categorization, the first section then describes a further concept that is relevant for the description of both types of a 'mixed economy', i.e. provision. For the purpose of this study, 'provision' is disentangled into three different, yet related elements, namely 'finance', 'production and/or delivery' and – introduced in this study – 'provider decisions'.

Section 2 then shifts the focus to examine changes of the welfare mix. Based on the dual concept of a 'mixed economy' elaborated in Section 1, it differentiates between two types of transformations. The first one concerns changes in the mix of welfare providers[14]. These comprise movements towards more public and less private provision, but also towards more private and less public provision. For the purpose of this study, only the latter type of change is of interest, which is discussed under the prominent notion of 'privatization', i.e. a reduced (or, indeed, altered) role of public actors in welfare provision and an increased role of private actors. The second type of shift concerns (i) changes in the modes of provision applied by both public and private welfare actors, and/or in the case of joint provision (ii) changes in the contractual arrangements between public and private welfare actors. However, this section only focuses on developments that lead to an increased 'marketization' of welfare provision. This term is widely used in the literature to describe a fashionable trend, according to which both public actors as well as nonprofits incorporate more 'market' characteristics (such as competition, choice, accountability, etc.) in both their modes of provision and – in case of joint provision – their contractual agreements. Section 3 finally summarizes the main findings of this chapter.

[14] Although there are transformations within the societal sectors (e.g. defederalization of the public sector, shifts towards more or less faith-based organizations in the nonprofit sector), these are not subject of this study.

1. What constitutes a 'mixed economy of welfare'?

Scholars broadly agree that welfare provision is not the exclusive task of the welfare state. Accordingly, many suggest to implement broader concepts such as 'welfare pluralism' (Evers and Olk 1996, Höck 1996), 'welfare democracy' (Leibfried 2003, Nullmeier 2003a), the 'welfare market' (Nullmeier 2003b), the 'mixed economy of welfare' (Pinker 1992, Ben-Ner and Van Hoomissen 1993, Wistow *et al.* 1994, Kramer 2004, Powell 2007), or the 'welfare mix' (Evers and Wintersberger 1988, Vogel 1999, Ascoli and Ranci 2002c, Taylor 2004, Bode 2006). However, what do these phrases stand for? I will argue that at least two different interpretations of these concepts prevail in the literature, which I categorize and discuss in Section 1.1. Section 1.2 is then concerned with examining a further concept upon which these interpretations are based, i.e. 'provision'.

1.1 A dual approach towards the 'welfare mix'

Across the literature, the 'mixed economy of welfare' and similar concepts are interpreted in several and often contradicting ways. I therefore propose to cluster the different interpretations, and argue that it is possi ble to differentiate between two approaches[15].

The focus of the first approach towards a welfare mix, which I label 'Type I welfare mix', is on welfare providers. These belong to at least two and up to four different societal sectors (see Section I.2.2) and engage in welfare provision either side by side or jointly. The focus of the second group of interpretations, which I label 'Type II welfare mix', is on both the modes of welfare provision applied by (different types of) welfare providers and their modes of cooperation. In what follows, the two approaches towards a 'welfare mix' are discussed in more depth.

1.1.1 Type I welfare mix

The first cluster of interpretations of the 'mixed economy of welfare' and similar concepts prevalent in the literature centres around a mix of wel-

---

[15] This duality is adopted mainly for reasons of analytic clarity rather than representational accuracy. As will be shown, there are some overlaps between the two interpretations identified. Thus, the boundaries between the two approaches are fuzzy.

fare actors from different societal sectors that provide cash, goods or services alongside each other or jointly. At the core of this approach is thus the issue of 'who provides (what share or which part of) welfare?'. This interpretation of a 'mixed economy' or a 'plural economy' is prominent, for example, in the literature of British scientists (Johnson 1999, Lewis 2004, Powell 2007). It is also a well-known approach within the discipline of economics in which it is usually termed the 'mixed economy of welfare' rather than the 'welfare mix' (e.g. Stiglitz 2000: 4, Samuelson and Nordhaus 2001: 8, Barr 2004: 4). I shall call this approach 'Type I welfare mix'.

It is widely accepted that actors from the public sector, the nonprofit sector, the informal sector and the for-profit sector engage in the provision of welfare. However, many empirical studies on welfare provision omit one or more of these providers. In one extreme case, they focus only on statutory bodies. However, even if private actors are considered, some types are ignored, such as third-sector organizations. For example, Gøsta Esping-Andersen (1990: 21) in his influential study on the three worlds of welfare capitalism, examines only the welfare contributions of the state, the family and the market. The large proportion of statutory funding might justify subsuming nonprofit activity under the statutory sector. However, if a distinction is made between financing, producing and/or delivering welfare (see below), the role of nonprofits becomes substantial in many countries.

According to Johnson (1999: 22f), the crucial consideration of a mixed economy of welfare is not the existence of up to four societal sectors in the welfare market, but the balance between them, which varies (i) between one country and another, (ii) between one time and another, (iii) between one service and another, and (iv) between one component of service and another. In relation to service delivery, Johnson distinguishes between three distinct elements, namely provision, finance and regulation (for the elements of provision adopted for the purpose of this study, see below). Adopting a concept elaborated by Anheier and Seibel (1998), he differentiates between four approaches towards service delivery[16] through public (government), nonprofit (voluntary agencies, self-

[16] Johnson (1999: 23ff) only considers welfare services in his assessment. Clearly, and as discussed in Section I.2.1, other in-kind goods and cash transfers are also relevant welfare, and indeed poverty relief, instruments.

regulated associations) and for-profit sectors (commercial providers, markets) (see table 6).

Table 6: Ideal-type approaches to service delivery

Approach	Provision*	Finance	Regulation
State-oriented	Government	Public sources	Government
Traditional mixed economy	Government Voluntary agencies	Public and private sources	Government Self-regulated associations
Contemporary mixed economy	Government Voluntary agencies Commercial providers	Public and private sources	Government Self-regulated associations Markets
Market-oriented	Commercial providers	Private sources	Markets

*Source: adapted from Johnson (1999: 24) based on Anheier and Seibel (1998); Note: * 'Provision' in this framework is equivalent with the element 'production and/or delivery' adopted in this study (see below).*

In the state-oriented approach, which was common in former communist countries of Central and Eastern Europe, the responsibility for service delivery lies with the public sector. In traditional mixed economies (such as the Netherlands or Germany), the public sector is joined by nonprofits, which rely on both public and private funding sources. For-profits enter the welfare market alongside public and nonprofit actors in the contemporary mixed economy. From the traditional form this model differs in two respects: the relationships are competitive rather than cooperative and roles are not specifically assigned. Examples of this welfare mix approach include Australia, the US, the UK or Japan. Finally, in the market-oriented approach, neither the public nor the nonprofit sector is involved in the provision of welfare, not even in a regulatory role. However, Johnson (1999: 24) admits that not even those most committed to the New Right consider a totally unregulated type of service delivery.

While Johnson differentiates between three sectors of a mixed economy of welfare, Gidron *et al.* (1992) focus on the relations between public and nonprofit organizations in (welfare) provision only, thus omitting the informal and the for-profit sector. However, it is mainly public and nonprofit organizations that are relevant in providing poverty relief instruments (on the role of the other two sectors in poverty relief, see Section I.2.2), which justifies including this model here. Gidron *et al.* (1992) distinguish between four models of relationship between these two types of actors, based on the theoretical division between the finance and the production of welfare instruments (see table 7).

Table 7: Models of relationships between public and nonprofit organizations

Models / Functions	Public sector dominant	Nonprofit sector dominant	Dual	Collaborative
Production	public	nonprofit	public / nonprofit	nonprofit
Finance	public	nonprofit	public / nonprofit	public

Source: adapted from Gidron et al. (1992: 18)

In the 'public sector dominant model', both finance and production of welfare are taken on predominantly by the state, whereas nonprofits play a minor role in society. In the 'nonprofit sector dominant model', third-sector organizations dominate both the finance and production of welfare. Both of these concepts are thus based on single-sector provision. In the 'dual model', both state and third-sector organizations finance and produce welfare instruments. Clearly, in a world with more than only two societal sectors, the dual model becomes a multi-sector model. Thus, I suggest renaming this model 'multi-sector provision'. Multi-sector provision may or may not involve differences between actors from different societal sectors in terms of the products they provide and/or the clients they target. If there are differences the result is product differentiation and/or client differentiation. For example, nonprofits might concentrate on the delivery of social services within a country, while the public sector specializes in providing cash transfers. This is product differentiation. Similarly, the public sector might target large population groups, while nonprofits concentrate on specific population groups only, such as religious fundamentalists. As mentioned earlier, it is often argued that the specific demands of these marginal groups might be neglected by government provision, if they do not represent the preferences of the median voters. This makes a case for nonprofit provision (see also Section I.2.2.4). This is called client differentiation.

Cooperation is vital for the 'collaborative model' in the framework described by Gidron *et al.*, which is commonly found in the conservative welfare states in Europe, and indeed also in the social services sector in Austria (Schneider *et al.* 2007). According to this model, public and private organizations share the task of providing a specific welfare instrument, i.e. there is joint provision. For example, public and nonprofit actors may agree that the former fund a social service that the latter deliver. Often, these forms of joint provision are termed 'public-private partnerships' (see, for example, Budäus and Grüning 1997: 46ff), which involve different types of collaboration – ranging from principal-agent models to bargaining models (see below).

To summarize: the first approach towards the 'mixed economy of welfare' presumes that actors from different public and private societal sectors engage side-by-side or jointly in the provision of welfare. In the framework developed by Johnson (1999), this refers to the 'traditional mixed economy' and the 'contemporary mixed economy'. In the framework put forward by Gidron *et al.* (1992) this applies to the dual model (renamed here as multi-sector provision) and the collaborative model (renamed here as joint provision). Table 8 sketches these two categories of Type I welfare mix.

Table 8: Categories of Type I welfare mix

Categories	Explanation
Multi-sector provision	Actors from at least two societal sectors engage in the provision of welfare (in case of differentiated provision: product differentiation and/or client differentiation)
Joint provision	Actors from at least two societal sectors provide welfare jointly, i.e. they share the tasks of providing a welfare product

Source: own illustration

Type I welfare mix is thus primarily concerned with the following issues: which actors engage in welfare provision and which tasks (such as funding, production, etc.) do they perform in case of joint provision? Consequently, preconditions for this first approach towards a 'welfare mix' are (i) the existence of a range of actors from different societal sectors, and – in the case of joint provision – (ii) the possibility to split different tasks of provision (such as funding, production, regulation) between actors. Potential outcomes of a specific balance of Type I welfare mix are – in the event of multi-sector provision – similarities and/or differences concerning welfare measures supplied or groups served by actors belonging to different societal sectors. In the event of joint provision, a potential outcome of this first approach towards a 'welfare mix' is a specific division of provisional tasks between welfare actors from different societal sectors (e.g. nonprofits as producers and/or delivers of services and public organizations as financiers). Consequently, a thorough analysis of the concept of 'provision' allows examining the characteristics of 'Type I welfare mix'. The former concept is discussed in more depth in Section 1.2. Prior to that, however, a second group of interpretations of the 'welfare mix' prevalent in the pertinent literature is described and discussed in the following section.

1.1.2 Type II welfare mix

A second group of interpretations of the 'mixed economy of welfare' does not focus – at least *prima facie* – on actors. Rather, it derives from arguments that concentrate on the values, norms and rationales which influence and explain the actions of groups and organizations engaged in welfare provision (e.g. Svetlik 1993). To illustrate this approach, Evers and Laville constructed a welfare triangle consisting of the cornerstones 'market', 'state' and 'community' (see figure 1).

The authors suggest that from "*a socio-political perspective the triangle highlights the plural nature of the resources that contribute to social welfare*" (Evers and Laville 2004: 15). Each of the cornerstones of the triangle represents dominant values. Welfare actors are positioned within this triangle depending on the character of their activities. For example, the dominant value of activities close to the cornerstone 'market' is profit. Thus, actors that engage in welfare activities to make profits would qualify as market actors (or for-profit organizations) – and be positioned at or close to the cornerstone 'market'. The main rationale for activities of actors close to the cornerstone 'state', according to Evers and Laville, is 'redistribution'[17], whereas for the 'community' (i.e. informal actors) it is

[17] Associating this rationale with the state implies a benevolent government. Several economic approaches to behavioural patterns of public actors differ from this view and suggest a utility maximizing behaviour of government agents (e.g. maximizing power, maximizing the likelihood to be re-elected etc.). Further rationales related to the state sector are thus 'power', 'compulsion', but also 'paternalism' or 'universalism' (e.g. Blank 2000: C37). In recent years, moreover, much reference has been made in the literature of a shift from government to governance (e.g. Sarker 2005, Bode 2006). This led to the introduction of new rationales into the state sector, as the often-cited metaphor of a public sector that no longer rows but steers the (welfare) boat

'personal responsibility' or 'reciprocity' (Evers and Laville 2004: 15). In this approach, nonprofits are positioned between different value systems. They have to balance a bundle of values and norms by which actors from the 'private' and the 'public', the 'formal' and the 'informal' and the 'for-profit' and the 'nonprofit' spheres are governed (e.g. Bauer 1993). The aggregate activities of some nonprofits are close to the dominant value of the market, which is why they may be described as 'market-oriented'. The aggregate activities of other nonprofits are closer to the cornerstone of the state, which makes them 'state-oriented'. The activities of yet other third-sector organizations are mainly characterized by values similar to those prevalent in community-based groups. These actors may thus be called 'community-oriented' nonprofits (Zauner 2007: 148ff).

Figure 1: The welfare mix triangle

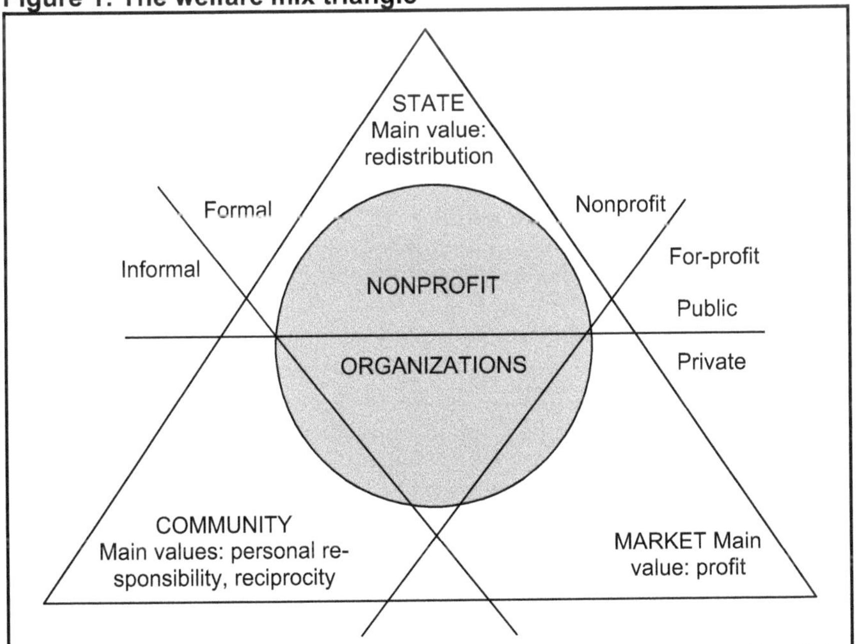

Source: adapted from Evers and Laville (2004: 19)

suggests (e.g. Newman 2004: 73).

However, nonprofits are not the only organizations to act as intermediaries in terms of their value structure. For example, for-profits engaged in corporate social responsibility (Pomper 2007) do not aim to make 'profits' with these actions. Similarly, public actors often apply management methods that are characteristic of for-profits, such as new public management. This involves management principles that consist of several inter-related components (such as increasing the autonomy of public managers, rewarding organizations and individuals on the basis of whether they meet performance targets, introducing competitive elements[18] in contracting etc.), and imitates features prevalent in for-profit organizations. Thus, the governance structure of public and for-profit organizations may be mixed as well – in the sense that most of their activities are state-oriented or market-oriented, while some are not. Whereas single actions of organizations follow one main rationale or norm, the aggregate of actions, and thus the character of the actor, is the complex result of a combination of different and sometimes conflicting values. Consequently, Evers (1993: 21) suggests to conceptualize organizations governed by multiple values as 'hybrid' or 'polyvalent organizations' (see also Evers 2005). For him, these intermediate types of organizations represent "*mixes in the welfare mix*" (Evers 1993: 21). Clearly, focusing on norms and values, rather than on, for example, legal forms or ownership structures, makes it more difficult to cluster organizations unequivocally into societal sectors. Kramer (2004: 220) even proposes to refrain from classification of organizations into sectors altogether.

The values, norms and rationales allow to understand why actors engage in the provision of welfare. However, these values, norms and rationales also determine (i) how actors engaged in the 'welfare market' complete their tasks and (ii) how they cooperate with their partners in case of joint provision. This implies that welfare providers have different options in complying with provision and in contracting with their partners. The very options chosen not only reflect, but also shape the norms, values and rationales by which welfare actors are governed (see figure 2).

---

[18] Instead of competition, contestability is a valid concept to enhance efficiency in markets. Characteristics of perfect contestability are the complete absence of any barriers to market entry and exit, and perfect information of both providers and demanders. Contestability might denote a middle way between planning (i.e. regulation) and competition (Johnson 1999: 94f).

Figure 2: Relationship between 'why' and 'how' actors provide welfare

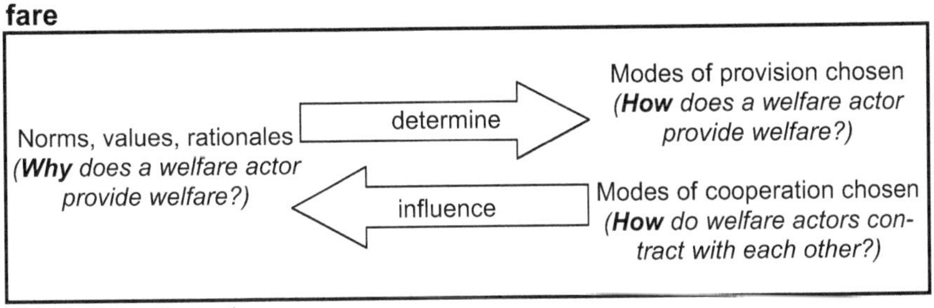

Source: own illustration

This study is interested in the specific mix concerning both (i) the modes of provision employed by welfare actors as well as (ii) the modes of cooperation chosen in case of joint provision (which is henceforth termed 'Type II welfare mix') – rather than in the combination of norms, values and rationales by which they are governed. This does not imply, however, that the latter need not be considered. Norms, values and rationales are particularly relevant when the characteristics of Type II welfare mix, and thus the modes of provision selected and/or the modes of cooperation chosen, change over time. Different actors, even though they may follow different rationales, may end up choosing the same modes of provision and contracting. For example, a welfare actor's decision to offer a social service (such as a child care facility) instead of cash transfer (such as a childcare allowance) may be based on different motivations, reaching from paternalistic attitudes (e.g. restricting the users' choice in terms of who takes care of children) towards more liberal attitudes (e.g. establishing a child care market and thereby increasing the choice for users). Thus, an understanding of changes of Type II welfare mix (and thus changes in the modes of provision chosen and/or the modes of cooperating in case of joint provision), necessitates assessing the motivations that have led to these shifts.

While one precondition for Type I welfare mix is the existence of a range of different types of welfare actors, one precondition for Type II welfare mix is the existence of different options actors have in providing welfare and in contracting. Most notably, welfare actors have to choose (i) which clients to target, (ii) which types of welfare transfers to provide, (iii) how to organize and administer the provision of transfers, and/or – in case of joint provision – (iv) how to cooperate with the contracting partner.

Which options do welfare actors have in complying with the very modes of provision and in cooperating with their contracting partners? In terms of targeting clients, different options are available, ranging from targeting through attributed needs towards targeting through means-tested needs (Gilbert 2001). For a more detailed description of these and other design options, see Section 1.2.3. Regarding welfare instruments, welfare actors have the choice of providing bounded or unbounded cash transfers, in-kind goods or services (see Section I.2.1). They decide whether benefits are granted for a limited time only or unlimited. They decide on the degree of user participation (e.g. in terms of financing services), etc. Regarding the organization and administration of provision, welfare actors have different options (i) to produce and/or deliver welfare instruments (e.g. in terms of how they handle excess demand), and (ii) to finance welfare transfers (e.g. whether they rely on, for example, donations or request fees from users).

In case of joint provision, cooperating partners have to decide on the very stipulations of the contract, which also determine the distribution of decision-making powers between the two partners. A multitude of concepts has been forwarded in the literature to circumscribe different forms of cooperation between public and third-sector organizations. For example, Johnson (1999: 152ff) differentiates between the 'parallel bar theory', the 'extension ladder theory' and 'partnership theories' to describe relationships between the two sectors[19]. It is also possible to conceptualize contractual relationships as being ranked on a continuum between two extreme forms, namely a principal-agent relationship and an equal partnership (see table 9). At one extreme, cooperation may denote a liaison by the two actors, in which nonprofits simply fulfil the tasks entrusted to them by public bodies. In this model, which is of a principal-agent type (e.g. Kräkel 1999), nonprofits are viewed by the state as decentralized agencies, which fully depend on their principal. They are not attributed any decision-making power by the principal (e.g. as to which clients to target or which products to provide), but rather function like a prolonged arm of the state or a "*third party government*" (Salamon 1995: 18). Nonprofit actors' dependence on their public principal is thus complete and not limited to the receipt of public resources. Rather, the state also decides on nonprofit production and/or delivery by, for example, determin-

[19] For further models of relationships between public and nonprofit actors, see, for example, Young (1999, 2000) or Galaskiewicz and Sinclair Colman (2006).

ing what to produce, which clients to target, what prices to set, etc. Depending on complete or incomplete contracts on which principal-agent relationships are based, the principal may more or less rely on the agent. Especially in the case of incomplete contracting (see also Shleifer 1998), there are specific problems of the so-called 'contract state' with regard to regulating the agent. In this context, Johnson (1999: 89) suggests that regulation is (i) time-consuming and costly, (ii) difficult to police as evasion is always possible, (iii) difficult to devise and to appropriately sanction, and (iv) difficult to balance (between too little and too much regulation).

Table 9: Cooperation between public and nonprofit providers: the two extremes

Nonprofit organizations as agents of the public sector	Nonprofit organizations as partners of the public sector
Principal-agent relationship or: third-party government	Equal partnership
e.g. public actors (co-)finance transfers, nonprofits produce or deliver them Public actors have decision-making power	e.g. public actors (co-)finance transfers, nonprofits produce or deliver them Decision-making power is either shared by public and nonprofit actors or obtained by nonprofits

Source: adapted from Heitzmann (2004c)

At the other extreme of cooperative relationships, public and third-sector organizations perceive each other as – more or less – equal partners. While the division of labour may still be the same as in the traditional principal-agent model, decision-making power is distributed more equally between the two actors or obtained by nonprofits. If the first type of partnership is of a 'principal-agent' type, this form of relationship may be termed 'equal partnership'. Whereas nonprofits are financed by the public sector (and thus depend on the statutory partner), they have some or full autonomy regarding decision-making powers. Nonprofits decide (either alone or together with the public financier) which and how much of an instrument to produce or deliver. They choose (again: either alone or together with the public financier) how to produce or deliver these measures. Nonprofits may decide (again: either alone or together with the public financier) who should get welfare benefits and how much each individual should get. The liberty granted to nonprofits may also include the freedom to create and implement innovative programmes without (or without much) public interference. Some authors even stress that the right of nonprofits to be innovative, experimental and irrational is their main function in society (e.g. Seibel 1992, 1997). Governments as well as bureaucracies often refrain from this innovative function in the welfare market – as their power depends, either directly or indirectly, on re-election, which might be jeopardized in case of obvious failures. Thus, there is some rationale for public actors to entrust nonprofits with high-risk tasks.

In between these two extreme forms of cooperation there is a wide range of intermediate forms. A variety of these characterizes the collaborative relationships between the national and local governments and third-sector organizations. It is the collaborative contract between the two actors that usually stipulates the conditions of the agreement, and thus the distribution of decision-making powers between the contracting partners. Johnson (1999: 73) stresses the differences in contracting across countries. For example, contracts in the UK are very detailed, whereas in France they are very brief and loosely defined. This implies a different relationship between purchasers and providers. In Sweden, three different forms of contracts have been identified, i.e. (i) the 'mixed market model', in which private producers and/or deliverers may be selected by the users; (ii) the 'public competition model', in which the choice of private producers and/or deliverers is restricted to public providers, and finally the (iii) voucher model (Johnson 1999: 73).

The stipulations of contracts in case of joint provision have implications on the functions of nonprofits, their organizational form, their degree of independence and, finally, their accountability. Contracts specify which transfers to provide, how much of these transfers to provide, which clients to target (and how) and at what cost (Johnson 1999: 194). For both public and nonprofit actors, moreover, contract compliance may be expensive and time-consuming (Johnson 1999: 194).

As has become clear from the discussion so far, a thorough analysis of welfare provision allows to capture the main building blocks of Type II welfare mix. Depending on the choices made concerning the provision of welfare (including the elements of production/delivery, finance and decision-making), provision by public and nonprofit actors may be either different or similar. Moreover, depending on both the modes of provision and the modes of cooperation applied, it is likely that welfare actors from different sectors become more alike (i.e. hybridization of welfare actions and actors).

Prior to introducing the concept of 'provision' in the following section, the two different approaches towards the welfare mix distinguished within this study, i.e. Type I and Type II welfare mix are summarized and contrasted in table 10.

Table 10: Type I and Type II welfare mix: preconditions, main issues, potential outcomes

Type I welfare mix
Precondition: Range of different types of welfare actors, possibility to split different tasks of provision between welfare actors Main issue: Who provides (what part of) welfare? Potential outcome: Division of labour regarding clients targeted and/or products supplied between actors from different societal sectors; in case of joint provision: division of labour with regard to the specific tasks taken over by actors from different societal sectors
Type II welfare mix
Precondition: Different options to provide welfare, different options to contract in case of joint provision Main issues: How are welfare clients targeted?; Which welfare instruments are provided?; How do welfare actors fulfil their tasks in provision? In case of joint provision: How do contracting partners cooperate? Potential outcome: Homogeneity or heterogeneity concerning the modes of provision applied across different welfare actors; hybridization of welfare actors from different societal sectors

Source: own illustration

The following section discusses the constituting elements of both interpretations of the welfare mix, i.e. the concept of provision. It first examines approaches towards the concept of provision prevalent in the literature. Second, I introduce a concept of provision elaborated for the purpose of this study. This concept consists of the elements (i) production and/or delivery, (ii) finance and (iii) provider decisions.

1.2 The concept of 'provision'

A key characteristic of Type I and Type II welfare mix is that public and private actors engage in the provision of welfare instruments. In case of joint provision, they even share the responsibility of providing specific welfare transfers. A fundamental requirement for such a division of labour is that the provision of these instruments may be split into several distinct elements. Some authors differentiate between two components of provision, namely finance (or: purchase) and production (e.g. Kolderie 1986, Gidron *et al.* 1992). Others set apart more pieces (e.g. Le Grand and Robinson 1984: 3, Burchardt 1997: 3, Barr 2004: 89ff). For example, Burchardt (1997: 3) adds 'decision' to the conventional split between provision and finance[20]. At the core of this element is the question of who makes the purchase decision. Two aspects are particularly relevant in this respect. The first involves the choice of the provider (i.e. the decision of who selects the provider), the second aspect refers to the choice of the (level of the) transfer (i.e. the decision of who selects the level of the welfare instrument received). Burchardt (1997: 3), while she admits that the "*distinction between public and private decision-making power is a fuzzy one*", justifies the selection of the element 'decision' in relation to potential alternative elements, such as 'regulation', by arguing that 'decision' allows (i) to see how different mechanisms to deliver welfare are related, and (ii) to portray the development of welfare policy as shifts from public towards private provision (Burchardt 1997: 9f).

A somewhat different approach to capture the concept of 'provision' is adopted by Barr (2004: 90), who insists that, in addition to finance and production as distinct elements of provision, regulation too has to be taken into account. Nullmeier (2003b: 965) emphasizes three functions of regulation, namely (i) its competitive function (i.e. regulations should hamper the foundation of monopolies and guarantee fair competition); (ii) its function to guarantee a certain quality standard in provision (which is especially relevant regarding the provision of social services); and (ii) its function to stabilize markets (which indeed allows consumers/clients to trust (market) activities and actors).

The concept of 'regulation' is structured and interpreted in various different ways in the literature (e.g. Knieps 2001). Nowotny (1999: 212ff), for example, differentiates between outside regulation (*Außenregulierung*) and inside regulation (*Innenregulierung*). The former type comprises

[20] The terminology relating to the different elements of provision differs in the literature. For example, Burchardt (1997: 5f) uses the term 'provision' to refer to the element that I call 'production and/or delivery' (see Section 1.2.1). She views 'finance' and 'decision' as two parts that make up the element 'purchase'.

public regulations of private companies, while the latter refers to direct market interventions, e.g. when the public sector owns and runs companies. In his model of provision, Barr (2004: 90) distinguishes between two types of regulation. The first involves decisions on the total quantity produced of a good. The second type refers to decisions on how much each individual consumer should receive (the latter aspect is thus similar to the concept of 'decision' forwarded by Burchardt). Barr (2004: 91) illustrates the complexity of a mixed economy (interpreted as Type I welfare mix) considering the four components of provision he distinguishes (see table 11). Obviously, the table would become much more complex, if a more detailed differentiation were applied with regard to (i) the types of societal actors engaged (i.e. informal actors, for-profit organizations, nonprofit organizations and public organizations) and (ii) the different levels at which these actors operate (e.g. public organizations of the local, the regional, the national or the supranational level might engage jointly in the provision of a specific welfare product).

With reference to the dual concept towards the welfare mix elaborated so far, I propose to adopt a somewhat different approach to distinguish elements of provision for the purpose of this study. First, I adopt the conventional split between the elements (i) production and (ii) finance, although I rename the element 'production' into 'production and/or delivery'. While goods need to be both produced and delivered (these tasks might be taken over by actors from different societal sectors), social services are 'produced' (in the sense of 'made') and 'delivered' (in the sense of 'handed over to consumers or users') at the same time by the same actor. As for cash transfers, the focus is also on the organization that delivers the transfer (rather than the organizations that produce the money, i.e. coins and banknotes). Second, I propose to add a third dimension, which I term (iii) 'provider decisions'. This element involves several separate decisions, including: 'who (i.e. in the case of this study: public or nonprofit welfare providers) decides which clients to target, and which decisions have been made in this respect?', 'who decides which welfare products to provide, and which decisions have been made in this respect?', and: 'who decides how to provide welfare, and which options have been chosen in this respect?'.

Table 11: Public and private provision according to the concept of Barr (2004)

Type of allocation	Production	Regulation		Finance	Examples*
		Decision about total production	Decision about individual consumption		
1. Pure private	Private	Private	Private	Private	Food purchased out of non-transfer income
2. Private market plus state finance (income subsidy)	Private	Private	Private	Public	Consumption of privately produced goods purchased of transfers, e.g. food stamps
3a. Private market plus regulation of individual consumption	Private	Private	Public	Private	Mandatory automobile insurance
3b. Private market plus regulation of total provision	Private	Public	Private	Private	Health care (Canada, approx.)
4a. Private production, state regulation and finance; provision wholly private	Private	Private	Public	Public	Education vouchers
4b. Private production, state regulation and finance; total provision determined by the state	Private	Public	Public	Public	Inputs for NHS and national defence
5a. Public production, private allocation and finance; total provision determined by private demand	Public	Private	Private	Private	Public transport

5b. Public production, private allocation and finance; provision wholly public	Public	Public	Private	Private	NHS pay bed
6.Public apart from private finance	Public	Public	Public	Private	National insurance (UK)
7.Public apart from private consumption decision	Public	Public	Private	Public	Post-compulsory education
8. Pure public	Public	Public	Public	Public	NHS, national defence

*Source: Barr (2004: 91, Table 4.1). Notes: * Examples are only approximate; they are drawn from the UK*

There are several reasons to introduce 'provider decisions' as a distinct element of provision instead of relying on similar elements of provision suggested by other researchers, such as Burchardt and Barr. For example, in contrast to the concept of 'decision' elaborated by Burchardt, the element 'provider decisions' introduced in this study focuses on the decision-making powers of welfare providers only. It does not consider the decisions taken by the consumers or users of welfare products, given that the latter are not at the core of the 'welfare mix' examined in this study. In contrast to the dual concept of regulation forwarded by Barr, 'provider decisions' is not only interested in eligibility criteria for transfers (which is a concept broadly similar to Barr's regulation of individual consumption). It also focuses on the choices made by the providers in terms of clients targeted and products provided as well as the specific modes of provision applied by them – which are all important characteristics of Type II welfare mix. In what follows, the three elements of provision are described in more depth.

1.2.1 The element of 'production and/or delivery'

An important component of provision is 'production and/or delivery'. 'Production' involves the physical making of goods and services using inputs, such as labour or capital. A production function reproduces the relationship between (fixed and/or variable) inputs employed in a given period of time and the quantity of the good or service that can thereby be produced (e.g. Mansfield and Yohe 2000: 198ff, Varian 2003: 320ff). Examples of welfare instruments produced in such a way include in-kind goods, such as a soup that is produced for a soup kitchen, or meals that are prepared for 'Meals on Wheels'. The production, delivery and consumption of in-kind goods usually take place consecutively. Thus, production and delivery might be a responsibility of different actors. For example, meals for 'Meals on Wheels' may be produced by (public, nonprofit or for-profit) hospitals but delivered by other (public, nonprofit or for-profit) social service organizations.

As discussed previously, personal social services follow the *uno actu* principle (see Section I.2.1.2), which implies that production, delivery and consumption of such goods occur simultaneously (Badelt and Österle 2001a: 90). In this study, I use the term 'delivery' (in the narrow sense described above) to imply this synchronism of production and delivery (as well as consumption). Indeed the notion of 'production' may be misleading in case of cash transfers (see above). Hence, this monograph uses the notion of 'production and/or delivery' to circumscribe this element of provision.

A crucial question regarding **Type I welfare mix** refers to the issue of who produces and/or delivers which share of welfare transfers. The range of potential actors producing in-kind goods and/or delivering cash transfers or social services to welfare recipients, which includes public and nonprofit actors, has been discussed earlier (see Section I.2.2).

The key issue in examining **Type II welfare mix** is how welfare transfers are provided. This requires identifying the different options welfare providers have in this respect. In the context of production and/or delivery, it is important to distinguish between the targeting design of a welfare transfer (which is a crucial issue of the element 'provider decisions'; see below) and the administration of its production and/or delivery. While eligibility criteria determine who has access to welfare transfers, the administration of their production and/or delivery determines the 'quality' of the products provided[21]. In this study, I am interested in the type of 'quality' that ultimately may affect utilization rates of welfare transfers (van Oorschot 1991, Riphahn 2001). This refers to the fact that even if specific groups or individuals have formal access to benefits they might not (be able to) utilize them (e.g. Heitzmann *et al.* 2002: 28f). Reasons for non-take-up include stigmatizing effects of benefits, the location or the timing of delivery as well as insufficient user information. For example, individuals who are not aware of transfers to which they are entitled to will not utilize them. Specific hospitals, health care centres or universities are often only available in major urban centres – a geographic constraint that makes it difficult for the rural population to access these services. Similarly, if the quantity demanded of a specific transfer exceeds the quantity supplied, the result might be a shortage and some form of rationing. Also, the very administration of transfer applications (e.g. is it possible to apply for a specific transfer online or is it necessary to show up personally at a specific agency?; how 'bureaucratic' is the application procedure for a specific transfer?; do opening hours of agencies make it easy or difficult for clients to turn to these agencies?, etc.) might nega-

---

[21] For differences regarding quality aspects of goods and services, see Blank (2000) and Jordan (2005).

tively affect utilization rates. Potential stigmatizing effects of benefit delivery may derive from disdainful procedures applied in determining eligibility or from disdainful procedures adopted in controlling compliance with eligibility criteria.

To sum up, for an assessment of Type I and Type II welfare mix regarding the element of 'production and/or delivery' it is important to examine (i) who produces and/or delivers (which share of) welfare transfers, and (ii) how welfare actors administer production and/or delivery. The latter covers procedures adopted in terms of transfer applications, in terms of the actual delivery of transfers and in terms of controlling compliance after delivery. The very modes of production and/or delivery chosen determine the 'quality' of production and/or delivery, i.e. the take-up rate of benefits. In what follows, a further element of provision – 'finance' – is discussed.

1.2.2 The element of 'finance'

'Finance' and 'production/delivery' are two distinct parts of provision. This does not only apply to goods and social services, but also to cash transfers. Often, the organization that finances a cash transfer also delivers it. In some cases, however, finance and delivery may be split. This is the case, for example, with regard to assistance for asylum seekers in Austria. Nonprofits are in charge of providing them with delivering statutory benefits (*Grundversorgung*), even though these benefits are fully financed by the state. Consequently, it is necessary to distinguish between finance and delivery also with regard to cash transfers.

Who funds the welfare transfers that are produced and/or delivered by public or nonprofit actors? Answering this question is relevant to identify **Type I welfare mix**. Burchardt (1997: 6f) differentiates between public and private finance in this respect. Funding sources qualify as public if they derive directly from the public budget, for example, from general taxation or earmarked taxation (e.g. social insurance contributions). If a public actor finances a service that is delivered by a nonprofit actor, the purchaser has several options. First, it might simply grant a subsidy to the nonprofit partner and rely on the mission being fulfilled by the latter. Second, it might fund the partner according to performance-related indicators, which are stipulated in the contracting agreement. A third option is to shift purchasing powers to the users of the service, who then decide from which providers to buy goods or services[22]. This is the standard voucher model, in which the government provides some redistribution of income among potential recipients, but the recipients themselves contract for services in private markets (Blank 2000: C38). Whereas the first two options qualify as public funding, the third option is defined as a private source in this study.

Further forms of private funding include membership fees, service fees or user charges, or other forms of commercial income (e.g. resources gained through merchandising or lotteries, etc.). An important way to finance welfare transfers delivered by nonprofits is to solicit donations (Hansmann 1987a: 39). This may involve both private giving from individuals (i.e. the informal sector) or corporate giving (i.e. the means derive from the for-profit sector). A further specific form of income-generating behaviour commonly used by nonprofits is cross-subsidization. This implies that one service is produced and sold by the organization at a profit, which is then used to finance provision of another service (e.g. Toepler 2006). All of these forms of finance are defined as private finance for the purpose of this study.

In many instances, nonprofits engaged in the provision of welfare are financed by a combination of both public and private sources. Since these sources are not always dedicated to specific purposes it may be difficult, and sometimes indeed impossible, to identify which funds have been used to finance a specific welfare transfer.

In contrast to Type I welfare mix, **Type II welfare mix** is primarily interested in the specific composition of the budget (i.e. the funding portfolio of providers), which also has repercussions on the resource management of the welfare actor (e.g. Bode 2006: 350ff). In this context, it is not the issue of 'who' funds the budget (which is a crucial issue to determine Type I welfare mix), but in which form it is funded. The specific types of funding sources chosen by welfare actors reflect their attitudes towards issues such as cost sharing between providers and users. For example, a nonprofit actor that relies on private funding sources can choose be-

[22] This is why Burchardt (1997: 3) differentiates between 'finance' and 'decision'. The latter aspect concentrates on the issue of who (i.e. the state or the consumer) decides on the purchase.

tween charging users of services and relying on donations – both of which are forms of private funding, albeit with different implications for the clients served.

1.2.3 The element of 'provider decisions'

'Provider decisions' is introduced here as a distinct element of welfare provision. This concept involves several decisions: (i) 'who decides which clients to target?'; (ii) 'who decides which welfare products to provide?'; (iii) 'who decides on the modes of production and/or delivery of provision?'; (iv) 'who decides on the composition of funding sources?'; (v) 'which decisions have welfare actors made in terms of clients targeted?'; and: (vi) 'which decisions have welfare actors made in terms of welfare products supplied?'.

Answers to the first four questions allow to identify the characteristics of Type I welfare mix (i.e. 'who decides?'), while Type II welfare mix may be identified by answering the two latter questions (i.e. 'which decisions have been made?')[23].

To understand **Type I welfare mix** it is thus crucial to examine who decides (i) which clients to target, (ii) which products to provide, (iii) how to produce/deliver the welfare products and (iv) how to finance the transfers. It is important to stress that answering these questions is particularly relevant (as well as difficult) in case of joint provision, i.e. when actors from at least two societal sectors share the task of providing a specific welfare product. In case of multi-sector provision (see Section 1.1.1), the actor that finances and produces/delivers a welfare transfer also makes the provider decisions. In case of joint provision, however, the distribution of the decision-making power between the cooperating partners becomes vital. It may be the actor financing a transfer that also decides which clients to target and/or which products to provide. However, these decisions may also be taken by the actor who produces and/or delivers the transfer. Similarly, the financier and the producer/deliverer may decide jointly on these issues, or they may agree

[23] Answers to the questions: 'which decisions have welfare actors made in terms of producing and/or delivering welfare?', and: 'which decisions have welfare actors made in terms of the composition of funding sources?' are discussed as part of the elements 'production and/or delivery' and 'finance' (see above).

that one actor determines the targeting criteria and the other one chooses the types of transfers that should be supplied, i.e. dual decision-making.

Whatever the agreement, its details are usually stipulated in the contract regulating the cooperation between organizations from different societal sectors. If the agreement is of a principal-agent type (see Section 1.1.2), it is likely that the financier – mostly the state – maintains the decision-making powers. If the two contractors are equal partners, (some of the) decision-making power might be shifted towards the delivery agency. A more equal distribution of decision-making power might, for example, apply to forms of joint provision, in which nonprofits are financed by the state through grants rather than performance-related payments, as contracts based on grants usually leave more autonomy to nonprofits (Zauner *et al.* 2006). Performance-related payments are often agreed under contracts that are the result of public procurement processes (Holoubek *et al.* 2007). These processes not only lead to increased competition between producers/deliverers, but also entail very detailed contracts with less autonomy left to the contractor (Zauner *et al.* 2006, Schneider and Trukeschitz 2007a).

As discussed previously, **Type II welfare mix** focuses on the actual choices made by welfare providers. Regarding 'provider decisions', this involves two features, namely: (i) 'which income poor groups have welfare providers chosen to target?', and: (ii) 'which welfare products have welfare providers chosen to provide?'. As these questions imply, welfare actors have different options concerning these decisions, which are discussed in the following paragraphs.

Regarding products supplied, welfare actors e.g. have the choice between delivering (bounded or unbounded) cash transfers, goods or social services. As discussed previously, unbounded cash transfers allow the recipient of the transfer to decide how to use the money received. Bounded cash transfers, in-kind transfers and services restrict this choice. In the most extreme case, the recipient can only choose to take-up the transfer or not. Thus, the decision on the type of transfer granted reflects providers' values and norms in terms of whether they want users to have some choice or not.

In terms of clients targeted, welfare actors can choose between a rather universal approach (in case of poverty relief this would involve targeting all income poor within a nation state) or a selective approach (e.g. providing transfers to a specific group of the income poor only, such as migrants, homeless people or single mothers, or limiting transfers to a specific region only). A variety of different targeting options is available to welfare actors, which define – based on these options – eligibility criteria. These criteria stipulate who qualifies for a welfare transfer.

Gilbert (2001: 216ff) differentiates between four different targeting designs, namely attributed need, compensation, diagnostic differentiation and means-tested need (see table 12). Transfers based on attributed need or compensation are targeted to specific groups of the population rather than individuals. In terms of attributed need, the groups targeted share common needs that are defined according to normative standards (e.g. the need for health care). Based on the definition of a common need, the group targeted may cover the total population or selected groups, such as single parents or the elderly. In case of compensation, benefits are targeted to those population groups that have made identifiable social contributions, such as war veterans, or who have made economic contributions, such as social insurance contributors. In addition, people having unfairly suffered harm, such as victims of racism, may be entitled to this type of benefits. In recent years, a variant of the compensatory method has emerged, which focuses not only on past contributions or harms suffered by groups, but also on the current behaviour of individuals. Linking eligibility for social welfare benefits to behavioural criteria is sometimes referred to as 'social engineering'. Through the use of sanctions and incentives welfare recipients are compensated for engaging in socially approved behaviours such as vaccination of their children, getting married, going to work (which is closely linked to the trend towards a workfare state, see Section 1 in the Introduction), or refraining from having additional children while on welfare (Gilbert 2001: 216f).

Transfers based on diagnostic differentiation or on means-tested need are not targeted to groups of the population but to individuals (or families/households). In case diagnostic differentiation is applied, eligibility is conditioned upon professional judgements of individual cases to determine need for social welfare provisions, as in the situation of the physically or mentally impaired. Targeting based on means-tested need is conditioned upon evidence regarding the financial circumstances of individuals, families or households. The means taken into consideration can be limited to income ('income test') or include both income and assets.

Gilbert holds that

> *"(t)hese four approaches to targeting are not mutually exclusive, even though their underlying promises may seem incompatible as, for example in the joint employment of (universally oriented) attributed need and (highly selective) means-tested need. Indeed, various combinations of allocative principles are found in the design of social welfare policies, reflecting the tug, pull, and eventual compromise over competing values." (Gilbert 2001: 218).*

Thus, targeting decisions are based on social values and political considerations, such as cost containment or preferences for certain groups and regions. This also applies to the means test, which is loaded with value judgements and political considerations (Gilbert 2001: 220ff). In this context, Gilbert (2004: 142f) insists that many of the negative effects associated with means-tested transfers are not a consequence of these transfers' very design, but the way they are administered. For example, when the methods of determining eligibility involve intrusive procedures, such as unscheduled home visits, or when interviews to assess income status are conducted in a disdainful manner, stigmatization may be high and take-up of welfare transfers may be low. As has been mentioned earlier, it is therefore important to distinguish between the very design of a transfer (which is a crucial issue within the element of 'provider decisions') and its administration (which forms part of the element 'production and/or delivery').

Table 12: Classification of targeting designs

Targeting design	Targeted at	Eligibility criteria	Examples
Attributed need	Groups	Normative criteria of need	NHS in the UK; benefits for lone parents
Compensation	Groups	Normative criteria for the restoration of equity	Affirmative Action Programmes; benefits for veterans, victims of crime
Diagnostic differentiation	Individuals	Technical diagnostic criteria of need	Benefits for the physically or mentally impaired
Means-tested need	Individuals	Economic criteria of need	Social assistance, income support

Source: based on Gilbert (2001: 216ff)

Through different combinations of the four targeting designs, there is a broad variety of options available to welfare actors in addressing specific clients. The eligibility criteria formulated mirror the targeting option chosen. In case of poverty relief: the choice of the criteria stipulates who of the income poor (groups) are entitled to a specific poverty relief transfer.

So far, this chapter has argued for a dual interpretation of the welfare mix. First, it is vital to understand which actors finance, produce and deliver welfare and which actors are entitled to make provider decisions. Second, it is critical to recognize which options welfare actors have chosen in financing transfers, in producing and/or delivering transfers, in targeting recipients and in providing welfare products. Table 13 summarizes the three elements of provision discussed and includes main features relevant for an identification of Type I and Type II welfare mix.

It is important to recognize that both Type I welfare mix and Type II welfare mix as well as the three elements of provision are intertwined. The actors responsible for each of the tasks in provision influence how or in which mode this task (but also other tasks) are performed. For example, if a welfare transfer produced and delivered by a nonprofit actor is financed by public actors, the latter may have the right to decide which products to produce and/or deliver and which clients to target with these transfers.

In what follows, Section 2 proceeds to discuss what a change of the mixed economy might imply. These changes are discussed against the background of the two types of interpreting a 'welfare mix'.

2. Selected shifts of 'Type I welfare mix' and 'Type II welfare mix'

However the 'mixed economy' and the 'welfare mix' are defined, one of their dominant characteristics during the last three decades has been that they have changed in virtually all areas of social security. A range of research studies accompanied many of these shifts (e.g. Burton 1987, Gurin 1989, Salamon 1993, Mitchell and Zeldes 1996, Kotlikoff *et al.* 1998, Boeßenecker *et al.* 2000, Megginson and Netter 2001, Scheil-Adlung 2001, Powell and Hewitt 2002, van Berkel and van der Aa 2005).

Table 13: The three elements of provision and main features to identify Type I and Type II welfare mix

	Main features of ...	
Elements of provision	**Type I welfare mix**	**Type II welfare mix**
Production and/or delivery	**Who** produces and/or delivers welfare products?	**Which modes of production and/or delivery** are applied?
Finance	Are welfare transfers financed through **public and/or private funding sources**?	**Which types of (public and/or private) funding sources** have been chosen to finance welfare transfers?
Provider decisions	**Who** decides which (group of) clients to target? **Who** decides which type of welfare transfer to provide? **Who** decides how to produce and/or deliver welfare transfers? **Who** decides how to finance welfare provision?	**Which clients** are targeted? (i.e. which eligibility criteria have been applied?) **Which welfare products** are provided?

Source: own illustration

The studies assessed the ideological background of the changes, their economic or political causes, the processes triggering and accompanying shifts, and the implications of the changes for various stakeholders, such as the economy, the public purse, private providers, the recipients of welfare measures, etc. Concepts such as 'welfare change' (e.g. Powell and Hewitt 2002), 'privatization' (e.g. Kamerman and Kahn 1989), 'marketization' (e.g. Ascoli and Ranci 2002c: 230), 'contracting' (e.g. Smith and Lipsky 1993) or 'hybridization' (e.g. Lloyd 2004: 192) have flourished. They circumscribe and conceptualize changes in the mixed economy of welfare (or outcomes of these changes), which have affected many areas of social security. The variety of terminology prevalent in the academic discourse suggests that the concept of a changing welfare mix is far from being clear-cut. It is the aim of this section to shed light on some of the many facets of change in the mixed economy. To achieve this aim, this chapter proceeds as follows: Section 2.1 concentrates on the dominant type of change relevant for Type I welfare mix, i.e. 'privatization'. Section 2.2 then focuses on a specific type of shifts of Type II welfare mix, i.e. 'marketization'.

2.1 The concept of 'privatization'

Much of the literature on social security within the last three decades has been concerned with the (perceived) crisis of the welfare state. Consequently, both political as well as academic elites have been concerned with elaborating and discussing possibilities to overcome the alleged crisis. One approach, which many governments have applied, has been to decrease the role of statutory actors in the provision of welfare while in parallel expanding the role of private provision, or, in other words, to reduce public responsibilities and to increase private responsibilities. It is particularly this type of shift that is of interest for this part of the study. At the core are changes that affect shifts from public sector provision towards provision by nonprofits rather than towards informal actors (who have also been primary addressees of retrenchment policies) or for-profit organizations. The latter have become prominent providers in various areas of welfare such as health care (e.g. Salamon 1993), or in the provision of (private) retirement pensions (Weller 2006). In terms of poverty relief, however, they continue to play a subordinate role.

Usually, the notion of 'privatization' is used to circumscribe shifts of Type I welfare mix that involve a decrease of contributions of the public sector in provision and an increase of private (and indeed nonprofit) responsibilities. Economic approaches towards privatization usually take the perfect market (i.e. the competitive market or for-profit sector) as the standard for judging efficiency and find that public organizations are deficient because they fail to measure up to that standard (e.g. Cullis and Jones 1998: 1f). Apart from cost-containment arguments, opinions on the value of privatization diverge with regard to the quality of the products supplied (Kolderie 1986: 287, Fershtman 1990, Shleifer 1998, Blank 2000). For example, proponents of public production are convinced that privatization means poorer services at higher costs. Proponents of the free market argue that privatization offers better services at lower costs. As mentioned in the introduction, nonprofits, owing to the profit-distributing constraint, are said to be less likely to renounce quality and are thus often a preferred choice in case of privatizing less marketable goods.

The politics of privatization gained wide circulation in the 1980s with the rise of the conservative governments in Great Britain and the USA, even though countries like Germany or Chile have introduced privatization policies much earlier (see, for example, Megginson and Netter 2001). The political movement towards privatization has been accompanied by a variety of scholarly assessments. In what follows, I discuss the concept of privatization in more depth and present various forms of privatization.

What exactly is 'privatization'? Seeking agreement on a single definition of this concept is, according to Schuster (1997: 263) "*an experiment that would be doomed to fail*". 'Privatization' is far from being a straightforward concept. The literature offers many different approaches to describe and categorize various forms of privatization. The definitions offered differ according to the criteria chosen to depict privatization. For example, Vickers and Yarrow (1991: 111f) distinguish between three types of privatization based on an empirical analysis of privatization programmes introduced in different countries: The privatization of competitive firms involves the transfer of state-owned enterprises operating in competitive product markets free from substantial market failures into the private sectors. The privatization of monopolies implies the transfer of state-owned enterprises with substantial market power (e.g. the telecommunication branch) to the private sectors. Finally, privatization also occurred in that the delivery of public services was contracted out to private organizations.

In this latter context, Bendick (1989: 98f) distinguishes between two 'faces of privatization': 'Load shedding' implies that both the means for financing and for producing and/or delivering a service are separated from the government. 'Empowerment' covers arrangements under which government retains some or complete responsibility for funding services while delegating production.

In one of the earliest assessments of 'privatization' in Europe, Le Grand and Robinson (1984: 3) suggest that privatization concerns a decrease of public intervention in at least one of three areas, namely production, finance or regulation. They also suggest that privatization differs in terms of what is proposed instead. While some favour a replacement of the state through for-profit organizations, others suggest to substitute one form of state activity (e.g. production) by another (e.g. regulation or finance), and yet others want to encourage the activity of nonprofits[24] (Le Grand and Robinson 1984: 6).

Based on the result of privatization processes, Trube and Wohlfahrt (2000: 22f) distinguish between three types of privatization. In the first case, parts of the public administration (such as employment services) are outsourced and produced/delivered by private companies, which are, however, founded and owned by the state (*formale Privatisierung*). In the second case, a specific public organization (e.g. a hospital) or a publicly provided service is purchased (often at a symbolic price) by a private company (*materielle Privatisierung*). In the third case, the public administration contracts with private actors who are charged with fulfilling a specific public task (such as delivering a specific social service). However, the state retains the responsibility for some part of provision, e.g. by maintaining decision-making powers and/or by financing provision (*funktionelle Privatisierung*).

[24] This latter focus on nonprofits has been unique (e.g. the contribution by Sugden 1984), given that the theoretical work on this type of organizations at that point of time – also in a comparative perspective – has still been quite limited (see also Section I.2.2.4).

Ascoli and Ranci (2002b: 6ff) present yet another approach to categorize different forms of privatization. Their definition does not derive from the actual results but rather from the objectives of privatization processes. In this context, they distinguish between 'demand-driven' and 'supply-driven privatization'. According to their reasoning, 'demand-driven privatization' includes measures which attempt to redirect demand for services towards private provision. Relevant (statutory) instruments to achieve this aim include regulations and tax allowances for the purchase of private insurances. 'Supply-driven privatization' implies that the state keeps its financial responsibility but aims at modifying the current mix of regulatory tools. According to the authors, measures aimed at expanding the degree of contracting out of state services and at supporting the growth of private providers financed by public programmes fall within this approach.

Within this study, I define, decompose and categorize the concept of privatization with reference to the concepts of (i) Type I welfare mix and (ii) provision (see Sections 1.1.1 and 1.2). This implies that shifts from public towards private provision may affect one, several or all of the three different dimensions of provision. Privatization, or shifts from public towards private actors in the provision of welfare, can thus affect the dimension of production and/or delivery and/or the element of provider decisions. Moreover, shifts from public towards private sources of funding qualify as 'privatization' (see figure 3). Consequently, the definition applied in this study focuses on the likely results of privatization processes (see, for example, Trube and Wohlfahrt 2000) rather than on its potential political or economic objectives (see Ascoli and Ranci 2002b).

Figure 3: The process of privatization

Production and/or delivery	Finance	Provider decisions
Public actor ↓ Private actor	Public sources ↓ Private sources	Public actor ↓ Private actor

Source: own illustration

Complete or 'total privatization' is achieved if all of the components of provision are shifted from public to private actors (or, in the case of finance, from public towards private funding sources). Every shift from 'public' to 'private' within only one or two of the three dimensions is a form of 'partial privatization'. In what follows, I illustrate the different elements of privatization in more depth. The focus is – as in the empirical part of this study – on shifts from public towards nonprofit provision.

2.1.1 The privatization of production and/or delivery

As discussed in Section 1.1.1, the crucial question regarding Type I welfare mix with regard to the element of production and/or delivery refers to the issue of who produces and/or delivers welfare. In recent decades, it has particularly been this element of provision that has become prominent in the context of privatization policies, and thus been in the focus of many research studies (e.g. Smith and Lipsky 1993, Lewis 1994, Deakin 1996, Taylor 2002, Huque 2005, Bifulco and Vitale 2006, Jahn and Ochel 2007, Nisar 2007). The terminology used to describe the privatization of production and/or delivery includes 'contracting', 'sub-contracting' or 'outsourcing' (Smith and Lipsky 1993). The description of the resultant form of the state varies in the literature, including phrases such as 'the enabling state', 'the contract state', 'the entrepreneurial state', or 'the managerial state' (Johnson 1999: 71). All of these suggest that the state keeps some role in provision, be it as a financier or by assuming responsibilities for provider decisions (Bendick 1989: 106). However, in case of total privatization, the role of the public actor in provision ceases to exist.

Figure 4: Shifts that qualify as privatization of production/delivery

Public production/delivery	→	Joint production/delivery (public and nonprofit providers)
Public production/delivery	→	Nonprofit production/delivery
Joint production/delivery (public and nonprofit providers)	→	Joint production/delivery (but: enhancement of nonprofit share)
Joint production/delivery (public and nonprofit providers)	→	Nonprofit production/delivery

Source: own illustration

As figure 4 suggests, several shifts between public and nonprofit actors qualify as privatization of production and/or delivery. For example, governments can purchase specific services from (or, indeed, contract for whole programmes with) nonprofits. Prior to this form of contracting there might have been public production/delivery or already joint production/delivery. Governments may also create private providers where they otherwise do not exist (Smith and Lipsky 1993: 9). For example, hostels for homeless females may be founded by the public sector, yet be organized in the form of a non-public agency. If the state shifts decision-making powers to this new agency and also relies on private funding, this is yet again a form of total privatization.

Assessing past forms of privatizing production and/or delivery from public to nonprofit organizations, Smith and Lipsky (1993: 43ff) regard the 1980s as the 'age of contracting', given the host of evidence they collected for this form of partial privatization for the USA[25]. Contracting has also increased as a form of privatization within social services in European countries (for Germany see, for example, Boeßenecker *et al.* 2000, for the UK see, for example, Smithies 2005).

2.1.2 The privatization of finance

One crucial feature of Type I welfare mix is the question of 'who finances welfare transfers?'. The main issue in terms of privatization is thus whether public sources of finance have been exchanged either completely or partially through private sources (figure 5). This implies that some form of public funding must have characterized the provision or welfare prior to the shift towards privatization.

Different forms of privatization are conceivable in this respect. For example, government can simply stop or reduce financial support for specific products produced and/or delivered by nonprofits. To achieve the latter, subsidies or performance-related payments to third-sector organizations are decreased or – provided the budget needs rise – limited. However, an over-proportional increase of private forms of funding (e.g. through increasing donations, user charges, or enhanced revenues from sales) – and thus a relative decrease of public finance as a proportion of total ex-

---

25 Especially in the USA, however, there has been a considerable increase of contracting between public and for-profit actors.

penditure – is also a potential form of this type of privatization (even though this might not be the result of a deliberate decision to privatize on the part of public agencies). Alternative financiers to the public sector are thus formal actors, such as nonprofit or for-profit organizations, but also consumers or users of services as well as (individual and corporate) donors. Especially in the last decade, user-charges were introduced or raised for a variety of different social and health services (e.g. hospital care, health care, etc.), which supports the hypothesis of a partial privatization concerning this element of provision. This also applies to an increase of fees from sales in various areas of welfare provision (Salamon 1993).

Figure 5: Shifts that qualify as privatization of finance

Public funding	→	Private funding
Public funding	→	Public and private funding
Public and private funding	→	Public and private funding (but: enhancement of private funding share)
Public and private funding	→	Private funding

Source: own illustration

2.1.3 The privatization of provider decisions

Section 2.1.3 introduced the concept of 'provider decisions'. This concept consists of several decisions that can be clustered into two questions, i.e. (i) 'who takes the provider decisions?', and (ii) 'which decisions have been taken?'. As discussed previously, it is the first of the two questions that is significant for identifying Type I welfare mix, while the second question refers to an identification of Type II welfare mix.

Since privatization is studied with regard to changes of Type I welfare mix, developments that involve a shift away from decision-making by public providers and towards decision-making by private actors are at the core of the privatization paradigm. While the state can shift decision-making powers towards nonprofits and for-profit providers as well as users of welfare transfers, this study is interested in shifts from public organizations towards nonprofits only.

Figure 6: Shifts that qualify as privatization of provider decisions

Public decision-making	→	Nonprofit decision-making
Public decision-making	→	Joint decision-making (public and nonprofit providers)
Joint decision-making (public and nonprofit providers)	→	Joint decision-making (but: enhancement of nonprofits' decision-making power)
Joint decision-making (public and nonprofit providers)	→	Nonprofit decision-making

Source: own illustration

As discussed previously, a static assessment of provider decisions is mainly relevant in terms of joint provision, as, in case of a pure public or a pure nonprofit provision, provider decisions are taken by these actors. In a dynamic analysis, however, it is not only joint provision that is crucial (see figure 6). Rather, privatization of provider decisions has occurred if there was a shift from pure public towards nonprofit provision. A shift from pure public provision towards joint provision qualifies as privatization concerning the element of provider decisions If decision making powers have been affected by this shift. Similarly, changes in joint decision-making that have led to a higher degree of nonprofit decision-making qualify as a privatization. Moreover, a development from joint provision, in which the public actor had some decision-making power, towards pure nonprofit provision qualifies as privatization.

In all of the above cases, the public provider gives up or limits decision-making powers regarding the issues of (i) which clients to serve and/or which targeting criteria to apply; (ii) which products to provide, (iii) how to produce and/or deliver welfare products and/or (iv) how to fund provision. Privatization of provider decisions therefore implies a reduction of government control (Starr 1989: 25).

So far, this section has discussed the concept of 'privatization'. Among others, Ascoli and Ranci (2002c: 240ff) suggest that the meaning of privatization has changed within the last decades. While in the 1980s it was associated with a return to market forces, 'privatization' has come to take on a more complex meaning in recent years. Rather than a one-dimensional shift from public towards private responsibilities, privatization policies attempt to restructure the role of the state and of private actors. This implies that the actors themselves change – which is not least mirrored in how they administer provision. This interpretation of a shifting mixed economy is at the core of the following section.

2.2 The concept of 'marketization'

An alternative view of changes of the welfare mix focuses on the pluralization and diversification of the values and rationales which shape the actions of (public and private) welfare providers. From a macro perspective, these shifts in plural welfare systems bring about changes in the roles and responsibilities of all actors participating in the provision of welfare (Svetlik 1993: 33). From an organizational perspective, they bring about changes in the governance structures of the actors involved (e.g. Williamson 1998, Bevir *et al.* 2003, Newman 2004, Evers 2005, Ahonen *et al.* 2006, Bode 2006, de Andrés-Alonso *et al.* 2006). Arguably, the main trend related to these changes and discussed in the literature is the trend towards 'marketization' of welfare provision (e.g. Salamon 1993, Mok 1997, Belfield 2002, Eikenberry and Kluver 2004, van Berkel and van der Aa 2005). This view of interpreting a shifting mix of welfare is not particularly new. Already early studies on the privatization of the welfare state include assessments that stress the increasing relevance of market ethics within organizations that do not belong to the for-profit sector. For example, Walker suggested already in 1984 that

> "(...) *privatisation is not simply a matter of the full transfer of ownership from the state to private enterprise (...). Privatisation may be said to take place when responsibility for a service or a particular aspect of service delivery passes, wholly or in part, to the private sector and when market criteria, such as profit or ability to pay, are used to ration or distribute profits" (Walker 1984: 25).*

In a more recent publication – a comparative study on the provision of social care services –, Ascoli and Ranci (2002a: 230ff) argue that marketization has become a dominant trend with regard to both public and nonprofit provision. They identify two different developments in this respect. First, supply-driven marketization has established greater competition and monitoring of efficiency between the state that finances social services and nonprofits that deliver them. As an example of this trend the authors consider the introduction of management by objectives implemented in both public administrations and in contracts between public and nonprofit organizations across Europe. The general idea behind the introduction of this management concept is to imitate market mechanisms in order to obtain more transparency in the comparative assessment of costs and results, as well as to encourage business type behaviour of nonprofits.

Another example of supply-driven marketization is the change from grants to contracts as a means of state funding. There is a tendency towards new performance-related contracts in which the individual components of a service are considered as products. Moreover, costs are reimbursed and services are delivered according to strict criteria established *ex ante*. These criteria also include procedures for assessing results.

A further example of supply-driven marketization mentioned by Ascoli and Ranci (2002a) is the introduction of tendering for state funding. European Union legislation has made tendering for government contracts compulsory, if contracts exceed certain monetary thresholds. The expected effects of tendering are an increase of both transparency and efficiency in the procedures for selecting and controlling private contracting partners. A precondition for tendering is that there are enough potential producers or deliverers to allow for some competition. However, even when competition occurs, resorting to tendering does not always guarantee the expected results. This is the case, for example, if public agencies fail to monitor costs and the quality of results purchased from their private partners, which made many governments shift purchasing (and monitoring) power to final consumers. This process, which is called demand-driven marketization, introduces competition and monitoring of results by the final beneficiaries of services (not least through the introduction of vouchers, which shift the purchasing power towards the beneficiaries of a service).

According to Ascoli and Ranci (2002a), the trend towards marketization thus concerns (i) new management forms implemented in both public agencies and nonprofit organizations, (ii) new contractual relationships between these two types of actors, and (iii) new (contractual) relationships between the providers and the final beneficiaries of welfare instruments. Salamon (1993: 17) describes the 'marketization of welfare' more generally as a penetration of essentially market-type relationships into the social welfare arena.

The implementation of market principles in the provision of welfare and in contracting arrangements also leads to important changes in the way how nonprofits are perceived: they are increasingly considered as 'real enterprises'. Much earlier, Le Grand and his collaborators forwarded a concept to circumscribe this specific outcome, which they termed 'quasi-markets' (e.g. Le Grand and Bartlett 1993, Bartlett *et al.* 1994). Prior to that, Bosanquet (1984: 64ff) already introduced the concept of a 'mixed enterprise', which circumscribes an organizational type that no longer represents the 'old-style' state organization, but a hybrid actor in terms of its functions (providing public goods) and the resources it obtains (private and public funds).

Figure 7: The processes of marketization and hybridization

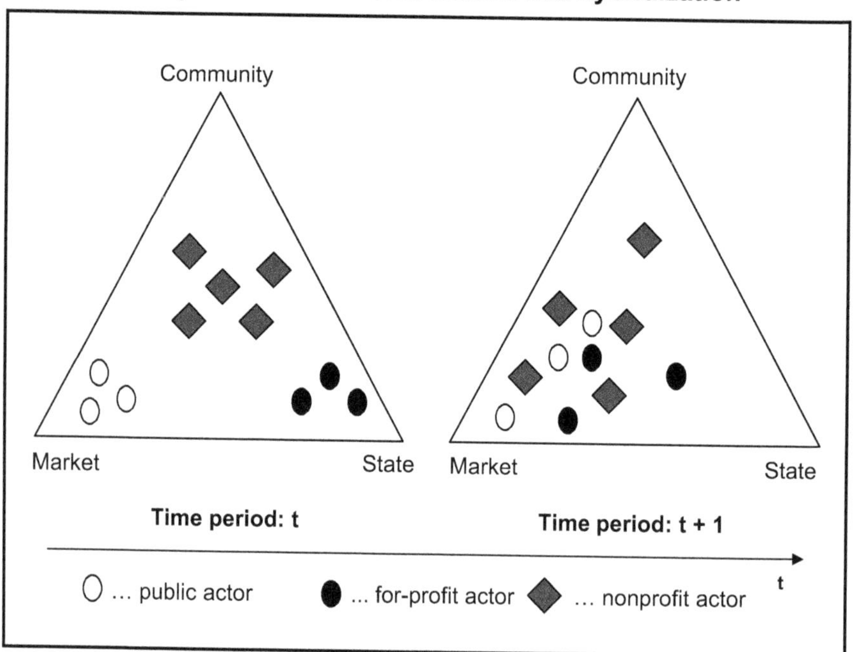

Source: own illustration

Indeed, 'hybridization' is one of the potential outcomes of 'marketization' (e.g. Evers 2003, Kramer 2004, Evers 2005): Organizations from the public and third sector function more like for-profits, as they all implement market ethics in their management, their cooperation and/or the administration of their provision. This makes it difficult to differentiate clearly between 'public' and 'private' actors. The developments thus lead to increasingly fuzzy boundaries between sectors – if they are characterized by their main norms rather than, for example, their ownership structure (e.g. Evers and Laville 2004: 14ff). Instead of distinct organizational types governed by one dominant norm, hybrids develop that follow a set of diverse norms (a development already relevant for nonprofits, if they are interpreted as intermediaries between different value systems, see figure 1). Figure 7 illustrates the dual development towards (i) marketization and – as a potential outcome of it – (ii) hybridization in terms of the values by which welfare actors are governed.

In what follows, I conceptualize the concept of marketization as it is used for the purpose of this study. It concerns specific types of shifts of Type II welfare mix and is based on the tripartite concept of provision introduced in Section 1.2.

2.2.1 The marketization of production and/or delivery

Regarding the element of production and/or delivery, the key issue in examining Type II welfare mix is how welfare transfers are produced and/or delivered. As discussed earlier, this refers to the procedures adopted in delivering welfare transfers, which not least determine whether or not welfare products are utilized by potential beneficiaries. Now, which are the changes in terms of these procedures that qualify as shifts towards an increasing 'marketization'?

In terms of **provision by public actors**, the introduction of management by objectives and similar management principles in public agencies is discussed in the literature as a chief way of implementing market principles[26]. As mentioned earlier, the new forms of governance in the public sector tend to imitate features of the market. In terms of production/delivery, this might lead to a shift away from strict bureaucratic rules

[26] Various authors discuss the end of the area of new public management, though (e.g. Noordhoek and Saner 2005, Drechsler 2008).

towards a stronger client-orientation through a professional quality and service-culture (e.g. Drechsler 2008: 22). Examples of the latter include a reduction of waiting times, an increase of opening hours of public agencies, a less bureaucratic application for transfers (e.g. through the implementation of e-government), an improvement of the information policy for clients, etc. Whenever these developments affect the delivery of welfare transfers, they ought to have positive effects on take-up rates. However, whether these changes of governmental procedures have been introduced to imitate market mechanisms needs to be judged by the motivations for their implementation, rather than by the measures alone. An increase of quality-orientation and service-orientation in governmental procedures might also be the result of a general drive towards a benevolent state (based on ethical reasons), rather than a trend towards increasing marketization.

In terms of **nonprofit provision**, the introduction of market principles is discussed in the literature in various ways. For example, there is a trend towards more professionalization, evidenced by a substitution of volunteers through professionals. However, this substitution usually affects the management of an organization rather than the staff actually delivering services (e.g. Meyer 2007). Moreover, the effects of this substitution in terms of efficiency gains are unclear (e.g. Brudney and Gazley 2002, Handy *et al.* 2008). Thus, it is once again crucial to examine the reasons and motivations behind changes in the administration of nonprofit production and/or delivery to judge whether or not the changes are due to a drive towards a more market-like provision.

2.2.2 The marketization of finance

In terms of finance, Type II welfare mix is interested in the composition of funding sources. Shifts that qualify as an increasing marketization (or: commercialization) of finance focus on very specific changes with regard to these funding sources.

In terms of **private funding sources**, a (relative) increase of service fees or other commercial income qualifies as 'marketization' or 'commercialization' concerning the element of finance. Johnson (1999: 56ff) identifies such a transfer of costs to the recipients of services and benefits as one of the prominent measures implemented in many welfare markets in the 1980s and 1990s. Not least, these developments may lead to significant shifts in the welfare mix. Salamon (1993: 23ff) suggests for the USA, for example, that there is evidence for a growing share of commercial incomes to be gained in various welfare areas, e.g. in health care (e.g. Salamon 1993)[27]. According to him, this change in funding sources only made many for-profits enter the market.

Concerning joint provision, in which **public** actors **finance** nonprofit production and/or delivery, 'marketization' refers to specific changes in the modes of public funding, namely from funding through grants to funding through performance-related payments. The latter are an important feature of tendering, the introduction of which leads to increased competition in the welfare market. This has led several nonprofits to invest in activities that are prominent in the for-profit world, such as PR or marketing (e.g. Bode 2006: 352ff). In performance-related contracts, costs are financed or reimbursed by public actors according to criteria established *ex ante* (Ascoli and Ranci 2002a). Purchase-of-service arrangements, last but not least, increase the accountability of nonprofits, which is considered as an important feature of for-profit provision.

2.2.3 The marketization of provider decisions

To examine whether 'marketization' is a dominant trend in the provision of welfare, changes of Type II welfare mix are once more at the core of the analysis. Regarding provider decisions, a static analysis of Type II welfare mix is concerned with two issues, namely: (i) 'which decisions have welfare actors made in terms of clients targeted?', and (ii) 'which decisions have welfare actors made in terms of products supplied?'. In terms of clients targeted, welfare providers may choose between different targeting designs, ranging from targeting through attributed needs towards targeting through means-tested needs. There is ample evidence of both (i) a reduction of benefits payable to welfare recipients (both in amount and duration) and (ii) a tightening of eligibility criteria, e.g. through the greater use of means-testing, so that fewer people qualify for benefits (Johnson 1999: 56ff). However, which changes qualify as an increasing 'marketization'?

---

27 For a framework that explains for-profit entry into welfare markets dominated by nonprofits, see, for example, Marwell and McInerney (2005: 9ff).

As mentioned in the introduction of this study, one trend closely connected with a revaluation of market ethics is the implementation of 'workfare benefits' (e.g. Lødemel and Trickey 2001). Workfare transfers are strongly linked to the willingness to search for and take on paid employment. In case of non-compliance, sanctions are used as a way of disciplining recipients of welfare transfers. As for other changes concerning clients targeted, it is difficult to judge *a priori*, whether these qualify as 'marketization'. This requires making such judgements *a posteriori*.

Section I.2.1 suggested that welfare actors have several options in terms of which welfare products to provide, i.e. cash transfers, goods or social services. Now, which changes in products supplied qualify as 'marketization'? This question is difficult to answer. For example, a shift away from in-kind towards cash transfers might qualify as a shift towards an increased marketization, as the latter increase the choice of beneficiaries. However, a shift from cash transfers towards in-kind goods or social services might also enhance client-orientation, especially in cases in which no 'market' has been established. Changes in terms of products supplied might also lead to an extension of the range of products supplied – a development which enhances the choice for consumers (e.g. Belfield 2002). However, there might also have been developments towards specialization of provision – and thus a decrease in the range of products offered. It is difficult to ascertain whether such changes may have followed the logics of the market economy (which suggests division of labour as a key way to increase efficiency and gain competitive advantages and profits), they may have been implemented for other reasons as well, such as the need for cost containment or a changing demand structure, etc. Consequently, it is once again vital to examine the motivations behind such changes to judge whether developments indeed represent a drive towards a more marketized provision.

3. Summary of this chapter

This chapter attempted to establish a conceptual framework that both (i) disentangles the concepts 'welfare mix', 'privatization' and 'marketization' and (ii) links these concepts sensibly together. To achieve this objective, two categories of 'welfare mix' have been distinguished at first: One cluster summarizes approaches that focus on a mix of welfare providers, which I termed 'Type I welfare mix'. A second cluster captures interpretations that are interested in the mix concerning the modes of provision chosen by welfare actors (which are shaped – among other things – by the value structures of the welfare actors). This second type of interpreting a mixed economy has been termed 'Type II welfare mix'.

A concept that helps to identify and examine both forms of the welfare mix is 'provision', which has been split into three distinct elements. Welfare transfers need to be produced and/or delivered and financed. Moreover, welfare actors need to decide (i) which clients to target (and how to target them) and (ii) which products to provide (and how to produce/deliver and finance them). In addition to the conventional split of the concept of provision into 'production/delivery' and 'finance', this study has therefore added the dimension of 'provider decisions'. In contrast to alternative elements offered in the literature, 'provider decisions' does not include decisions made by users or consumers of services (an aspect which is considered in the element 'decision' forwarded by Burchhardt). It does, however, include decisions of providers concerning issues such as which products to provide or which clients to target (i.e. decisions not considered by the two elements of 'regulation' forwarded by Barr).

As regards welfare provision, Type I welfare mix is concerned with the issue of who provides (what part of) welfare transfers. This implies that there is a range of different welfare actors available that might provide welfare either solely or jointly. Type II welfare mix is concerned with the question of how welfare actors comply with their tasks. This implies that different options in providing welfare are available to them. In terms of transfers supplied, they can, for example, choose between producing and/or delivering (unbounded or bounded) cash transfers, in-kind goods or social services. In terms of clients targeted, they may choose between a universal and a selective approach and select from a variety of different eligibility criteria. In terms of production and/or delivery, providers have different options on how to complete this task – with, for example in the case of income-tested transfers, quite some potential to stigmatize clients and negatively affect utilization rates. In terms of finance, welfare provision is financed either through public or private sources – with a variety of different options available within each of these two funding sources.

As a second step, the chapter attempted to identify the consequences of a changing welfare mix. Based on the clarifications made before, which distinguished between two types of a welfare mix, two types of change have been differentiated. First, the mix of welfare providers may change. The dominant type of shift regarding such changes is 'privatization', a concept this study also applies to denote a change towards increased nonprofit in contrast to public provision and/or more private rather than public sources of financing provision. It has been shown that privatization is a more complex concept than it may seem at first sight: If privatization takes place this might affect only one or two elements of provision (referred to as 'partial privatization') rather than all of them (referred to as 'total privatization'). Regardless of whether shifts lead to partial or total privatization, a key issue is that changes enhance (i) the role of private actors in provision and/or (ii) the role of private sources of funding. Privatization thus refers to specific changes of Type I welfare mix.

'Marketization' – a trend widely discussed in the literature – concerns only specific kinds of changes of Type II welfare mix. Marketization implies that market ethics and principles become more important in the provision of welfare and shape both (i) the actions of, as well as (ii) the interactions between public and third-sector organizations. In terms of provider decisions, marketization is, for example, evidenced by the substitution of welfare benefits through workfare benefits. Regarding production and/or delivery of welfare transfers, an improvement of client-orientation may, for example, be the result of marketization – albeit only if changes have been implemented to imitate market mechanisms rather than, for example, some ethical considerations. In terms of finance, an increasing share of commercial income (including user fees) qualifies as an increasing marketization of provision. In case of joint provision, evidence for an increased marketization is, for example, a rising share of performance-related funding.

Tables 14 and 15 summarize the conceptual framework elaborated in this chapter to identify the concepts of 'Type I welfare mix' and 'privatization' as well as 'Type II welfare mix' and 'marketization'.

As has been shown, there is a variety of different developments that qualify as increasing 'privatization' and/or 'marketization'. Figure 8 illustrates potential pathways of change in this respect.

Figure 8: Privatization and marketization: potential pathways of change

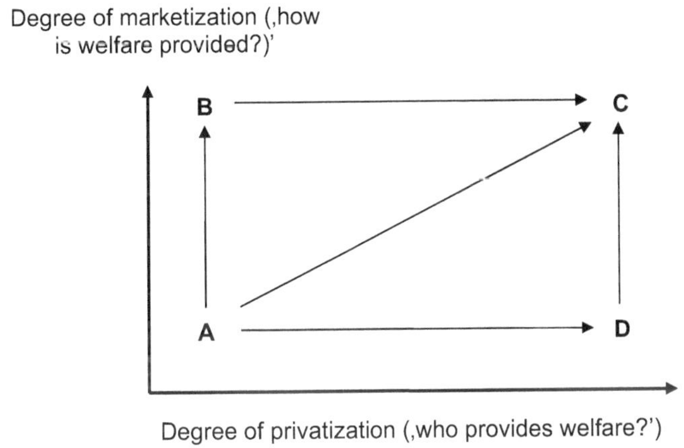

Source: own illustration

Depending on the point of departure (see also Section 1 in the Introduction), several shifts qualify as increased 'privatization' or 'marketization'. If the point of departure is A, developments may lead to new balances at points B, C or D. All of these new balances denote shifts towards an increased privatization and/or marketization of poverty relief. If the point of departure is B, a movement towards C or D represents a development towards more privatization. However, a shift towards D implies a decrease of marketization. If the point of departure is D, a movement towards C implies an increase of marketization, whereas a movement towards B implies an increase of marketization but a decrease of privatization. If C is the point of departure, movements towards A, B, or D imply a reduction of both privatization and marketization. The figure thus illustrates the pathways this study focuses on (sketched as arrows): from A to B, C or D; from B to C; and from D to C. Any other movements indicate a decrease of either privatization and/or marketization.

Table 14: Type I welfare mix and privatization

<table>
<tr><th colspan="3">Type I welfare mix</th></tr>
<tr><td colspan="3">Main issue: which types of actors provide (what part of) welfare?
Precondition: range of welfare providers belonging to different societal sectors, possibility to split provision
Potential outcome: single-sector provision; multi-sector provision (→ coordinated or uncoordinated forms of product and/or client differentiation), joint provision (→ sector-specific division of labour in terms of which type of provider conducts which task of provision)
Identification / operationalization: through tripartite framework of provision</td></tr>
<tr><th>Production and/or delivery</th><th>Finance</th><th>Provider decisions</th></tr>
<tr><td>Who…
… produces (goods) and/or
… delivers (cash, goods, services) welfare?</td><td>Who finances welfare products?</td><td>Who decides …
… which clients to target; which products to provide,
… on the modes of production/delivery,
… on the types of funding sources?</td></tr>
<tr><th colspan="3">Privatization</th></tr>
<tr><td colspan="3">Main issue: (only) shifts from (i) public towards nonprofit production/delivery, (ii) from public towards nonprofit decision-making in provider decisions, and/or (iii) from public towards private sources of funding
Potential outcome: Partial or total privatization
Identification / operationalization: through tripartite framework of provision</td></tr>
<tr><th>Production and/or delivery</th><th>Finance</th><th>Provider decisions</th></tr>
<tr><td>PO → NPO
↘ ↗
PO/NPO
↓
↓ PO/NPO ↑</td><td>public sources → private sources
↘ ↗
public / private sources
↓
↓ public / private sources ↑</td><td>PO → NPO
↘ ↗
PO/NPO
↓
↓ PO/NPO ↑</td></tr>
</table>

Source: own illustration; Notes: PO: public organizations; NPO: nonprofit organizations

Table 15: Type II welfare mix and marketization

Type II welfare mix		
Main issue: which options do providers from different societal sectors choose in providing welfare? Precondition: different options of welfare provision Potential outcome: similarities and/or differences in the modes of provision applied Identification / operationalization: through tripartite framework of provision		
Production and/or delivery	**Finance**	**Provider decisions**
How is production and/or delivery administered by welfare actors?	Which forms of public and/or private funding sources have actors chosen?	Which decision have been made in terms of … …clients targeted, …products provided?
Marketization		
Key issue: (only) shifts from a less marketized to a more marketized provision Potential outcome: a hybridization of welfare actors and welfare actions Identification / operationalization: through tripartite framework of provision		
Production and/or delivery	**Finance**	**Provider decisions**
Have there been changes in the administration of production/delivery that account for an increase of take-up rates (e.g. more client and service orientation, such as longer opening hours, etc.)? Have these changes been implemented to imitate mechanisms of for-profit organizations?	Has the proportion of user fees or commercial income increased as a means of funding? In case of joint provision: has the share of performance-related funding increased?	Has there been a shift away from welfare and towards workfare benefits? (other types of shifts: it is not possible to judge *a priori* whether shifts qualify as marketization)

Source: own illustration

Having presented answers to the theoretically oriented research question, this chapter concludes the conceptual and theoretical part of the book. Chapter III contains the empirical information collected to answer the last research question posed in this study, i.e. in how far the conceptual framework elaborated helps to study both (i) the characteristics of the prevalent mixed economy of poverty relief and (ii) recent shifts that might qualify as privatization and/or marketization of poverty relief in Austria.

Part B: Empirical evidence

III. The mixed economy of poverty relief in Austria -- and recent changes thereof

This chapter aims to answer the empirical research question guiding this study: In how far does a conceptual framework that organizes and links the concepts 'welfare mix', 'privatization' and 'marketization' help in illustrating both (i) the characteristics of the current 'welfare mix' as well as (ii) recent shifts thereof that qualify as 'privatization' and/or 'marketization' in an empirical investigation? As discussed in the introduction, Austria has been selected as the geographical focus for this exercise. But given the dominant role of public actors and nonprofits in the provision of poverty relief in Austria, only their contributions are considered in this study.

Since sketching the welfare mix and changes thereof requires empirical data, the conceptual framework, in addition to guiding the execution of this exercise, is also tested as to its appropriateness in completing the empirical investigation. The framework is particularly apt if it meets several requirements. For example, it must ensure the possibility to operationalize the concepts elaborated in the theoretical part of this book. Moreover, data needs must be deductible from the indicators chosen for operationalization, and data sources must be available. Section 1 therefore explains the research approach adopted. Section 2 presents the information collected in order to illustrate the prevalent welfare mix in poverty alleviation in Austria. Section 3 proceeds to scrutinize recent changes that may qualify as privatization and/or marketization of poverty alleviation. Section 4 summarizes the main findings of this chapter.

1. The empirical research approach

An empirical assessment that is interested in portraying the contemporary mixed economy of poverty alleviation and recent changes thereof and that is guided by the conceptual framework elaborated in the first part of this book is confronted with a variety of practical challenges, the solution of which will also determine the framework's adequacy in tackling this exercise. First, it is necessary to operationalize the framework's crucial concepts ('poverty', 'poverty relief', 'nonprofit organizations', 'public organizations', 'welfare mix', 'privatization', 'marketization'). While scientific concepts have to be clear, simple and universally applicable to allow for theoretical analysis, real-world phenomena are usually ambiguous, complex, country-specific and/or they change over time. Through operationalization, academic concepts are translated into one or more dimensions or indicators able to represent these concepts clearly and comprehensively and allowing for potential country-specifics and/or time-specifics (Atteslander 2008: 33ff). Second, and based on the dimensions and/or indicators chosen to operationalize the concepts, data needs have to be deducted and data sources containing relevant information have to be identified. In principle, data sources may include secondary data, i.e. information already collected for various purposes, or – if data are not readily available – primary data. An empirical analysis that relies on secondary data has a variety of advantages over an analysis that necessitates the collection of primary data, most notably in terms of research costs and time – provided the existing information is complete with regard to the data needs and of good quality in terms of how it has been collected. If it is possible to complete the empirical analysis with the help of secondary data only, the conceptual framework that guides the empirical assessment thus proves to be particularly suitable for such an exercise. Should the analysis require primary data, it is, third, crucial to decide how to collect relevant information.

It is the aim of this section to tackle the first two tasks described above (the third task, i.e. deciding on methods for collecting primary data, is discussed in the conclusion of this book). To achieve this aim, this section proceeds in the following way. Section 1.1 is concerned with operationalizing the concept of 'poverty relief actors'. Section 1.2 concentrates on the dual model of the 'mixed economy of poverty alleviation' and Section 1.3 focuses on the concepts of 'privatization' and 'marketization'. Section 1.4 then summarizes the data needs deriving from the indicators chosen and identifies and selects secondary data sources that contain relevant information.

1.1 Operationalizing 'poverty relief actors'

This section operationalizes the concept of 'poverty relief actors'. This requires both (i) translating the concepts 'poverty' and 'relief' into indicators that allow for their empirical reflection and (ii) differentiating between 'public' and 'nonprofit actors' that provide poverty relief in Austria.

1.1.1 'Poverty'

Section I.1.1.3 has defined **'poverty'** for the purpose of this study rather narrowly as income poverty. The German equivalent for this concept is *Einkommensarmut*. A prominent term used as well is *Armutsgefährdung* (Lutz *et al.* 1993, Steiner and Wolf 1996, Lamei and Till-Tentschert 2005), which is synonymous to the Eurostat concept 'at-risk-of-poverty'. The notion of *Armut* (i.e. poverty) is commonly understood as a multi-dimensional disadvantage, with income poverty being a key element, but not the only element considered. Common German terms for this notion of deprivation used in the Austrian debate are *akute Armut* (acute poverty) or, since more recently, *manifeste Armut* (manifest poverty, e.g. Statistik Austria 2006b, 2007a, 2008, 2009a).

Even if poverty is interpreted as 'income poverty', as is the case in this study, many decisions are necessary to precisely define what constitutes poverty – which is an important prerequisite for it to be measured (e.g. Coudouel *et al.* 2002, Eiffe and Heitzmann 2006, Eiffe 2009). This study uses the Laeken indicator 'at-risk-of-poverty' elaborated by Eurostat as the dividing line between the income poor and the non-poor (see also Atkinson *et al.* 2002), thereby operationalizing 'income poverty'. This indicator contains a relative definition of poverty based on the distribution of disposable income[28]. The poverty threshold is set at 60 per cent of the median income (after social transfers) which is calculated based on the national income distribution. The unit of analysis is the household, which is equivalized according to the Eurostat scale. This attributes a weight of

[28] On the basis of EU-SILC data (see below), Eurostat suggests that the *"(…) total disposable income of a household is calculated by adding together the personal income received by all household members plus income received at household level (…) In other words, the total disposable income of each household is calculated: EITHER by adding together the net income received by all members of the household from all the specified component sources. This includes monetary and in-kind income from work (employment and self-employment), private income (from investments, property, etc. including imputed rent from owner-occupation), transfers received from other households, pensions and other social benefits less payments made to other households and payment of loan interest. OR by adding together the gross income received by all members of the household from all the specified component sources, and deducting taxes and social security contributions (…)"* (http://epp.eurostat.ec.europa.eu/cache/ITY_SDDS/EN/tsisc010_sm1.htm, last accession date: September 2009)

1 to the first adult within a household, of 0.5 to every additional adult and of 0.3 to every child (below the age of 14). Household income is assumed to be distributed equally across all members of the household[29].

The main rationales for this pragmatic approach in operationalizing 'income poverty' through the Laeken indicator are twofold. First, the adoption of the Laeken indicator 'at-risk-of-poverty' allows for a simple differentiation between the income poor and the non-poor. This differentiation is more difficult to achieve if other, more complex concepts of 'poverty' are applied, such as 'social exclusion'[30] (see Section I.1.1.2). Second, the Laeken indicator has been utilized in several studies on income poverty in Austria, including official publications of the Ministry of Social Affairs (Förster and Heitzmann 2002, Till-Tentschert *et al.* 2004, Till *et al.* 2009) or the Austrian Statistical Office (Statistik Austria 2005, 2006a, 2006b, 2007a, 2008, 2009a). The poverty threshold derived from the Laeken indicator is also used in political documents as the official poverty line (e.g. Bundeskanzleramt Österreich 2007). This suggests that this definition of poverty is widely accepted in Austria, which is an important requirement when it comes to operationalizing it.

Section I.1.2 has introduced the social risk management framework to distinguish between two approaches to combat poverty. Strategies of *ex ante* risk management include instruments which are organized for people not (yet) hit by income poverty. By contrast, only income poor people are eligible for *ex post* management instruments. **'Poverty relief'** has been defined according to the second set of measures. This implies that in the context of this study only those transfers or programmes qualify as poverty relief measures that exclusively target the income poor. Consequently, poverty relief actors include all actors that provide poverty relief instruments. Thus, instruments requiring an income test are particularly relevant for this study. In what follows, I discuss whether this approach

[29] Several researchers have criticized this assumption. Many arguments have been brought forward claiming that women and girls are disadvantaged in the distribution of household resources as compared to men and boys (e.g. Millar and Glendinning 1989, Jenkins 1991, Heitzmann 2002). Even though some anecdotal evidence (Sen 1981, Middleton *et al.* 1997) confirms this hypothesis, poverty studies continue to assume that the distribution of resources across household members is equal.

[30] Berghman (1995: 20ff) has defined social exclusion as a process (and deprivation as its outcome). Since the concept of relief as defined for this study focuses on situations after poverty has materialized, the focus is on an outcome.

suffices to identify those types of actors that are at the core of this study, namely public and third-sector organizations.

1.1.2 'Public' poverty relief actors

Prior to identifying poverty relief actors from the public sector, it is vital to identify organizations that add up to the **'public sector'**. Following Stiglitz (2000: 12ff), Section I.2.2.3 defined organizations as public if two criteria applied. First, individuals responsible for running public agencies need to be appointed directly or indirectly through an electoral process. Second, public actors can use compulsion, and thus take actions private actors are not entitled to perform. How appropriate is this definition for the organizational landscape in Austria? Does it cover all organizations considered as 'public' in this country?

Whereas in Austria a variety of organizations qualifies as 'public' according to the definition forwarded above – e.g., legislative bodies, executive authorities, the judiciary, but also the Austrian Public Employment Service (*Arbeitsmarktservice*, or in short *AMS*), which is responsible for the administration of means-tested unemployment assistance (*Notstandshilfe*) –, there are also organizations that fulfil only one of the conditions necessary to qualify as a 'public' organization. This includes, for example, the social insurance institutions in Austria, which provide an important type of poverty relief transfer, namely compensation supplement (*Ausgleichszulage*), i.e. a minimum pension for those entitled to retirement pensions. While the social insurance institutions may use compulsion, their managing board is not appointed directly or indirectly through an electoral process. Rather, these organizations are self-governing bodies. The members of the management board are appointed by the social partners, rather than by the political elites. Nonetheless the social insurance institutions are perceived as 'public', rather than 'private' bodies in Austria. For the purpose of this study, therefore, organizations that fulfil only one of the two criteria identified earlier, i.e. the right to use compulsion, are also defined as 'public' actors[31].

[31] The Viennese school on nonprofit sector research (Badelt *et al.* 2007b), however, suggests that the proportion of sovereign tasks executed by an organization should exceed a certain level (i.e. 5 per cent of all tasks performed by this organization) to qualify as 'public'. This is the case with the Austrian social insurance institutions.

As mentioned earlier, only actors that provide *ex post* instruments to combat poverty are considered to be poverty relief actors in this study. Section II.1.2.3 has forwarded four different options for targeting. These include attributed need, compensation, diagnostic differentiation and means-tested need. While income poor people may be entitled to transfers organized according to all of these types of targeting, only income-tested transfers are granted exclusively to the income poor – provided the income considered is equal to or below the income poverty threshold calculated for a country. In case of a single person household, for example, in Austria this threshold amounted to € 912 per month in 2007 (see table 16).

Table 16: Income poverty thresholds for selected household types, Austria, 2007

Household types	Income poverty threshold in € per month
Single person household	912 €
Household with 2 adults	1,368 €
Household with 2 adults and 1 child	1,641 €
Household with 2 adults and 2 children	1,915 €
Household with 2 adults and 3 children	2,189 €
Household with 1 adult and 1 child	1,186 €

Source: Statistik Austria (2009a: 30)

In general, in Austria means-tested or income-tested transfers are regarded as *Fürsorgeleistungen*, i.e. transfers for the needy. However, due to differences in how these transfers are financed, (mostly) tax financed social assistance (*Sozialhilfe*) may be more closely perceived as a typical transfer targeted to the poor than are insurance-based transfers such as unemployment benefit or compensation supplement, which are financed at least in part through insurance contributions. Nonetheless, public organizations that provide income-tested transfers (which are granted based on a maximum income at or below the poverty thresholds calculated for specific household types) are operationalized as **public poverty relief actors** for the purpose of this study.

As this study is interested not only in the public sector's contributions to poverty alleviation but also in those made by the nonprofit sector, the following section is concerned with operationalizing nonprofit poverty relief actors in an Austrian context.

1.1.3 'Nonprofit' poverty relief actors

Section I.2.2.4 proposed to define **'nonprofits'** according to three criteria, i.e. (i) they must be organizations, (ii) they must not qualify as 'public' actors, and (iii) they must not be allowed to distribute profits to owners or shareholders (except for small amounts). This definition combines the structural-operational definition elaborated by the Johns Hopkins Comparative nonprofit project with the European approach to third-sector organizations (Evers and Laville 2004: 11ff). Is it possible to identify existing organizations in Austria unambiguously as nonprofits according to this definition? Indeed, several obstacles hamper this exercise. First, no single legal organizational form exists that captures nonprofits according to this definition. Second, the sector of the private not-for-profit organizations included in the national accounts is defined in a different way than proposed here (Schneider and Hagleitner 2005, Haider *et al.* 2008). As I focus on the activity field of poverty alleviation, however, one concept is particularly apt to differentiate nonprofit organizations from actors of other societal sectors, i.e. charitable status. Austrian tax law awards a charitable status to those entities that primarily serve purposes of public interest. This status allows for tax alleviations. To achieve public benefit status, profits must remain within the organizations and not be distributed to the shareholders or owners of the company. For-profit organizations therefore do not qualify.

Charitable status is not a form of legal personality for organizations, though, nor is there sufficient information on all (private) organizations to which this tax status is granted (Schneider and Hagleitner 2005), even though former research on nonprofits in Austria presented evidence that those organizations are mostly incorporated as associations (Heitzmann 2001: 70ff, Schneider *et al.* 2007). Thus, associations as well as other public benefit organizations in Austria are operationalized as nonprofits for the purpose of this study. A variety of publications applied broadly the same definition concerning these types of organizations (e.g. Bachstein 1997, Heitzmann 2001, Trukeschitz 2006, Schneider *et al.* 2007, Haider *et al.* 2008, Dimmel *et al.* 2009b). Not least, this definition of third-sector organizations is widely accepted in Austria (e.g. Litschel and Wetzel 2004).

Following the operationalization of nonprofits, the next step necessary is to differentiate third-sector organizations engaged in poverty alleviation from other nonprofits. This proves to be more difficult than with regard to public poverty relief actors: In contrast to social security measures provided by the state, information on the provision of poverty relief by nonprofits is much scarcer in Austria. There are only some (outdated) official estimates relating to the overall extent of nonprofits engaged in welfare and relief activities. For example, data on the number of associations engaged in this field suggest that 6,649 organizations existed in Austria in 2001 (Statistik Austria 2002: 158). Associations providing 'welfare and relief' include a broad variety of different actors, though. It remains unclear how many of them engage in poverty alleviation. Assistance by nonprofits tends to be idiosyncratic and not couched into pre-defined programmes or transfers (Dawid and Heitzmann 2006a: 55). For example, the Austrian *Caritas* or the *Volkshilfe*, i.e. large nonprofit welfare actors in this country, as well as many other third-sector actors organize social advice centres in many of their local establishments. People in need of support – regardless of whether this is a need for information, for counselling, for social services or for material help – turn to these organizations. While many of the clients belong to the low-income sector of the population, others do not. Moreover, often, no means test is required in order to receive support by nonprofits, even though there are exceptions. This implies that a classification of the transfers provided by nonprofits into *ex ante* or *ex post* instruments based on the approach forwarded above for public actors is not feasible.

Therefore, this study takes a more pragmatic approach in operationalizing **nonprofit poverty relief actors,** relying on a selection made by two (nonprofit) network organizations – the Austrian Poverty Network (*Österreichische Armutskonferenz*) and the Austrian Committee for Social Work (*ÖKSA*). They recently commissioned a study on the activities of those of their member organizations that primarily engage in combating poverty in Austria (Dawid and Heitzmann 2006b, 2006a). For this purpose, they selected 561 nonprofits among their members and classified them as being primarily engaged in combating poverty. For pragmatic reasons, these nonprofits are defined as poverty relief actors for the purpose of this study, too. This operationalization of nonprofit poverty relief actors is a second-best solution, as it may (i) include instruments provided by these actors that would qualify as *ex ante* rather than *ex* *post* measures, (ii) exclude *ex post* measures of nonprofits that are – according to the two network organizations – not primarily engaged in poverty alleviation or (iii) miss out third-sector organizations providing poverty relief that are not known by the two network organizations. Nonetheless, this selection of nonprofits is a good proxy as it should cover the majority of poverty relief actors.

1.2 Operationalizing 'Type I welfare mix' and 'Type II welfare mix'

As argued in the conceptual framework, a thorough analysis of the three elements of provision allows to describe the characteristics of the dual concept of a 'mixed economy of poverty alleviation', i.e. 'Type I welfare mix' and 'Type II welfare mix'. In what follows, potential indicators that allow for an empirical assessment of these three elements are identified.

1.2.1 Production and/or delivery

One distinct element of provision is production (in case of goods) and delivery (in case of goods, services and cash transfers). To illustrate **Type I welfare mix** regarding this element, it is particularly vital to identify those public and nonprofit actors that engage in the poverty relief 'market' (on their operationalization, see above). However, poverty relief actors in Austria differ in size, their regional relevance and their product portfolio (see Section 2). Thus, the relative roles of these sectors in the welfare mix may be better captured by comparing their overall transfer expenditures and number of clients served, rather than by simply comparing the number of public and nonprofit poverty relief actors. These two indicators are therefore chosen to operationalize production and/or delivery concerning Type I welfare mix.

A variety of different indicators may be scrutinized to describe how production and/or delivery is administered, and thus to operationalize **Type II welfare mix** with regard to this element of provision. As discussed in the conceptual framework (see Section II.1.2.1), the quality of production and/or delivery varies due to potential stigmatizing effects related to benefit delivery, the location of delivery, the timing of delivery, or the extent of user information. The administration of production and/or delivery not only refers to the actual delivery of transfers, but includes all procedures implemented by the producers/deliverers ranging from (i) the application for benefits, (ii) the determination of eligibility, (iii) the actual delivery of the transfers and (iv) the controlling of *ex post* compliance with eligibility. There are indicators that may capture at least some of the aspects concerning these different dimensions of production/delivery (e.g. availability of internet application, location of transfer delivery (i.e. at the domicile of the user or the delivery agency), the number and distribution of delivery agencies across the country, opening hours of delivery agencies, waiting times, the time period needed by delivery agencies to complete a transaction, etc.). Since the very procedures adopted to produce/deliver transfers influence take-up rates, take-up rates of poverty relief transfers are chosen as a proxy indicator to operationalize Type II welfare mix concerning the element of production and/or delivery. Even though take-up rates are not only influenced by the administration of production and/or delivery, this indicator provides for a general impression concerning its quality, whereas the indicators mentioned above only capture small parts of the overall picture.

1.2.2 Finance

Poverty relief transfers may be financed through public and/or private funding sources. According to the conceptual framework (see Section II.1.2.2), an assessment of the relative share of these two types of funding allows capturing the characteristics of **Type I welfare mix**. This requires identifying the relative proportions of public and private funding sources as a share of total transfer funding for both public and nonprofit poverty relief actors. Consequently, these proportions are chosen as indicator to operationalize this element of provision.

To assess **Type II welfare mix**, the conceptual framework first suggests focusing on an analysis of the different forms of funding. This requires identifying the relative shares of the different components of the funding portfolio (e.g. donations, user charges, taxes, social insurance contributions, etc.) of poverty relief transfers provided by public and nonprofit actors. These shares are therefore selected as one indicator to operationalize the element of finance regarding Type II welfare mix. A second indicator chosen covers financial requirements in case of joint provision. As discussed earlier, public actors can finance nonprofit production and/or delivery through subsidies (or *ex post* cost coverage) or through performance-related funding models (which stipulate concrete conditions for the receipt of pre-defined funds). The relative proportions of these two forms of funding are therefore selected as a further indicator to operationalize this element of provision.

1.2.3 Provider decisions

For an empirical assessment of **Type I welfare mix** in the context of 'provider decisions', it is first vital to identify whether there is multi-sector provision or joint provision (see Section II.1.1.1). As discussed earlier, the question of 'who takes the provider decisions?' is easy to answer in case of multi-sector provision: the same organization that finances, produces and/or delivers poverty alleviation also takes the provider decisions. In case of joint provision, however, the tasks of finance and production/delivery of poverty relief are split between different types of actors. In these cases, the issue of 'who takes the provider decisions?' in fact involves four different decisions: (i) 'who decides which income poor (groups) to target?'; (ii) 'who decides which poverty relief products to provide?'; (iii) 'who decides on the modes of production and/or delivery?'; and: (iv) 'who decides on the composition of funding sources?'.

The following approach is adopted to examine empirically who is in charge of decision-making. As discussed earlier, the type of financial agreement stipulated in the contract between public actors and nonprofits allows some inferences to be drawn on the distribution of decision-making powers: Cooperation based on performance-related funding suggests that the financier (which is usually a public actor) is likely to make provider decisions. Cooperation based on funding through subsidies suggests that the producer/deliverer (which is usually a nonprofit actor) is in charge of decision-making. Consequently, the type of financial agreement stipulated in the contracts between public and nonprofit actors is chosen as a proxy indicator to operationalize Type I welfare mix. It assumes, however, that one of the actors takes decisions on all of the four different decisions mentioned above.

For an empirical analysis of **Type II welfare mix**, it is vital to find answers to the following two questions: (i) 'which decisions have been taken with regard to income poor (groups) targeted?', and: (ii) 'which decisions have been taken with regard to poverty relief products provided?'.

As for income poor (groups) targeted, the following two indicators are utilized. First, eligibility criteria are examined, as they determine who in principle has access to poverty relief transfers. As discussed earlier (see Section II.1.2.3), poverty relief actors have the choice between a rather 'universal' approach and a 'selective' approach. Poverty relief transfers are – by definition – income-tested (see above). However, further targeting designs may apply as well. It is the sum of these criteria that determines whether or not income poor individuals have formal access to a specific transfer (Heitzmann *et al.* 2002: 28f). While an assessment of eligibility criteria allows to examine *ex ante* which clients have been targeted, an assessment of income poor (groups) served by welfare actors allows for an *ex post* analysis. Thus, the composition of the client groups served is chosen as well as an indicator for this element of provision. Based on the results of this assessment, it will also be possible to see whether public and nonprofit actors target the same or different groups of the income poor.

The second relevant question for identifying Type II welfare mix regarding provider decisions refers to the issue of 'which decisions have been taken regarding poverty relief products provided?'. As discussed earlier, poverty relief actors have the choice between providing (bounded or unbounded) cash transfers, in-kind transfers or social services. The relative proportions of these types of instruments provided by poverty relief actors describe the characteristics of Type II welfare mix – and are chosen to operationalize this element of provision. Based on the data collected, it will, moreover, be possible to see whether there are similarities and/or differences concerning the products provided by public organizations and nonprofits.

1.3 Operationalizing 'privatization' and 'marketization'

This study is interested not only in portraying the current balance of the welfare mix in Austria but also in examining whether this balance has been the result of recent shifts towards privatization and/or marketization of poverty alleviation. Section II.2 has argued that, conceptually, 'privatization' involves specific shifts of Type I welfare mix, while 'marketization' refers to specific changes of Type II welfare mix. It has further been argued that a thorough examination of shifts in the three elements of provision allows capturing both privatization as well as marketization. In what follows, both of these concepts are operationalized according to this tripartite framework.

1.3.1 Production and/or delivery

If **privatization** of poverty alleviation has affected the element of production and/or delivery in recent years, the contributions of public actors must have decreased and the contributions of nonprofits must have increased in this activity field (see also figure 4 in Section II.2.1.1). To evaluate empirically whether such shifts have taken place in Austria, it is vital to examine changes with regard to the indicators identified earlier to capture Type I welfare mix, i.e. (i) the number of clients served by these actors, and (ii) the amount of transfer expenditures produced and/or delivered by public and nonprofit actors. To account for shifts towards privatization, the proportions of nonprofit provision ought to have increased in contrast to those of public provision.

To identify shifts that qualify as **marketization**, it is necessary to examine specific types of changes of Type II welfare mix. It has been mentioned earlier (see Section II.2.2.1) that the implementation of management principles in both public and nonprofit organizations that imitate market mechanisms is one potential sign of marketization. Thus, evidence of a recent implementation of organizational restructuring (e.g. introduction of management by objectives) hints towards increased marketization. In case marketization has increased, moreover, there should be evidence for more service-orientation and/or client orientation (even though this might also be the result of changes other than imitating market principles). A more service-oriented approach in terms of public provision requires, for example, delivery agencies' opening hours to be expanded, bureaucratic procedures in applying for a poverty relief transfer to become more client-friendly, or procedures applied for determining eligibility to be stripped of their stigmatizing power. As discussed earlier, take-up rates of welfare transfers give a general impression regarding their acceptance. Thus, a reduction of non-take up may hint towards an improved 'quality' of transfer delivery and thus towards marketization. Consequently, increases of take-up rates of poverty relief transfers are operationalized as one indicator to operationalize marketization. However, this only applies if the motivations that account for the changes in the administration of production and/or delivery indeed suggest that an imitation of market mechanisms has been the driving force for the changes. It is therefore crucial to examine the underlying motivations that have caused these changes.

Increased marketization concerning the element of production and/or delivery may also manifest itself in an increase of professionalization. With regard to nonprofit provision, this may, for example, be evidenced through an increase of paid staff (substituting volunteer work). Consequently, changes regarding this dimension are qualified as a further indicator to operationalize this element of provision. As mentioned earlier, however, the motivations that have led to such changes need to be examined: Only if changes have been implemented to copy market mechanisms, developments will qualify as evidence for increased marketization.

1.3.2 Finance

Privatization regarding the element of finance implies that there must have been a decrease of public funding sources and an increase of private funding sources of poverty relief transfers. For an empirical examination of privatization concerning this element of provision data need to be collected on the proportions of public and private funding sources in public and nonprofit provision over time. Whereas the former ought to have decreased, the latter ought to have increased to qualify as privatization.

Marketization concerning the element of finance is captured by two indicators. First, there should have been an increase of specific forms of private funding sources, namely user fees and commercial income. This transfer of costs towards the beneficiaries of services and benefits has been argued as being a chief way of 'commercialization' (see Section II.2.2.2). Second, there should have been a substitution of grants as a form of public finance of nonprofit production and/or delivery through performance-related payments. If there is evidence for this latter development, this is usually the result of prior changes – most notably, an increased competition among the state's contracting partners. This ought to be reflected in an enhanced rate of tendering as a method to choose contracting partners. Related to this development, the very relationships between contracting partners in poverty alleviation should have changed:

These relationships ought to have become more professionalized, as evidenced, for example, through shifts from opaque and non-transparent agreements between public and private actors towards a professional and business-like partnership, more transparency in terms of contracts as well as enhanced accountability requirements. Such changes should be reflected, at least in part, in the stipulations of the contracts. These two indicators (increased shares of user fees and/or commercial income as a proportion of total funding; increased share of performance-related payments and decreased share of subsidies in case of joint provision) are therefore selected to operationalize this element of provision with regard to Type II welfare mix.

1.3.3 Provider decisions

Privatization in provider decisions involves four types of changes (see figure 6 in Section II.2.1.3), which all involve a decrease (or a discontinuation) of public decision-making and an increase of nonprofit decision-making. An increased role of nonprofits concerning provider decisions is evidenced by (i) an increased share of nonprofits engaged in joint provision with the public sector and (ii) an increased share of contracting arrangements, in which public finance is based on subsidies rather than performance-related payments – given that the former type of financial agreement is likely to allow the producer/deliverer of poverty relief transfers to make provider decisions. Consequently, these two indicators are selected to operationalize this element of provision.

'Marketization' of provider decisions refers to specific changes of Type II welfare mix. As discussed earlier, two decisions are particularly relevant when it comes to identifying Type II welfare mix, i.e. decisions taken in terms of (i) clients targeted and (ii) products provided. However, only specific changes concerning these two dimensions qualify as a trend towards marketization of provider decisions. In terms of clients targeted, an increase of workfare benefits has been identified as being linked to the revaluation of market ethics (see Section II.2.2.3). Two indicators are selected to capture this development. First, changes with regard to eligibility criteria have to be assessed in terms of whether the willingness to search for and take on paid employment is demanded to a greater extent and/or with regard to a greater number of poverty relief transfers than compared to the past. Second, it needs to be examined whether there has been a rise of transfer payments suspended due to inappropriate behaviour. If there has been such an increase, this supports hypotheses suggesting that 'social engineering', including compliance with work obligations, has become more important.

As has been argued earlier, it is not possible to identify *a priori* whether other changes that affect Type II welfare mix (most notably (i) shifts in the proportion of cash and in-kind transfers and (ii) shifts in terms of the range of poverty relief products provided) qualify as trends towards increased marketization. So if there is evidence for changes concerning the type or the range of poverty relief products provided, the motivations that brought about these changes need to be assessed as well, as they might allow for some inferences on whether or not these shifts qualify as a 'more marketized' provision.

1.4 Data needs and data sources

So far, the study has been concerned with operationalizing the basic concepts of the framework elaborated in Part A of this book, which implied identifying indicators that operationalize and thus help measure the mixed economy of poverty relief and changes thereof. In what follows, the data needs deriving from these indicators are summarized. Then, data sources that contain relevant information are discussed. In this context, it is also vital to decide which of these sources to utilize in the empirical assessment.

1.4.1 Data needs

The above sections have presented a variety of indicators that have been selected to operationalize the crucial concepts elaborated in the first part of this book. These indicators, which determine the data needs for the empirical assessment, are summarized in table 17.

Whereas some of the indicators chosen (e.g. Laeken indicator 'at-risk-of-poverty') allow for a fairly precise operationalization of concepts, others are only proxies that will help shed some light on the mixed economy of poverty relief and changes thereof in Austria, rather than reveal the whole picture.

1.4.2 Secondary data sources

After having summarized the data needs for the empirical assessment, the next step necessary is identifying information sources that contain relevant data. As mentioned earlier, both secondary and primary data may be utilized to complete the empirical analysis. Secondary data have important advantages over primary data in terms of research costs and time. In this study, only the former type of information is utilized, as it allows for some conclusions on the capability and appropriateness of the conceptual framework in assisting the empirical analysis. However, available data sources are limited in terms of both (i) quantity and (ii) quality. Regarding the former, information is available only on selected poverty relief transfers or actors and/or on some of the indicators mentioned. Regarding the latter, a large amount of available data has been collected for specific (and usually non-scientific) purposes and/or only includes 'anecdotal evidence'[32]. This often leads to biased results that do not meet scientific requirements for secondary data. It thus becomes necessary to select among secondary information sources to ensure only data are utilized that allow for an objective reflection of the empirical reality. In what follows, secondary data sources that contain relevant information and have been selected for the empirical exercise are identified. The latter requirement has made it necessary to include some information on the provision of poverty alleviation in Austria already in this section.

Concerning **public poverty relief actors**, only some data sources hold information on all poverty relief transfers provided in Austria. First, publications of the European Statistical Office contain aggregate information on means-tested transfers (e.g. Eurostat 2007, 2008), which are a close proxy to public poverty relief transfers as operationalized for the purpose of this study (see above). The publications include information on (the development of) total transfer expenditures, divided into cash and in-kind transfers.

---

[32] This type of evidence derives from experts and/or staff from selected poverty relief providers. The 'anecdotal evidence' has been made public in the form of presentations, round-table discussions and other forms of debates. However, it is not based on information that is collected in a way to meet scientific requirements.

Table 17: Indicators chosen to operationalize the theoretical concepts

Income poverty
Laeken-indicator 'at-risk-of-poverty'
Public poverty relief actors
Public actors providing income-tested transfers (level for income test ≤ Laeken indicator 'at-risk-of-poverty')
Nonprofit poverty relief actors
561 nonprofits that have been selected by two large network organizations and defined as 'primarily engaged in combating poverty'
Production/delivery
Type I welfare mix: (i) transfer expenditures; (ii) number of clients served Type II welfare mix: (i) take-up rates of poverty relief transfers Privatization: (i) number of clients served (public actors ↓, nonprofits ↑); (ii) total transfer expenditures (public actors ↓, nonprofits ↑) Marketization: (i) introduction of new management principles (e.g. MBO) in public and nonprofit organizations; (ii) reduction of non-take up rates of poverty relief transfers (if changes are motivated by market ethics); (iii) relative increase of paid staff in nonprofits (if changes are motivated by market ethics)
Finance
Type I welfare mix: (i) proportions of public and private funding sources as a share of total transfer funding Type II welfare mix: (i) proportions of different components of the total funding portfolio; (ii) proportions of nonprofits in joint provision financed through performance-related payments and subsidies Privatization: (i) decreasing proportion of public funding sources and increasing proportion of private funding sources Marketization: (i) increase of user fees, commercial income; in case of joint provision: (ii) substitution of grants through performance-related payments

Provider decisions
Type I welfare mix: (i) proportions of nonprofits in joint provision financed through performance-related payments and subsidies
Type II welfare mix: (i) eligibility criteria applied; (ii) composition of income poor groups served; (iii) portfolio of products provided
Privatization: (i) increased share of nonprofits engaged in joint provision; (ii) increased share of nonprofits relying on subsidies rather than performance-related payments
Marketization: (i) changed eligibility criteria (increase of workfare benefits); (ii) increase of transfer payments suspended due to inappropriate behaviour; (iii) shifts in the proportion of cash and in-kind transfers provided (if changes are motivated by market ethics); (iv) changes in the range of poverty relief products provided (if changes are motivated by market ethics)

Source: own illustration

Second, a compendium published annually by the Austrian Chamber of Labour includes information on most social security transfers provided by the Austrian welfare state (Kammer für Arbeiter und Angestellte 2005, 2006, 2008). Among others, the overview contains information on most of the means-tested transfers provided by the public sector in Austria, including data on expenditures per transfer, the number of clients served, eligibility criteria, etc.[33] A considerable amount of different income-tested programmes provided by the welfare state exists in Austria. Indeed, about a third of all welfare state instruments listed in the mentioned encyclopaedia are either means-tested or include a means-tested supplement. Many of these programmes are rather small, both in terms of overall expenditures and/or in terms of clients served.

Belonging to the family of the 'continental', 'conservative', and strongly 'corporatist' welfare state regimes (Esping-Andersen 1990: 26ff, 1999: 81ff, Esping-Andersen *et al.* 2002: 16f), Austria strongly relies on social insurance and universal support for families – both forms of *ex ante* risk management. However, even within these schemes, there are means-tested transfers or supplements that qualify as poverty relief instruments as defined in this study. Speaking of **means-tested insurance transfers**, this refers, for example, to unemployment assistance, i.e. an insurance benefit that may be granted after (non-means-tested) unemployment benefit has expired. Unemployment assistance is delivered by one of the many local offices of the *AMS* located throughout Austria. The average level of unemployment assistance paid in 2007 amounted to € 19.3 per day, which is an amount well below the income poverty threshold (i.e. € 912 per month in 2007) (Kammer für Arbeiter und Angestellte 2008: 139). A further means-tested insurance benefit is compensation supplement, which targets pensioners who receive an income from the pension insurance that is below a certain threshold. In 2008, this sum amounted to € 747 for a single-person household[34]. Even though this benefit is paid 14 times a year, it is still below the income poverty threshold calculated for 2007. Compensation supplement is delivered by the pension insurance institutions in Austria. Means-tested transfers are also incorporated in the Austrian health insurance scheme.

---

33 Additional publications contain some further information on selected transfers provided by the Austrian welfare state (e.g. Dimmel and Pfeil 2009, Steiner 2009).

34 The average level of compensation supplement paid in 2007 amounted to only € 238, though (Kammer für Arbeiter und Angestellte 2008: 250).

These include exemptions from the annual fee for the electronic sickness insurance card, exemptions from prescription fees for pharmaceuticals, exemptions from costs for thermal cure or exemptions from costs for medical rehabilitation measures (Kammer für Arbeiter und Angestellte 2008). Applications for these transfers need to be filed with the health insurance institution with which the applicant is insured. Some **means-tested** supplements top up **universal benefits** in Austria. For example, families on low income may qualify for a means-tested supplement to universal childcare allowance, applications for which need to be filed with the health insurance institutions (Kammer für Arbeiter und Angestellte 2008: 25).

In addition to means-tested transfers embedded in the Austrian social insurance and universal transfer scheme, several instruments are constructed as a **second social net** and granted in addition to insurance and universal transfers. Different national, regional or local authorities deliver these transfers. For example, the Federal Ministry for Social Affairs grants means-tested family hardship compensation (*Familienhärteausgleich*) on a discretionary basis (Kammer für Arbeiter und Angestellte 2008: 45ff). Applications for means-tested exemptions from radio and television licence fees and a reduction of telephone charges need to be directed to a subsidiary of the Austrian Broadcasting Company (Kammer für Arbeiter und Angestellte 2008: 309ff). A means-tested housing benefit (*Mietzinsbeihilfe*) may be granted upon application via the local tax offices (Kammer für Arbeiter und Angestellte 2008: 289). Means-tested allowances granted by national authorities also include scholarships for students, for which applications have to be filed with one of 15 agencies (*Studienbeihilfenbehörden*) located throughout Austria (Kammer für Arbeiter und Angestellte 2008: 104ff).

Yet the most prominent transfer within the second social net provided by the nine federal provinces[35] (*Länder*) rather than by the nation state is social assistance (*Sozialhilfe*) – with differences between the *Länder* being profound in some cases (Pfeil 2001, Pratscher 2008, Dimmel and Pfeil 2009). Nine different legal acts serve as applicable statutory basis for social assistance. In recent decades, there have been several attempts to harmonize the nine laws across the country, which for a long

---

[35] The nine provinces are Burgenland, Carinthia, Lower Austria, Salzburg, Styria, Tyrol, Upper Austria, Vienna and Vorarlberg.

time failed not least due to resistance from the provinces[36]. Thus, social assistance does not offer a uniform nationwide minimum income. Rather, the nine regional governments fix reference rates autonomously – with differences being profound at times. However, it is not only the reference rates that differ across Austria but also the number of clients served (see table 18).

Table 18: Reference rates of social assistance benefits (in € per month) and number of beneficiaries, Austria and Austrian *Länder*, 2006 and 2008

Provinces	Support for a single person household (2008)	Beneficiaries in private house-holds (2006)	Beneficiaries in institutions (2006)
Burgenland	455.40 1)	846	1,212
Carinthia	490.00 1)	1,352	3,734
Lower Austria	515.80	11,342	10,557
Salzburg	449.00	11,062	3,432
Styria	522.00	4,786	6,470
Tyrol	444.10	10,009	4,132
Upper Austria	552.00 1)	4,472	10,819
Vienna	439.00 1)	83,523	17,579
Vorarlberg	490.00	3,926	1,991
Austria	---	131,318	59,926

Sources: Pratscher (2008: 600ff), Kammer für Arbeiter und Angestellte (2008: 350f). Notes: 1) higher rate for those unavailable for the labour market, e.g. old-aged people, disabled people

The reference rates for temporary cash benefits to subsist on varied between € 439 and € 552 per month for one-person households in 2008. While they are thus all well below the income poverty threshold of € 912 calculated for 2007, there are various supplements granted for housing, heating and various other needs. In Vienna, for example, several types of social assistance transfers are available for income poor citizens, including citizens of the European Union and the EFTA, recognized refugees and citizens from other countries (*Drittstaatsangehörige*) in case

[36] The social assistance schemes will be replaced in 2010 by a means-tested minimum income scheme (*Bedarfsorientierte Mindestsicherung*), which aims primarily at harmonizing the different laws on social assistance and thus at providing for transfers to be comparable across the country (Dimmel 2009).

they have obtained a legal right of residence[37]. These include temporary financial assistance (*Geldaushilfe*). Different reference rates apply to temporary assistance, which mainly depend on household composition. For example, the reference rate for a one-person household in Vienna amounted to € 439 in 2008. In case of need, an additional heating allowance (€ 42 per month) and a rent allowance (at a maximum of € 263 for a one-person household) may be granted as well (Kammer für Arbeiter und Angestellte 2008: 350f). In case of further needs, recipients of temporary financial assistance can apply for a supplement (*Sonderbedarf*). Special needs that may be covered include clothing, furniture or household repairs. However, while eligibility for temporary financial assistance is based on a legal right, entitlement to this supplement is subject to discretion.

Temporary financial assistance is limited in duration. Some population groups, however, may be entitled to permanent assistance (*Dauerleistung*). These include individuals above state retirement age and those unfit for paid work due to health-related reasons. Consequently, this type of transfer from the social assistance scheme is targeted to subgroups of the income poor. The benefit level of permanent support is considerably higher than compared to temporary transfers: in 2008, it amounted to € 710 in Vienna (Kammer für Arbeiter und Angestellte 2008: 350). Moreover, the receipt of permanent support may be linked to a rent supplement and a catalogue of reductions (*Sozialpass*, which includes reductions for public transport etc.).

Income poor individuals who are not covered by health insurance may apply for a health-related support (*Krankenhilfe*), which is a further transfer regulated within the Viennese social assistance scheme. It covers the costs for health-related expenditure such as hospital care (it does not, however, allow for full inclusion into compulsory health insurance). Additionally, a variety of further transfers is incorporated in the Viennese social assistance scheme, including in-kind transfers targeted to the elderly (mainly accommodation in nursing homes) and social services.

While persons in need have a legal right to social assistance, the amount of discretion is high. This leads to different coverage rates across the

[37] For this latter group, specific stipulations apply for the application of social assistance.

country. For example, in Vienna almost 83,600 people in private households received social assistance in 2006. In Lower Austria, a federal province with a comparable population size and comparable economic performance to Vienna[38], only 11,300 people were granted such benefits in the same year (Pratscher 2008: 602).

Provinces do not only differ in terms of the number of clients served but also in terms of administration of this benefit. For example, in Vienna, applications for social assistance have to be filed with one of ten social centres (*Sozialzentren* or *Sozialreferat*). These centres are local offices of the municipality department 40 (or in short: *MA 40*), and established throughout the capital city. People in need of non-monetary help have to turn to the social centres of the *MA 40* as well, although only in case they do not have dependent children. Members of households with children have to address one of the 18 regional offices (*Regionalstellen*) of the *MA 11*, which is the responsible administrative authority for the organization of support to families and children on behalf of the City of Vienna. While cash transfers of social assistance are delivered by the statutory agencies, production and/or delivery of non-monetary support, e.g. family counselling or family care, is often contracted out to nonprofits, such as entities of the *Caritas Wien* or the *Wiener Hilfswerk* (on these actors, see also below).

In addition to social assistance, the nine federal provinces and the 2,358 communities (*Gemeinden*) grant (usually by discretion) further benefits in case of hardship (e.g. housing benefit, means-tested allowances for families, means-tested allowances for students, etc.) – again with marked differences between them. The latter are a result of both the significance of federalism in Austria (Nowotny 1999: 122ff, Genser and Holzmann 2001: 222ff), but also of differences with regard to population groups perceived as particularly threatened by income poverty (and/or perceived as deserving public support).

Unfortunately, secondary information on all of the indicators identified for the operationalization of the welfare mix and its changes is not available for all of the many means-testes transfers. Despite these information

---

[38] http://www.stat.at/web_de/statistiken/volkswirtschaftliche_gesamtrechnungen/regionale_gesamtrechnungen/nuts2_verfuegbares_einkommen_und_verteilungskonten_der_privaten_haushalte/index.html (last accession date: September 2009)

gaps, however, preliminary evidence suggests that the majority of expenditures (more than 85 per cent) accrued by means-tested transfers provided by the welfare state in Austria has been caused by three transfers only (see Section 2.1.1). These are (i) social assistance, (ii) unemployment assistance and (iii) compensation supplement. This justifies – in case of information gaps concerning the aggregate of poverty relief transfers provided by the state – concentrating on secondary information for these three types of transfers only. Whereas unemployment assistance and compensation supplement are delivered throughout Austria, social assistance is – as mentioned earlier – a responsibility of the nine provinces. The transfers included in this programme thus vary across the country. Thus, in case information on these transfers are not comparable across Austria, it has been decide to concentrate on one province only concerning the social assistance scheme, i.e. Vienna. Austria's capital city, with roughly 1.6 million inhabitants, is the country's cultural, political and administrative centre. Apart from being the capital city, Vienna is the largest of the Austrian communities and one of the country's nine federal provinces. Devoting part of the empirical study to one province only seems justified, given the fact that stylized facts on income poverty in Austria suggest that its extent varies considerably across the country.

Table 19 includes data on the extent of income poverty in the nine Austrian provinces in 3-year average (2005-2007). From this it becomes apparent that the Viennese population is particularly threatened by income poverty. However, in contrast to other federal provinces of Austria there are no urban-rural differences in terms of poverty risks either, as Vienna has only an urban population[39].

As there is hardly any information available on the composition of the income poor in Vienna, two data sources (the European Community Household Panel, ECHP, and the EU-Statistics on Income and Living Conditions, EU-SILC) covering the period from 1995 to 2005[40] have been

[39] This does not imply that there are no variations in terms of the distribution of incomes across the 23 Viennese districts (*Bezirke*): In 2007, the range of average net employment income – compared to the Viennese average – amounted from 80 per cent in the 15th district to 157 per cent in the first district (http://www.wien.gv.at/statistik/daten/pdf/einkommen.pdf; last accession date: September 2009).

[40] Earlier information on income poverty in Austria is hardly available (exceptions are,

referred to in order to identify the income poor population of Vienna, since only transfers granted to them are at the core of the empirical analysis. The results of the data analysis that has been conducted utilizing the SPSS programme are listed in the *Annex* of this book.

Table 19: At-risk-of-poverty rates, Austrian provinces, 3-year average (2005-2007)

Austrian provinces	At-risk-of-poverty rate
Vienna	16 %
Burgenland	14 %
Carinthia	14 %
Styria	12 %
Vorarlberg	12 %
Lower Austria	12 %
Tyrol	11 %
Salzburg	10 %
Upper Austria	9 %

Source: Statistik Austria (2009a: 31)

In terms of **nonprofit provision**, the pragmatic definition of nonprofit poverty relief actors chosen (see above) has an important advantage, i.e. the availability of at least some secondary data on a large sample of this group. In 2005, all of the 561 Austrian nonprofit organizations delivering poverty relief were invited to participate in an empirical study on the tasks and provision of their organizations (Dawid and Heitzmann 2006a, 2006b). In gathering data the study relied on two methods. First, staff running the organizations was addressed by e-mail and invited to answer an internet-based questionnaire, which covered six different topics, including a profile of the organization, a description of the client groups served, or reflections on the relationships between the organization and public actors (Dawid and Heitzmann 2006b: 4). Questionnaires were completed by 187 organizations. Consequently, (secondary) information is available for a third of all nonprofits operationalized as poverty relief actors in this country.

for example, Steiner and Wolf 1996) and difficult to compare with ECHP and EU-SILC data. There is only restricted access to Austrian tax data (Biricz and Kniesz 2005, Kniesz 2005) or social insurance data. Income data from the Austrian microcensus do not cover all sources of household income, which is why they cannot be considered a perfect supplement to the survey data of the ECHP (Heitzmann and Wallner-Ewald 1999) and the EU-SILC.

Based on the first results of the internet-based questionnaire, expert interviews have been conducted with staff from 12 of the participating nonprofits across Austria. The selection of the interviewees was based on a joint effort by the aforementioned two network organizations (*Armutskonferenz* and *ÖFSE*) and the authors of the study. It has been made sure that at least one organization from each of the federal provinces was covered by the interviews. The expert interviews focused on a variety of topics, including perceived gaps in terms of the provision of poverty relief, attitudes concerning the interactions between nonprofits and their contracting partners, or experiences and ideas on how to enable participation of clients (Dawid and Heitzmann 2006a: 2). Based on a semi-structured questionnaire, interviews were conducted in the first half of 2006. The transcripts of the interviews were then assessed with the help of content analysis (Atteslander 2008: 181ff). In what follows, I quote the results of this study as 'NPO study' (Dawid and Heitzmann 2006a, 2006b). Moreover, given the author's involvement in the NPO study, it was possible to further utilize the raw data that had been collected through the internet-based questionnaire. This additional data analysis, which helped close some information gaps, was completed by using the SPSS programme. Information deriving from this additional analysis is henceforth referred to as a result from the 'NPO dataset'.

Even though both the NPO study and the NPO dataset include some of the data needed to complete the information requirements for the empirical exercise, information gaps remain. It has therefore been necessary to utilize further information sources. However, aggregate information on all nonprofit poverty relief actors does not exist. Information on some of the indicators identified earlier to operationalize the welfare mix and changes thereof are available only for some organizations or programmes provided by nonprofits. Sources that include information on these organizations and their provision refer to annual reports, bylaws or information from websites. In case umbrella organizations exist, these may hold aggregate information on their subsidiaries. On the vast majority of organizations, however, there is hardly any further information available except for that provided in the NPO study.

Rather than utilizing information from those nonprofits across Austria for which data are available, this study uses a more selective approach: A preliminary analysis of nonprofit provision suggests that – similarly to statutory welfare – nonprofit activity also varies across Austria. In many instances, nonprofits active at a federal level operate autonomously and are independent from their national umbrella organization (Schneider *et al.* 2007: 56). Moreover, many of the former hardly resemble their sister organizations in other federal provinces, which not only shows in terms of provision, but also in terms of their relationships with public actors (e.g. Dawid and Heitzmann 2006a: 38ff). The main reason for these regional variations is yet again the relevance of federalism in this country, which is an important principle not only with respect to the organization of statutory welfare, but also of nonprofit provision (Schneider *et al.* 2007: 56f).

Given regional variations across Austria in terms of poverty relief programmes provided by nonprofit actors, secondary information on nonprofit poverty relief programmes (for which no information from the NPO study or dataset exists) have been collected only for one of the nine Austrian provinces, i.e. Vienna. Yet there are a large number of poverty relief actors active in this city. For example, 66 of the 187 nonprofit organizations that have responded to the internet-based questionnaire for the NPO study are located in Vienna. Since secondary information (other than that collected for the NPO study) is not available for all of these actors, the focus of the empirical assessment is limited to those organizations that grant their support to large groups of the income poor (such as the *Caritas Wien*, the *Volkshilfe Wien* and the *Wiener Hilfswerk*); not least as this compares with the transfers included in the Viennese social assistance scheme.

In what follows, Section 2 includes the information selected to capture the characteristics of the contemporary mixed economy of welfare. For comparative reasons, information presented in the following section refers to the year 2005 – as this is the year referred to by the principal source covering aggregate information on all public means-tested transfers (Eurostat 2008). This also applies to most of the data included in the NPO study (and thus the information source that includes data on the largest sample of nonprofit poverty relief actors).

2. The mixed economy of poverty relief in Austria

Income poor individuals or families have a variety of different options to cope with their disadvantaged situation, many of which do not necessitate the engagement of either public agencies or nonprofits. In this study, however, only the contributions of the latter types of organizations in alleviating income poverty are considered to answer the first part of the empirical-oriented research question: In how far does the conceptual framework help to illustrate the characteristics of the current welfare mix in poverty relief? To answer this question, information needs to be collected for a broad range of indicators. In what follows, Sections 2.1 to 2.3 summarize the information collected in order to illustrate Type I and Type II welfare mix in poverty alleviation in Austria, based on the tripartite concept of 'provision'.

2.1 Production and/or delivery

Who produces and/or delivers poverty relief transfers to the income poor in Austria, and which modes of production/delivery are applied by these actors? This section aims to answer this question concerning the contributions of public actors and nonprofits.

2.1.1 Type I welfare mix

Type I welfare mix is concerned with the question, 'who produces and/or delivers poverty relief transfers to the income poor?'. As noted in Section 1.2.1, two indicators have been selected to operationalize the element of production and/or delivery – total transfer expenditures and the number of clients served by public and nonprofit poverty relief actors.

Despite their large number, means-tested transfers provided by the public sector (see above) play only a minor role in terms of social security **expenditures**. According to recent data published by Eurostat (2008: 44), the Austrian welfare state spent € 4.459 billion on means-tested benefits in 2005. As mentioned earlier, the majority of these expenditures is caused by three transfers only, namely social assistance, unemployment assistance and compensation supplement. Expenditures for social assistance in 2005 amounted to € 2.188 billion in Austria (Pratscher 2007: 738). Expenditures for unemployment assistance and for compensation supplement amounted to € 818 million (Arbeitsmarktservice Österreich 2006: 34) and € 812 million, respectively, in 2005 (Haydn 2006: 263).

Means-tested transfers provided by the welfare state in Austria only made up 7 per cent of the total expenditures spent on welfare transfers in 2005. This does not imply that the Austrian welfare state is not effective in combating income poverty (Statistik Austria 2007a: 43): The income poverty rate in 2005 would have amounted to 43 per cent (instead of 12 per cent), if no public transfers had been paid. Yet the main means-tested transfers of the public sector, i.e. social assistance including housing allowance, only account for a reduction of the income poverty rate from 13 to 12 per cent. The majority of the effect thus derives from other, primarily non-means-tested, transfers such as pensions or universal social security programmes, which largely qualify as *ex ante* measures of combating income poverty.

Regarding nonprofit provision, no aggregate data on total transfer expenditures is included in the NPO study. Secondary information on this indicator is available only for some of the larger poverty relief actors. For example, the *Caritas Wien*[41] provides three social advice centres (*Sozialberatungsstellen*) in Vienna to which people in need of support may turn to apply for cash or in-kind support[42]. These centres spent almost € 554,000 in support of their clients in 2005 (Caritas Erzdiözese Wien 2006: 7). The social advice centre (*Sozialberatungsstelle*) maintained by the *Volkshilfe Wien*[43], which offers low-level access to all peo-

[41] The *Caritas Wien* is one of the largest nonprofit organizations providing welfare in the Vienna region. (The region of 'Vienna' in this diocesan context differs from the federal province of Vienna – the *Erzdiözese Wien* also includes the eastern parts of Lower Austria.) Some 3,000 employees and 5,000 volunteers engage in delivering social services and support. The range of provision of the *Caritas Wien* includes assistance to the elderly, refugees, the homeless, families with children, the unemployed and many more (Caritas Erzdiözese Wien 2006).

[42] Migrants are excluded from applying for help at these centres – for them, the *Caritas Wien* provides specific programmes.

[43] Members of the Socialist Party (now Social-Democratic Party, SPÖ) founded the *Volkshilfe Wien* in 1947 (Volkshilfe Wien 2007). Similar to the *Caritas*, the *Volkshilfe Wien* is engaged in a variety of social activities in Vienna, focusing on long-term care, homecare and assistance for the homeless. About 1,100 employees and 500 volunteers assist it in complying with its tasks (Volkshilfe Wien 2007: 9).

ple in need of help, spent € 108,580 in 2006 (Volkshilfe Wien 2007: 20). Further secondary information is available for ten neighbourhood centres (*Nachbarschaftszentren*) operated by the *Wiener Hilfswerk*[44], which provide a variety of different services across Vienna (Wiener Hilfswerk 2005). One programme within these centres is particularly relevant in terms of poverty relief, namely the project '*guat beinand*', which supplies poverty relief transfers directly to its clients (Wiener Hilfswerk 2005: 39). Total transfer expenditures for support provided by this organization amounted to € 147,000 in 2005.

Even though the number of nonprofits providing poverty relief in Vienna and across the country is much larger, secondary information on their total transfer expenditures is not available. However, compared with the expenditures on means-tested transfers provided by the welfare state, the proportions of nonprofits concerning this indicator are likely to be considerably smaller than of statutory actors.

In addition to data on transfer expenditures, data on the total number of **clients served** is needed to capture the characteristics of Type I welfare mix with regard to the element of production and/or delivery. Aggregate information on this indicator concerning public provision is not available, though. There is, however, evidence on the number of clients served with regard to the three largest, in terms of expenditures, transfers: In 2005, roughly 182,000 citizens in both private and institutional households were entitled to support under the social assistance scheme (Pratscher 2007: 734). 96,500 unemployed people received unemployment assistance in the same year (Arbeitsmarktservice Österreich 2006: 35) and almost 227,000 citizens were entitled to a compensation supplement (Haydn 2006: 263). Whereas unemployment assistance and compensation supplement target different population groups, both the unemployed and the elderly may qualify for social assistance. Hence the total number of clients receiving at least one of these public transfers can not be calculated based on the available data.

---

[44] The *Wiener Hilfswerk* was founded in 1947 by members of the Austrian People's Party (ÖVP). At present, it engages in a variety of social activities, including home care, family care, etc., employing more than 600 employees and almost 500 volunteers (Wiener Hilfswerk 2006).

Information on the number of clients served by nonprofits derives from the NPO study (Dawid and Heitzmann 2006a: 5ff). The results point towards a considerable heterogeneity across nonprofits concerning this indicator: the number of people who asked for assistance at nonprofits ranged from a minimum of 4 individuals to a maximum of 8,500 in 2004 (163 organizations provided data on this issue, i.e. 29 % of all nonprofit poverty relief actors), although the support granted often assists persons other than those directly addressing the organizations, such as close relatives (e.g. children). Information on the total number of clients served was provided by 99 nonprofits. From these data it may be concluded that more than 223,000 persons were supported by those nonprofits. On the one hand, these data may include double counts (if clients turn to two nonprofits they are counted twice). On the other hand, however, only a relatively small number of nonprofits reported data on the number of clients served. A projection of the total number of people supported, based on the average number of clients served, suggests that approximately 950,000 people were provided assistance by poverty relief actors from the third sector in Austria (Dawid and Heitzmann 2006a: 7). This roughly corresponds with the total number of income poor individuals in this country (see *Excursus* in *Annex*). Based on median values, the projection suggests that the number of clients served totalled 225,000 (a difference as compared to the projection calculated on the basis of average values which underlines the skewed distribution of the nonprofit sample).

Compared to the number of clients served by public actors regarding the three main transfers under the means-tested scheme (social assistance, unemployment assistance and compensation supplement) this indeed underlines that, measured in terms of clients served, nonprofits have a considerable role in supporting the income poor in Austria.

2.1.2 Type II welfare mix

In addition to identifying the producers and/or deliverers of poverty relief transfers (which is a key concern of Type I welfare mix), Type II welfare mix requires identifying how production and/or delivery is administered by the poverty relief actors. As discussed previously (see Section 1.2.1), take-up rates of poverty relief transfers are utilized as a proxy indicator to capture this element of provision.

In terms of public provision, problems concerning **non-take-up** are particularly discussed concerning social assistance. A recent study conducted on the basis of micro simulation models suggests that more than 50 % of households that would have been entitled to social assistance did not apply for these transfers in 2003 (Fuchs 2003). The reasons are manifold and include ignorance, pride, fear of stigmatization, and unwillingness to burden relatives – given the requirement for recovery of paid assistance (Dimmel 2000: 407f, Badelt and Österle 2001b: 243ff).

A recent study confirms the relevance of these problems concerning the delivery of social assistance in Austria[45]: Based on the results of a questionnaire targeted to experts in nonprofits that work with recipients of social assistance, several problems have been identified[46]. First, the degree of discretion executed by staff in social assistance agencies is perceived to be particularly high, allegedly leading to different decisions on largely the same problems. Only some agencies implemented internal instructions to harmonize decision-making among staff. Second, the nonprofit experts observed that specific income poor groups are treated differently – with some groups being identified as more 'deserving' than others (including ex-cons, homeless people, but also migrants). Third, notifications on whether or not someone is entitled to social assistance are given in written or oral form – with the latter apparently being the rule rather than the exception. However, only a written notification allows for an appeal against it. Fourth, social assistance is (with a few exceptions) only granted to people willing to enter employment; otherwise transfers are reduced or refused. Usually, it is the *AMS* that decides whether or not a person is willing to take on paid employment. Experts criticize that in most cases, social assistance agencies accept this decision without examining further whether this 'unwillingness' is due to a lack of capability or possibility. Fifth, an important reason for the high non-take-up rate of social assistance is the requirement to pay back transfers either through the beneficiaries (in case of future capital) or through close relatives. Especially the fear to burden relatives makes many potential beneficiaries refuse to apply for social assistance transfers. Further aspects that have

---

[45] http://www.armut.at/Anford_ARMUTSKONFERENZ_Stand_23.1.08_end_06_druck.pdf (last accession date: September 2009)

[46] However, these are potentially biased results, as information has been collected only from experts from nonprofit organizations that represent a lobby of those applying for social assistance.

been criticized in connection with the delivery of social assistance refer to problems in calculating the level of the transfer or concerning an alarming behaviour of staff towards applicants. A specific problem is the long period it takes to decide whether or not social assistance should be granted, which may amount up to 6 months: this counteracts one of the main aims of the social assistance programme, i.e. to serve as a fast support of last resort.

While there are thus many problems connected with the delivery of social assistance in Austria, these problems are largely unknown with regard to other means-tested transfers provided by the public sector, most notably compensation supplement but also unemployment assistance: take-up of these transfers does not appear to be a particular problem.

What about the administration of production and/or delivery of nonprofit provision in poverty alleviation? As compared to social assistance, delivery of poverty relief transfers by nonprofits is usually perceived as less problematic. However, information from the NPO study suggests that support granted by nonprofits might be viewed as stigmatizing as well. For example, results of the interviews conducted suggest that potential clients of nonprofits hesitate to enter organizations that are known for supporting the disadvantaged – out of fear they might be observed by fellow citizens. This problem has particularly been identified for rural areas (Dawid and Heitzmann 2006a: 28). While this evidence does point to the fact that individuals feel embarrassed to depend on assistance – regardless of whether this help is offered by public or by nonprofit actors, no estimate on the 'non-take-up rate' concerning nonprofit provision does exist.

The evidence presented so far suggests that there are hurdles associated with the delivery of selected poverty relief transfers provided by both public and nonprofit actors. Although the facts presented only offer a snapshot based on limited evidence, it becomes clear that there is quite some room for improvement for both types of actors.

2.2 Finance

Following the illustration of the mixed economy of poverty alleviation concerning the element of 'production and/or delivery', this section turns to the second element relevant for the analysis, i.e. 'finance', and summarizes evidence collected to capture the characteristics of the mixed economy of poverty relief in Austria.

2.2.1 Type I welfare mix

Who finances poverty relief transfers in Austria? Finding answers to this question is key for assessing Type I welfare mix. In terms of public provision, funding derives exclusively (e.g. in the case of unemployment assistance or compensation supplement) or almost exclusively from the public budget. The latter applies, for example, to social assistance, which is mainly financed through resources from the budget of the federal provinces and communities. However, there are some possibilities to recover paid assistance from the recipients (e.g. in case of future capital or inheritance) or from relatives[47]. In Vienna, for example, recovery may be required from the recipient's partner and his/her parents, if they are obliged to pay maintenance. The obligation for recovery is limited to 3 years. Anecdotal evidence suggests that these recoveries are also utilized to deter potential recipients from applying for social assistance – rather than being a prominent proportion of total funding. For example, total expenditures for general social assistance in Vienna amounted to roughly € 211 million in 2005, while income generated through recovery from beneficiaries and regress payments from relatives amounted to € 15.5 million in the same year (Pratscher 2007: 738ff), i.e. a proportion of roughly 7 per cent.

Evidence for Austria suggests that there are quite some differences concerning the relative share of public and private funding within the third sector: While some poverty relief products are completely financed by public or private sources, the portfolio of others consists of a combination of both (Dawid and Heitzmann 2006a: 13f). Data analysis from the NPO dataset suggests that 31 per cent of nonprofits for which data is available (n=173, i.e. 31 % of all nonprofit poverty relief actors) financed their whole budget by public sources in 2004. In contrast, only 10 per cent noted that they financed their expenditures fully by private income, such as own revenues or donations. 59 per cent of third-sector organizations were financed by a mixture of public and private funding sources. The average organization (which does not correspond to a representative or-

[47] Except from recovery are certain benefits (e.g. transfers for educational purposes).

ganization, given the heterogeneity of nonprofit poverty relief actors) financed three quarters of its budget through public sources and the rest through private sources.

The results suggest that public transfers are almost exclusively financed by public sources (including social insurance contributions), whereas nonprofits rely to a larger proportion on private funding sources.

2.2.2 Type II welfare mix

Two indicators are utilized to operationalize Type II welfare mix concerning the element of finance. First, the very composition of public and private funding sources needs to be assessed. Second, the relevance of subsidies versus performance-related forms of payments in case of joint provision must be examined.

As regards the **composition of public and private funding sources**, poverty relief transfers produced and/or delivered by the public sector rely almost exclusively on public funding sources. However, some transfers – most notably social assistance – also rely on private funding in the form of recovery payments. For example, and as mentioned above, 7 % of the total income for general social assistance in Vienna derived from recovery payments financed by (former) beneficiaries and/or relatives.

As mentioned earlier, most nonprofits providing poverty alleviation in Austria for which data is available (n = 173, i.e. 31 % of all nonprofit poverty relief actors in Austria) rely on public funding sources as well. Information included in the NPO dataset suggests that 79 per cent of this sample financed at least half of their budget through public sources. In terms of private funding sources, the 'average' third-sector organization financed roughly 11 per cent of its overall budget in 2004 through commercial income, and another 13 per cent through other forms of private income, such as donations or membership fees (Dawid and Heitzmann 2006a). Further results derived from an analysis of the NPO dataset suggest that 58 per cent of the sample of nonprofit poverty relief actors in Austria for which information is available (n = 173) did not rely on commercial income at all, whereas only 2 per cent were fully funded by this type of income (which includes, for example, user fees). As for other sources of private income (such as donations or membership fees), 54 per cent of nonprofits that have reported data stated that they did not gain income from these sources, whereas 5 per cent funded their entire budget through this type of funding source.

From the few pieces of information available on the composition of funding sources it appears that nonprofit activity is financed by a broad range of different (private) forms of funding. However, their heterogeneity becomes once more apparent.

Information on the **form of financial agreements** in case of joint provision is included in the NPO study and dataset – and thus available for a large proportion of nonprofit poverty relief actors. Data suggest that 84 per cent of those nonprofits in Austria for which information is available (n = 155; i.e. data exist for 28 % of all nonprofit poverty relief organizations) relied on resources derived from public subsidies in 2005 (Dawid and Heitzmann 2006a: 14). 75 per cent noted that they have received performance-related payments (based on a sample of 169 organizations, i.e. 30 % of all nonprofit poverty relief organizations). As these figures indicate, most nonprofits (six out of ten) in the sample relied on a combination of subsidies and performance-related payments. This suggests that they hold several contracts with public actors – with different forms of financial agreements. In terms of organizations that exclusively relied on one or the other form of funding (n = 39, i.e. only 7 % of all nonprofits providing poverty relief in Austria), one third was financed solely by subsidies and the remaining two thirds by performance-related payments (NPO dataset).

2.3 Provider decisions

In what follows, information on provider decisions is summarized. As discussed earlier, four indicators are utilized to operationalize this element of provision. In terms of Type I welfare mix, this refers to the proportion of nonprofits in joint provision that are funded through subsidies or performance-related payments. Regarding Type II welfare mix, eligibility criteria applied, income poor groups served and types of products provided serve as proxy indicators to capture provider decisions.

2.3.1 Type I welfare mix

The key questions for examining Type I welfare mix in the context of 'provider decisions' are: 'which actor(s) decide(s) on (i) clients targeted, (ii) products provided, (iii) the modes of production and/or delivery, and (iv) the composition of funding sources?'. As discussed previously, the question of which actor(s) take(s) the provider decisions is relevant mainly in case of joint provision. The question is, however, to what extent is there multi-sector or joint provision between public and nonprofit actors providing poverty alleviation in Austria?

In terms of multi-sector provision, this category comprises a multitude of (mostly cash) transfers provided by the welfare state (including compensation supplement and unemployment assistance). Public actors both finance and deliver these transfers – and consequently also take the provider decisions. In terms of nonprofit delivery, information from the NPO study suggests that only 10 per cent of all nonprofits for which information is available (n = 173) have not been financed through public sources (which include resources from institutions of the European Union, national, regional and local authorities as well as social insurance institutions or the Austrian employment service). This implies that 90 % of third sector organizations included in this sample engaged in poverty relief jointly with public financiers to provide support to the income poor. Whenever public actors finance nonprofit production and/or delivery, the division of decision-making powers between the two cooperating partners becomes vital.

As discussed earlier, public subsidies are arguably a mode of finance that leaves decision-making to the nonprofit partner, whereas funding based on performance-related payments suggests that the financier makes provider decisions (see Section II.1.2.3). As mentioned above, however, six out of ten nonprofits in Austria for which information on the **financial agreement** in case of joint provision is available relied on both types of funding. This makes it impossible to draw inferences as to who has the regulatory power.

In those cases in which nonprofits are funded by a combination of public and private sources, moreover, it is necessary to differentiate between funding the organization and funding the transfers delivered. With regard to the latter, there is anecdotal evidence that nonprofit transfers are largely financed through private income such as donations. A further piece of evidence confirming this behaviour is the fact that even though nonprofits have the legal right to recover some of their transfer expenditures through the social assistance scheme, they hardly ever execute this option. This allows nonprofits to maintain decision-making powers (such as determining eligibility criteria).

2.3.2 Type II welfare mix

For an analysis of Type II welfare mix it is vital to examine which provider decisions welfare actors have made in terms of (i) eligibility criteria applied, (ii) clients served and (iii) products provided.

Which **eligibility criteria** do public and nonprofit actors in Austria apply and which **income poor (groups)** are **served** by them? Income-tested transfers provided by public actors target either all income poor groups (and thus incorporate a universal approach) or accrue to specific groups only (thus following a selective approach). Examples of the latter are those benefits integrated in the Austrian social security system that only target victims of crimes (*Hilfeleistungen nach dem Vebrechensopfergesetz*), participants of World War I and/or II (e.g. *Unterhaltsrente*), or citizens with health problems incurred while in military service (*Erhöhungsbeitrag Beschädigtenversorgung*). Thus, in addition to an income testing or means testing, these transfers are further limited to specific groups. This also applies to unemployment assistance (which is only available for individuals who have received unemployment benefit previously) and compensation supplement (which is only available for individuals entitled to a retirement pension). Only a few instruments are organized on a broader scale to cover larger population groups. The main transfer in this respect is social assistance. However, social assistance is subject to subsidiarity. This implies that individuals or families have a legal right to social assistance only if their material and social security cannot be guaranteed by other sources. These include income from employment, social security transfers and other assets of their family. The basic requirement for people applying for temporary financial assistance is their willingness to take on paid employment (in case they are not employed already). Thus, they need to be registered as unemployed with the *AMS*. Some groups are excluded from this requirement, though. In Vienna, for example, this includes minors, pupils that have not yet completed a secondary education (*Matura*), lone parents, if their youngest child is not two years old yet, people above state retirement age (which is 65 years for men and 60 years for women) as well as disabled or sick individuals classified as unfit for paid work by a medical examination. Migrants without a legal residence are excluded from provision[48]. Permanent social assistance, which is provided in some provinces (e.g. in Vienna), is only granted to people who are not able to integrate in paid employment (e.g. because they are above state retirement age or unfit for paid work due to health-related reasons).

More detailed information on the income poor groups served are available only for recipients of social assistance transfers provided to private households in Vienna. Data suggest that slightly more women (53 per cent) than men (47 per cent) living in private households received transfers under the social assistance scheme in the Austrian capital city in 2005. 24 per cent were under the age of 15, another 23 per cent were between 15 and 29 years old. 11 per cent were 60 years or older. Of the latter group, 69 per cent were females. Regarding citizenship, data for 2005 suggest that 76 per cent of social assistance recipients in private households in Vienna were Austrian citizens. In terms of educational attainment, the majority of social assistance recipients above the age of 18 years (61 per cent) had only elementary schooling – suggesting a close link between educational level and low income. In terms of household types, among those entitled to social assistance transfers one-person households slightly outnumbered multi-person ones (Pratscher 2007: 735f).

In terms of nonprofit provision, information on eligibility criteria concerning the transfers provided is not available – except for a few organizations. Anecdotal evidence relating to some nonprofits engaged in poverty relief in Vienna suggests that these only grant transfers to income-poor people on the basis of a means test. Like in the public sector, a variety of nonprofit provision is targeted to specific population groups only. This includes care services for the elderly, social services for the disabled, support for sick people, assistance targeted to the long-term unemployed and families, etc. However, a majority of nonprofits included in the NPO

[48] For them, separate programmes are available, which are financed by the state and delivered by agencies of the *Caritas*.

study did not specialize on selected risk groups. Rather, they granted low-level access to allow large groups to turn to them for help (Dawid and Heitzmann 2006a: 10ff).

In terms of demographic and socio-economic characteristics of income-poor (groups) served, data from the NPO study suggest that 16 per cent of their clients (n = 106) were below the age of 19. Eight per cent were above the age of 65 (n = 147). More than half of the clients served by nonprofits in Austria for which data is available (n = 144) noted that elementary schooling was their highest educational level – similar to the recipients of social assistance. Approximately 60 per cent of their clients (n = 150) were unemployed (Dawid and Heitzmann 2006a: 7f).

As regards **products provided**, welfare states differ in terms of their portfolio. Austria belongs to those welfare states that chiefly deliver monetary rather than in-kind benefits. Indeed, in 2005, 71 per cent of all social security transfers granted by the Austrian government were cash benefits (Eurostat 2008: 44). This large proportion is put into perspective by the fact that nonprofits provide many social services: Estimates suggest that 80 per cent of all social services in Austria are delivered by nonprofits (Trukeschitz 2006).

When considering solely means-tested benefits granted by statutory agencies, the proportion of cash transfers amounts to only 48 cent of all means-tested expenditures in 2005 (Eurostat 2008: 44). Statutory provision of poverty alleviation is thus less cash-dominated than suggested by the overall distribution of social protection expenditures. Both compensation supplement and unemployment benefit are (unbounded) cash transfers. Social assistance is granted both in cash and in kind. Whether cash transfers under the social assistance scheme are granted bounded or unbounded depends on regional legislations and administration. In Vienna, for example, most of the cash transfers that form part of the social assistance scheme are granted unbounded – even though for specific transfers clients have to document *ex post* that they had used the funds properly.

As regards in-kind transfers, the largest proportion of all of these transfers provided by public actors derives from the social assistance scheme. It includes funding accommodation of persons in institutional care (e.g.

homes for the elderly). In 2005, expenditures for this largest part of social assistance amounted to € 1.19 million in Austria (Pratscher 2007: 739), i.e. roughly 60 % of total expenditures for means-tested in-kind transfers (Eurostat 2008). Means-tested transfers under the social assistance scheme in Austria also include social services such as home care or outpatient care (which are often delivered by nonprofits). In terms of expenditures, these transfers added up to a total of € 325 million in 2005 (Pratscher 2007: 739).

Aggregate information on the proportions of cash and in-kind transfers delivered by nonprofits is not available for Austria. Whereas these actors primarily provide in-kind goods, and particularly social services (see above), evidence from the NPO study implies that almost one third of those nonprofits engaged in poverty alleviation in Austria for which data is available (n = 170) also granted cash transfers to their clients (Dawid and Heitzmann 2006a: 10). Even though this proportion is high, the total amount of these expenditures is – in comparison to statutory transfers – likely to be lower. The extent of in-kind transfers provided, and particularly the variety of social services offered, is, however, impressive. Information from the NPO study suggests that one of the main tasks of nonprofits in this respect is counselling the income poor (Dawid and Heitzmann 2006a: 9f). This ranges from legal and financial advice to social counselling. Many nonprofits engage in offering training, for example, to increase social skills. Poverty relief actors of the third sector also offer language courses for migrants, etc. An interesting finding from the NPO study suggests that hardly any third-sector organization in Austria concentrates on the provision of one specific activity only, e.g., debt counselling. Rather, most organizations provide a mix of several services, such as debt counselling, family counselling and legal counselling. Moreover, many nonprofits engage in lobbying activities to improve the situation of their clients. A large number of third-sector organizations assist clients in applying for social assistance, unemployment assistance or other types of support delivered by public agencies. Indeed, often these organizations do not deliver assistance or services themselves but rather help their clients to address other (public, for-profit or nonprofit) agencies. According to data from the NPO study (Dawid and Heitzmann 2006a: 10), this is the case mainly with regard to medical, psychological or psychotherapeutical needs as well as requirements of clients for legal counselling.

Thus, many nonprofits offer support that enables them to respond specifically to the needs of their clients, without losing sight of their – often manifold and very heterogeneous – problems. Rather than providing a clear, pre-defined and thus often very specialized assistance, which might enhance efficiency, the provision of many nonprofits engaged in poverty relief in Austria therefore tends to be more holistic. While this might hamper the efficiency of their operations, it might prove valuable concerning the effectiveness of nonprofit help in terms of a needs-based and high-quality support of income poor and socially excluded population groups (Dawid and Heitzmann 2006a: 55).

These results suggest that in poverty alleviation there is no clear division of labour between public and nonprofit actors. Whereas the former are primarily responsible for supporting the income poor with material resources, many nonprofits offer cash transfers, as well. The latter do specialize in providing social services. However, public sector organizations also deliver in-kind goods.

3. Privatization and marketization of poverty relief in Austria

Section 2 presented (some) evidence on the current balance of the mixed economy of poverty alleviation in Austria. This section is guided by the second part of the empirical research question of this study: It seeks to assess in how far the conceptual framework elaborated helps in empirically assessing changes that might qualify as 'privatization' or 'marketization' in the provision or poverty relief. As discussed in Section II.2, 'privatization' implies that responsibilities in the provision of poverty alleviation are shifted from public towards private (i.e. in the context of this study, nonprofit) actors and/or – in terms of finance – from public towards private funding sources. Growing importance of market ethics and principles in the provision of welfare, and thus 'marketization', has been defined as a key type of change of Type II welfare mix.

As indicated earlier, the balance of the welfare mix is continuously subject to change – not only at present times. This also applies to the mixed economy of poverty alleviation in Austria, in which the burden of alleviating poverty has been shifted several times within the last centuries (Heitzmann 2004b). This section focuses on the most recent adjustment processes that have led to the current balance of the mixed economy of poverty relief in Austria. Section 2 presented ample evidence that in this country, both public and nonprofit actors engage in the provision of poverty alleviation. Have the responsibilities and/or the role of these types of actors changed in recent years? Have there been shifts towards an enlargement of nonprofit responsibilities in poverty relief and/or an increase of private funding sources? Did poverty relief actors in the past comply with their tasks in poverty alleviation in a different manner than today? Finally, in how far does the conceptual framework elaborated in Chapter II help in answering these questions? In what follows, evidence for recent shifts in the provision of poverty relief in Austria is summarized. Section 3.1 assesses developments in terms of the production and/or delivery of poverty alleviation. Section 3.2 illustrates shifts in terms of financing poverty relief and Section 3.3 considers changes concerning provider decisions.

3.1 Production and/or delivery

Changes in the element of production and/or delivery of poverty alleviation may be manifold. This study, however, is interested in two specific types of shifts only. One type are developments that involve a decreasing contribution of public actors in the production and/or delivery of poverty relief transfers and/or an increase of nonprofit contributions. Only such changes qualify as (partial) privatization. The other type are changes that led to a more marketized type of production and/or delivery of poverty relief transfers.

3.1.1 Privatization

Changes in the element of production and/or delivery qualify as ‘privatization’ in the following cases (see figure 4 in Section II.2.1.1): shifts from public production/delivery towards (i) nonprofit production/delivery or (ii) joint production/delivery, as well as shifts from joint production/delivery towards (iii) nonprofit production/delivery or (iv) joint production/delivery with an increasing share of nonprofit production/delivery. For an empirical investigation that is interested in assessing whether the element of production and/or delivery of poverty relief transfers has been privatized in recent years it is vital to examine (i) whether and to what extent the number of income-poor (groups) served by public and nonprofit actors has changed, and (ii) whether and to what extent the amount of transfer expenditures has changed in recent years with regard to these two types of providers. These two indicators have been chosen for operationalizing this element of provision (see Section 1.3.1).

Have transfer expenditures of public and nonprofit poverty relief actors decreased or increased in the period analyzed? Information on developments of **transfer expenditures** is available only for some nonprofits. For example, in its annual report *Caritas* stated that in 2004 it had offered help to more than 10,000 clients in Vienna, and spent € 667,000 in the form of monetary relief. Only two years earlier, expenditures of the same organization had amounted to € 531,000, and the number of clients served to roughly 7,400 (Till and Till-Tentschert 2003: 3). There is only anecdotal evidence suggesting that increases in transfer expenditures have occurred also with regard to other nonprofit poverty relief actors. A further indication of considerable expansion of nonprofit providers refers to the number of associations providing welfare and relief, which increased quite substantially: Between 1991 and 2001[49], their number rose by 48 per cent in Austria. However, as mentioned earlier, it remains unclear how many of the associations providing welfare and relief are indeed poverty relief actors.

Available data on public provision suggest that between 1995 and 2005, social protection expenditures of the Austrian welfare state did not change in relative terms. Even though (nominal) expenditures increased by 40 per cent[50] (Eurostat 2007: 42, 2008: 44), so did GDP. Thus, social protection expenditures as a proportion of GDP remained stable at 28.8 per cent (Statistik Austria 2007b: 219). What has indeed changed are the relative proportions of means-tested versus non-means-tested transfers. In 1996 (comparable data for 1995 is not available), 4 per cent of all expenditures in Austria were due to means-tested transfers. Up until 2005, this proportion rose to 7 per cent (Eurostat 2008: 44). This suggests that the public sector has enhanced – rather than decreased – its (relative) contributions in poverty alleviation.

---

[49] From 2001 onwards, the Austrian Home Office has omitted information that would allow to differentiate between associations belonging to different activity fields.

[50] Inflation rose by 17 per cent between 1995 and 2005 (http://www.statistik-austria.at; last accession date: September 2009).

Further information suggests that there were quite some variations within the category of means-tested expenditures, though. Steiner (2009: 168), for example, notes that means-tested cash transfers granted by provinces or communities in Austria increased by 154 per cent between 1995 and 2006. This implies that the relevance of Austrian provinces and communities as poverty relief actors has grown in the new millennium as compared to the mid-1990s. Data on selected benefits confirm the increasing relevance of local poverty relief transfers (see table 20).

Between 1995 and 2005, expenditures for (regional) social assistance in Austria increased by 87 percent (in current prices). Expenditures for unemployment assistance and compensation supplement, which fall within national, rather than regional legal competence, did not rise to such an extent. Expenditures for the latter transfer even decreased slightly. The benefit levels of social assistance and compensation supplement rose by 18 per cent, which compares to the aggregate inflation rate for the period of 1995 to 2005[51]. This, however, implies that the average benefit paid in unemployment assistance even declined in real terms.

Table 20: Development of key indicators of selected poverty relief transfers of the public sector, Austria, 1995-2005

	Expenditures	Recipients	Benefit levels
Social assistance in Austria	+ 87 %	+ 63 %	+ 18 %[2)]
Unemployment assistance[1)]	+ 26 %	+ 35 %	+ 10 %
Compensation supplement	- 0.3 %	- 17 %	+ 18 %

Sources: BMAS (1996: 44ff); BMAGS (1997: 47, 1998: 37); Haydn (2006: 253ff); Pratscher (2007: 732ff); http://www.bmsk.gv.at (last accession date: September 2009); http://www.ams.or.at (last accession date: September 2009); own calculations. Notes: 1) recipients are an average per year; benefit levels based on average per capita transfers; 2) average calculated from the reference rates of the nine Austrian provinces

Data on these selected public benefits suggest that it has rather been the increase (or, in case of compensation supplement: decrease) in terms of **recipients** than an increase of benefit levels that led to the growth (decrease) of expenditures regarding the main poverty relief transfers provided by the public sector. For example, in Austria, the number of recipients of social assistance has increased by 63 per cent between 1995 and 2005 (Pratscher 2007: 734). The number of recipients of unemploy-

[51] http://www.wifo.at (last accession date: September 2009)

ment assistance rose by over a third in the same period, while the number of beneficiaries entitled to compensation supplement declined by 17 per cent (Haydn 2006: 263).

Given the considerable increase of recipients of social assistance, it seems appropriate to include some more information on this poverty alleviation transfer. The number of recipients in private households (who usually receive cash transfers) increased by 98 per cent between 1995 and 2005 (table 21) and thus to a much greater extent than the number of recipients in institutions (+ 17%). This also implies that, compared with data on transfer expenditures, *per capita* expenditures of in-kind transfers increased to a much higher degree than *per capita* expenditures of cash transfers.

Table 21: Development of social assistance expenditures and beneficiaries, Austria, 1995 – 2005

Social assistance	1995	2000	2005	1995-2005 in %
Number of beneficiaries				
...in private households	63,369	81,054	125,670	98%
...in institutions	48,496	62,680	56,785	17%
...total	111,865	143,734	182,455	63%
Expenditures (in mio. €) for				
... general social assistance	366	384	484	32%
... institutions	528	871	1,190	125%
... social services	187	318	325	74%
... assistance for refugees	52	13	123	134%
... other measures	36	37	67	85%
... total	1,169	1,624	2,188	87%

Sources: Pratscher (2007: 734ff); own calculations

The development of social assistance in Vienna was even more pronounced both in terms of the number of the income-poor targeted but also in terms of the growth of expenditures. In the capital city, the number of social assistance beneficiaries living in institutions, such as nursing homes, was about the same in 1995 and 2005 (see table 22). However, expenditures for people in institutions increased by 70 per cent, i.e. a profound increase of *per capita* expenditures.

A considerable variation in the last decade has also occurred regarding the distribution of temporary and permanent assistance delivered to private households. Between 1995 and 2005, the number of recipients of permanent assistance increased by 12 % in Vienna, while the number of clients receiving temporary assistance more than tripled in the same period. In 1995, moreover, about half of the clients entitled to temporary assistance could rely on additional income in the household. The other half did not obtain any household income other than social assistance. For them, this type of welfare transfers constituted the only income source. Ten years later, the situation is quite different. While the number of clients fully relying on social assistance increased by 11 %, the number of people receiving social assistance as a supplement to household income increased by 400 per cent. This suggests that the very function of social assistance in Vienna has changed: Rather than being a last resort for people without either employment income or income from social insurance or universal transfers, it is obtaining the role of supplementing those income sources that do not suffice to shift a person above the (comparatively low) social assistance reference rates (see also table 18).

Table 22: Development of social assistance benefits, Vienna, 1995 – 2005

Social assistance	1995	2000	2005	95-05 in %
Number of beneficiaries				
total	48,566	70,078	97,021	+ 100 %
...in institutions	17,090	24,041	17,067	0 %
...in private households	31,476	46,037	79,964	+ 154 %
......with permanent support	9,520	10,083	10,684	+ 12 %
......with temporary support	21,956	35,954	69,270	+ 215 %
.........full assistance	10,431	12,402	11,616	+ 11 %
.........partial assistance	11,525	23,552	57,654	+ 400 %
Expenditures (current prices)				
total in mio. €	486	61	740	+ 52 %
... for institutions (in mio. €)	187	255	318	+ 70 %

Sources: Pratscher (2007: 732ff); own calculations

What about the number of clients served by nonprofit poverty relief actors? Has this indicator changed recently? Results derived from the NPO dataset support the hypothesis of a growing demand for nonprofit provision in Austria (table 23).

Four out of five organizations for which data is available noted that both the number of clients served as well as the products provided has increased between 2000 and 2005 (Dawid and Heitzmann 2006a: 8) – the size of this expansion is unknown, though.

Table 23: Development of key indicators (in per cent) of nonprofit provision, Austria, 2000 and 2005

	Amount of products provided	Number of clients served
in 2005 > in 2000	80 %	82 %
in 2005 = in 2000	18 %	15 %
in 2005 < in 2000	2 %	3 %
Total	100 %	100 %

Sources: NPO dataset; own calculations. Notes: sample size (n): 175-176

3.1.2 Marketization

In contrast to Type I welfare mix, which mainly focuses on the issue of who produces and/or delivers poverty relief transfers, there have been quite some changes both in the public and the third sector in terms of how production and/or delivery has been administered. The following paragraphs will seek to evaluate in how far these changes qualify as 'marketization'. As discussed earlier (see Section 1.3.1), three indicators have been selected to operationalize this element of provision with regard to marketization. It needs to be assessed whether organizational reforms (such as management by objectives) have been implemented in the provider organizations, whether take-up rates have increased, and also whether tendencies to enhance commercialization have led to increased professionalization in nonprofits, which, in turn, would have enhanced the proportion of paid staff and decreased the proportion of volunteers.

Organizational reforms have affected a variety of public poverty relief actors. This also applies to those public agencies that offer the three main poverty relief transfers in Austria, namely unemployment assistance, compensation supplement and social assistance. For example, the public employment service law replaced the tripartite *Arbeitsamt* by a bipartite Public Employment Service (*AMS*) in 1994, which at present is responsible for delivering unemployment assistance. It was outsourced from the Ministry of Labour and organized as a separate legal entity under public law (*Dienstleistungsunternehmen öffentlichen Rechts*). As it is still publicly owned, this outsourcing also qualifies as a formal type of privatization (see also Section II.2.1). Service-orientation has become a key goal of the *AMS* in the late 1990s. For example, easier access to the services of the *AMS*, especially with regard to job search, has been granted through the enhanced use of internet. Moreover, within the last decade, the *AMS* introduced new management methods, including management by objectives (Arbeitsmarktservice Österreich 2004). These changes suggest that an enhanced market-orientation is indeed an identifiable trend concerning this actor.

The pension insurance institutions responsible for delivering compensation supplement were also subject to reform in the recent past. Most notably, the formerly separate institutions for blue-collar and white-collar workers merged into the *Pensionsversicherungsanstalt* (*PVA*), which was established in 2003. It delivers the vast majority of compensation supplements in Austria (smaller pension institutions are responsible for delivering compensation supplement to selected professional groups, including farmers or notaries). The merger of the two institutions has been motivated by a drive to reduce costs and increase efficiency. Forming part of a more general reform of public administration (*Verwaltungsreform*), these changes do support shifts towards a higher valuation of market ethics.

Restructuring has also been a key issue with regard to the third important poverty relief transfer provided by the welfare state, namely social assistance. However, given provincial responsibilities, this does not apply to all *Länder* alike. Restructuring has, for example, affected the public sector in Vienna, which is responsible for providing social assistance in Austria's capital city. A first organizational reform was implemented in 1999: 21 agencies that handled the applications for cash transfers under the social assistance scheme so far and 6 agencies concerned with delivering social work have been replaced by 10 social centres. In addition to establishing these centres, new public management was introduced as a management strategy, which has brought about less hierarchy, decentralized decision-making, and new governing principles through controlling and quality management. The 10 social centres at present serve as one-stop shops in which clients apply for social assistance and receive counselling and support through social workers (including an initial clearing to identify the specific problems of the clients). Prior to this reform, there were several problems associated with the old organizational structure and the delivery of transfers. For example, client-orientation was perceived to be weak. The amount of discretion in granting transfers varied widely across the city. Moreover, there were long waiting periods for clients and hardly any cooperation between agencies that delivered cash transfers, and agencies that delivered support through social workers.

Following this first organizational restructuring, a second reform was implemented in 2004. The previous municipal department *MA 12* (which was responsible for social assistance, assistance for the homeless and assistance for the disabled) and *MA 47* (which was responsible for care services and social services) merged into *MA 15*. This department was responsible for social welfare, nursing and care services. Meanwhile this municipal department has been split again, with *MA 15* being responsible for health-related aspects, and *MA 40* being responsible for social and legal issues and thus also for the administration of social assistance. Private tasks (including contracting with third-sector organizations) have, however, been delegated to the *Fonds Soziales Wien* (*FSW*). In terms of its legal form, this entity has been established as a foundation, i.e. a private organization (which entitles the *FSW* to employ private employees instead of civil servants). Since the managers of the *FSW* are appointed by the local government, however, it still qualifies as a 'public' rather than a 'private' organization for the purpose of this study (see also Section 1.1.2). The main tasks of this foundation involve the administration and organization of a broad variety of social services in Vienna, including, for example, provisions for the homeless. The establishment of the *FSW* has brought along important changes for the contracting partners of the City of Vienna. Most importantly, the *FSW*, and no longer the local administration, cooperates with nonprofits delivering social services in Vienna.

Concerning the social assistance scheme, organizational reforms implemented in Vienna from the 1990s onwards have brought about some changes for the applicants and beneficiaries of social assistance. Some of them have increased client-orientation. For example, it is now possible to arrange appointments with social assistance staff. Waiting periods for these appointments are still long, though, amounting to several weeks.

This is mainly caused by the considerable increase of applicants that Vienna has seen in recent years (see above). Information on social assistance and application procedures are now provided via the internet, which enhances transparency and makes application easier. Moreover, Vienna is among the federal provinces that introduced internal directions to harmonize decision-making of staff with regard to transfers granted on a discretionary basis, which also reduces bureaucratic arbitrariness. Service-orientation thus appears to have improved, which should have had positive effects on **take-up rates**. However, comparable data to support this hypothesis is not available (however, see Dimmel 1997: 47, Dimmel 2000: 399ff, Fuchs 2003, 2009). Even though the methods to achieve these rates differ, the results suggest that take-up rates have not (yet?) been affected by the organizational reforms implemented.

In terms of nonprofit provision, there is no information on organizational restructuring available for poverty relief actors[52]. However, there is ample evidence for an implementation of for-profit management techniques in a variety of Austrian nonprofits – not least as a consequence of contracts with performance-related payment forms (e.g. Zauner *et al.* 2006, Meyer 2007, Schneider and Trukeschitz 2007b).

Anecdotal evidence available for some poverty relief programmes shows that the increase in the number of clients served has led to an enhancement of waiting periods as compared to the past. In many instances, these waiting periods are as long as in the case of applying for social assistance. Moreover, given excess demand, clients with 'minor' problems are sometimes asked to return when their problems have become more severe. This implies that one of the main advantages of nonprofit provision, i.e. granting access at a very low level, can not be maintained by (some) nonprofit providers. Interestingly, these changes point towards a more technocratic mode of doing business (e.g. Meyer 2007: 90ff).

[52] Interestingly, data from the NPO study point to the fact that nonprofits offering poverty relief programmes are comparatively young: Only 39 per cent of all organizations in the Austrian sample (n = 128) were founded prior to 1991. Every fifth organization was founded in the year 2000 or afterwards. This may reflect an increase of demand for poverty alleviation provided by these types of organizations and/or a particularly high fluctuation of third-sector organizations in this activity field. The latter development suggests that it is more common to found organizations on a new basis than restructuring existing ones.

It has been argued earlier that an increase of professionalization in nonprofits qualifies as a change towards marketization. Indeed, data from the NPO study and additional analysis of the NPO dataset suggest that the majority of nonprofits in Austria enhanced the **number of paid staff** (as well as their workload, measured in working hours) between 2000 and 2005 (see table 24). This has not been the case with regard to voluntary work. Rather, the majority of nonprofits, for which data are available, noted that both the number of volunteers employed as well as their workload had remained stable in the period analyzed. This suggests that rather than relying on (low-cost) volunteers, many nonprofits invested in paid employees, which could be interpreted as a tendency towards more professionalization, and thus a marketization in the provision of poverty alleviation. However, since information on the motivations for these shifts is not available, the hypothesis of an increased marketization cannot be confirmed.

Table 24: Development of number of paid and unpaid staff and working hours within nonprofits, Austria, 2000 and 2005

	Paid staff	Working hours paid staff	Unpaid staff	Working hours unpaid staff
in 2005 > in 2000	57 %	56 %	27 %	35 %
in 2005 = in 2000	33 %	31 %	67 %	58 %
in 2005 < in 2000	10 %	13 %	7 %	8 %
Total	100 %	100 %	100 %	100 %

Sources: NPO dataset; own calculations. Notes: rounding errors occur; sample sizes (n): between 132 and 173

3.2 Finance

The element of finance may have changed in a variety of ways. Indicators chosen to capture those changes, which are of relevance concerning privatization and/or marketization of poverty relief include (i) shifts in the proportion of public and private funding sources, (ii) shifts in the relative importance of user fees and commercial income as a proportion of the total budget and, in case of joint provision, (iii) a substitution of grants through performance-related payments. In what follows, secondary information collected on these indicators is summarized.

3.2.1 Privatization

The following changes qualify as 'privatization' of finance (see figure 5 in Section II.2.1.2): shifts from public sources of funding towards (i) private sources of funding or (ii) public and private sources of funding, and shifts from public and private sources of funding towards (iii) private sources of funding or (iv) public and private sources of funding, with an increased share of private sources in relation to public sources. Evidence that helps identify such changes includes an assessment of the relative proportions of public and private funding sources within both public and nonprofit provision.

On closer examination of developments concerning the **composition of funding** of public poverty relief transfers, it becomes evident that these have been and still are financed through public sources either fully (e.g. unemployment assistance and compensation supplement) or to a large extent (social assistance). As mentioned earlier, possibilities to co-finance social assistance through users or relatives (via regress payments) are viewed in some provinces, including Vienna, primarily as a possibility to deter potential applicants from applying for social assistance rather than a source of funding. This might explain why the proportion of this private form of funding has not changed between 1995 and 2005 (Stolitzka 1997: 652ff, Pratscher 2007: 738ff) concerning general social assistance (*Allgemeine Sozialhilfe*). Thus, an increase of private funding does not appear to be a dominant trend in the provision of poverty alleviation from the public sector (in contrast to other areas of social security, such as health care).

Information on the development of the proportions of public and private funding sources concerning nonprofit provision is included in the NPO dataset. The data only suggests marginal shifts in this respect. In both 2000 and 2004, only 10 per cent of Austrian nonprofits for which information is available (n = 137 and 173) noted that none of their expenditures had been financed through the public sector. In contrast, the budget of 31 per cent of the organizations was fully funded through public sources in both 2000 and 2004. This suggests that the relative role of the public sector as a financier has not changed much within the third sector. These findings thus do not support hypotheses of a privatization of the element of finance in poverty relief – at least not for the period examined.

3.2.2 Marketization

Changes that qualify as 'marketization' or poverty alleviation concerning the element of finance involve (i) shifts towards specific forms of private funding sources (user fees, commercial income) and (ii) shifts from subsidies to performance-related payments in case of joint provision.

According to data from the NPO study and an additional analysis of the NPO dataset, the proportion of nonprofits with public contracts remained, with 90 to 91 per cent, broadly the same between 2000 and 2005 in Austria (see table 25). This does not imply a shift away from public towards private funding sources in nonprofits – let alone an **increase of user fees or commercial income**. Some 11 per cent of the budget of the 'average' nonprofit poverty relief actor included in the NPO study was made up of commercial income both in 2000 and 2004 (Dawid and Heitzmann 2006a).

Table 25: Development of contracting in nonprofits, Austria, 2000 and 2005

	2000	2005
Nonprofits with public contracts	90 %	91 %
... based on subsidies	84 %	84 %
... based on performance-related payment	62 %	75 %
... based on both of the above	43 %	60 %
Sample sizes (n)	*72-80*	*169-186*

Source: NPO dataset; own calculations. Notes: rounding errors occur

Further evidence suggests that a large number of Austrian nonprofits that contract with public actors in poverty alleviation could rely on subsidies – without much change between 2000 and 2005 concerning this type of funding. However, the proportion of third-sector organizations relying on **performance-related payments** (including project-related payments) has increased in Austria in this period (by 13 percentage points; see table 25). These results do not indicate a shift away from subsidies. Rather, the former type of funding remains crucial for nonprofits, even though the performance-related modes of paying for welfare purchased by the state have gained in importance. Indeed, the extent of nonprofits relying on both types of funding appears to have increased considerably between 2000 and 2005 (from 43 to 60 per cent). Small sample sizes on this variable (especially for the year 2000) suggest that this result be interpreted with caution, though: Information for the year 2000 is available only for 13 % of all nonprofit poverty relief actors in Austria.

In how far is the increase of contracts based on performance-related payments due to enhanced competition in terms of choosing contracting partners by the state? Regarding enhanced competition, which is a projected result of, for example, EU regulations on public procurement policies (Holoubek *et al.* 2007), there is no evidence available for poverty relief actors (for evidence for nonprofits providing programmes for the unemployed, see, for example, Schneider and Trukeschitz 2007a: 17f). In Vienna, however, competition among contracting partners is basically limited to nonprofits, as only public benefit organizations qualify for financial support through the *FSW*[53].

Reforms concerning the Viennese social assistance scheme have brought along important changes for nonprofits in terms of contractual relationships. As mentioned earlier, a newly introduced foundation, the *FSW*, has become the new contracting partner for nonprofits that cooperate with the City of Vienna. For third-sector organizations, this not only implied a change of their contracting partner. The *FSW* replaced the old contracts through new ones with other than the hitherto valid contract stipulations. This has also enhanced the transparency of contracts. These shifts, including enhanced proportions of performance-related payments as a source of funding delivery in case of joint provision, might thus qualify as an increased marketization.

3.3 Provider decisions

As discussed earlier, provider decisions may have changed in a variety of ways. This study is interested in two particular types of developments. One concerns shifts of Type I welfare mix, more precisely, developments involving a decrease of public decision-making and an increase of nonprofit decision-making. Only these changes qualify as (partial) privatization. The second type of change refers to shifts of Type II welfare mix, i.e. shifts in terms of (i) income poor (groups) targeted[54] and (ii) poverty

[53] http://www.fsw.at/export/sites/fsw/fswportal/downloads/foerderwesen_anerkennung/foerderrichtlinien/FRL_allgemein.pdf (last accession date: September 2009)

[54] In this context, it is vital to consider that the very composition of income poor groups might have changed and led to adaptations in terms of clients served. How-

relief products provided. As discussed earlier, only shifts that qualify as an increasing marketization are considered in this study.

3.3.1 Privatization

Developments that account for privatization of provider decisions include (see figure 6 in Section II.2.1.3): changes from pure public decision-making towards (i) nonprofit decision-making or (ii) joint decision-making, as well as changes from joint decision-making towards (iii) pure nonprofit decision-making or (iv) joint decision-making with an increased share of nonprofit decision-making. Indicators that help evaluate whether a privatization of provider decisions has occurred in the activity field of poverty alleviation in Austria include (i) an increased share of nonprofits engaged in joint provision, and (ii) an increased share of nonprofits relying on subsidies rather than performance-related payments.

As shown earlier, neither the proportion of nonprofits that rely on public funding nor the modes of public funding in case of joint provision have changed considerably within Austria. Even though there is evidence for an increase of contracts based on performance-related payments, this does not allow making inferences on potential shifts concerning the provider decisions, given that the majority of nonprofits relies on subsidies as well. Thus, data do not support hypotheses of privatization (given enhanced proportions of performance-related payments, evidence rather supports hypotheses that suggest a reduction of private responsibilities).

3.3.2 Marketization

The following paragraphs include information on changes that might qualify as a more marketized provision concerning the element of provider decisions. However, it is difficult to select *a priori* shifts that qualify as marketization (see Section II.2.2.3). This requires examining the changes as well as the motivations which brought them about to then determine whether they qualify as an increase of marketization.

---

ever, as analyses of data from the ECHP and the EU-SILC for the period of 1995 to 2005 show, the composition of income poverty has not changed much in the decade examined (see the *Excursus* on the development of income poverty in the *Annex*).

One indicator identified to operationalize marketization of provider decisions refers to changes of **eligibility criteria** and especially changes towards an increased relevance of workfare benefits. In terms of eligibility criteria applied, some means-tested transfers provided by the welfare state indeed have been closer linked to conditionality in recent years – shifts that qualify as an increased marketization. This applies, for example, to benefits paid as part of unemployment insurance. Regulations to accept paid work have become stricter in recent years, obliging the unemployed to accept jobs that require a lower qualification, or are located further away from home than those held so far[55].

Since the NPO study does not include information on the issue of eligibility criteria linked to transfers provided by nonprofits, we must rely yet again on anecdotal evidence from a few nonprofit poverty relief providers. According to these pieces of information, provider decisions have not changed in recent years. Support which was, and is, offered both in cash and in-kind was, and is, granted based on a means test.

'Social engineering' and thus a closer **link between benefit receipt and social behaviour** appears to have become more of an issue in recent years concerning public provision (no evidence is available for nonprofit poverty relief actors). For example, whereas the average number of people receiving a benefit from the unemployment insurance scheme increased by 48 per cent between 2000 and 2005, the number of benefits frozen due to some form of inappropriate behaviour (e.g. unwillingness to work or decline of job offer) rose by 65 per cent in the same period (Arbeitsmarktservice Österreich 2002: 35, 2006: 35). These developments support the hypothesis of increasing marketization – interpreted as a decrease of de-commodification (Esping-Andersen 1990: 21ff), i.e. a requirement to gain economic security through paid work rather than the welfare state.

In addition to eligibility criteria applied and developments concerning benefits frozen, changes concerning provider decisions also may have affected the **products provided**. In terms of public provision, the proportion of means-tested in-kind transfers provided by the Austrian welfare state increased from 20 per cent in 1996 to 52 per cent in 2005, whereas

55 http://www.arbeiterkammer.at/bilder/d72/kurzstudie_arbeitsmarktpolitik.pdf (last accession date: September 2009)

the proportion of cash transfers decreased from 80 per cent to 48 per cent in the same period (Eurostat 2008: 44). This suggests quite some dynamics in terms of the poverty relief products provided by the public sector. However, regarding the three largest poverty relief transfers of the public sector, neither unemployment assistance nor compensation supplement were affected by these changes, as both of these transfers have been delivered – at present and in the past – as unbounded cash transfers. Social assistance transfers, however, are not only paid in cash but also in-kind. The latter type of transfer mainly targets people living in institutions. Their accommodation is often financed fully or in part through social assistance payments. As mentioned earlier, the number of social assistance recipients in institutions increased by 17 per cent between 1995 and 2005. However, expenditures rose by 125 per cent during that period. Expenditures for social services, another in-kind transfer embedded in the social assistance scheme, increased by 74 per cent, and thus to a much larger extent than the cash transfers defined as general social assistance, i.e. temporary and persistent assistance, which only rose by 32 per cent in this period. These data confirm a shift away from cash transfers and towards in-kind transfers, even though this shift is not mirrored in the number of clients entitled to these benefits (see table 21).

In terms of products delivered by nonprofit organizations, anecdotal evidence from a few Vienna-based actors suggests that there has been an increase of both cash and in-kind transfers (see also table 23). No further information is available on whether the relative share of these two types of products has changed within recent years. However, anecdotal evidence suggests that the purposes for which support has been granted have changed. Rather than providing measures that allow for social inclusion (such as granting transfers to allow pupils attending school trips), transfers at present are granted, to a larger proportion than in previous years, to cover necessities such as housing and heating costs.

4. Summary of this chapter

This chapter aimed to answer the second research question posed in this study, i.e. to examine how the conceptual framework elaborated helps in illustrating the current balance of the welfare mix of poverty relief in Austria and recent shifts towards 'privatization' and 'marketization'.

To achieve this aim, the chapter started by explaining the **empirical research approach**. First, the concepts had to be operationalized, which involved identifying and selecting indicators that represent the concepts clearly and comprehensively and allow for potential country specifics and time-specifics. Then, data sources containing information on the data needs had to be identified. It has been decided to rely on secondary information to illustrate the welfare mix and changes thereof. However, only some sources contain data on all public poverty relief transfers (or, to be more precise, on means-tested transfers, which is a close proxy to poverty relief transfers). In terms of nonprofit provision, information on some indicators was available only for a sub sample (amounting to a third) of all poverty relief actors. Data for a variety of indicators had to be derived from only a few public and nonprofit programmes. Since the three public transfers considered in this respect make up the vastest proportion of all public transfer expenditures, they may deemed to represent total public provision. This is not the case with regard to nonprofit programmes. Given regional differences concerning the legal framework, moreover, the analysis focused on some programmes located in Vienna only. This also applied to the largest public transfer, i.e. social assistance: detailed information on these transfers derived partly from the Viennese social assistance scheme – which in part varies considerably from regulations in other provinces (Pfeil 2001, Pratscher 2008).

Section 2 presented evidence on the **current balance of the welfare mix**. Table 26 includes the results of this assessment for each of the indicators chosen (including the data basis from which the results have been deducted). Concerning Type I welfare mix, it could be seen that both public actors and third-sector organizations engage in the poverty relief market in Austria. The 'market share' in terms of transfer expenditures appears to be higher concerning public provision. However, in terms of clients targeted, the balance between the two sectors seems to be more evenly distributed. Public transfers are predominantly financed through taxes and/or social insurance contributions, whereas nonprofit provision relies to a larger extent on private funding sources (even though public finance is the dominant funding source within the majority of nonprofits). Most nonprofits for which information was available relied on both subsidies and performance-related payments from public actors. This dual form of funding nonprofits did not allow to make inferences concerning the question of who takes the provider decisions.

Regarding Type II welfare mix, take-up of important public poverty relief transfers (e.g. compensation supplement) appears to be no particular problem, whereas 50 % of households entitled to social assistance did not take up this transfer. One of the reasons for non-take up – stigmatization – also appears to be a problem concerning the provision of third-sector organizations, even though there is no estimate on their non-take up rates. The dependence of nonprofits on public funding is impressive: The average organization finances three quarters of its budget with public money. The rest is funded equally through commercial income and donations (incl. membership fees). Concerning provider decisions, available data do not support either the hypothesis of a clear client differentiation or that of a distinct product differentiation regarding the two sectors. However, while nonprofits provide a heterogeneous mix of instruments, public sector support appears to be less idiosyncratic.

Section 3 continued to present empirical information on shifts that might qualify as **privatization and/or a marketization** of poverty relief in Austria. Table 27 summarizes the evidence collected for each of the indicators selected. Regarding privatization, evidence suggests a considerable increase of clients served by the social assistance scheme in Austria between 1995 and 2005, a – less considerable – rise concerning unemployment assistance and a stagnation concerning the number of recipients of compensation supplement. Overall expenditures for means-tested transfers as a proportion of total social security expenditures rose between 1996 and 2005 from 4 % to 7 %. The number of clients has also increased within every fifth nonprofit actor, for which information has been available. The NPO study also suggests an increase of products provided between 2000 and 2005. Both developments should have led to an enhanced level of nonprofit expenditures. Confirmation of this development, however, could be provided only for one (large) nonprofit actor in Vienna.

Table 26: Characteristics of Type I and Type II welfare mix in the activity field of poverty relief in Austria

Type I welfare mix	Results	Data basis
1. Total transfer expenditures	Public: € 4.459 billion, i.e. 7 % of total social security expenditures (85 % caused by 3 transfers) Nonprofit: ~ € 810,000	Public: Σ means-tested transfers (Eurostat 2008) Nonprofit: 3 programmes in Vienna
2. Number of clients served	Public: social assistance: 182,000; unemployment assistance: 96,500; compensation supplement: 227,000 Nonprofit: 223,000 (projected number for total: up to 950,000)	Public: 3 (in terms of expenditures largest) means-tested transfers (Arbeitsmarktservice Österreich 2006, Haydn 2006, Pratscher 2007) Nonprofit: NPO study (n=99, 18 % of total)
3. Proportions of public and private funding sources as share of total transfer funding	Public: unemployment assistance and compensation supplement: 100 % public funding (taxes or social insurance contributions); general social assistance in Vienna: 7 % private funding, 93 % public funding Nonprofit: average organization: ¾ public and ¼ private funding (however: considerable heterogeneity within the third sector)	Public: 3 (in terms of expenditures largest) means-tested transfers (Arbeitsmarktservice Österreich 2006, Haydn 2006, Pratscher 2007) Nonprofit: NPO dataset (n=173, 31 % of total)
4. Proportions of nonprofits financed through performance-related payments and subsidies	Nonprofit: 84 % of organizations: subsidies: 75 % of organizations: performance-related payments; ~ 6 out of 10 organizations: both forms of finance	Nonprofit: NPO study and dataset (n=155 (28 %) – 169 (30 % of total))

Type II welfare mix	Results	Data basis
1. Take-up rates of poverty relief transfers	Public: social assistance: 50 % of entitled households Nonprofit: NA (however, some evidence that non-take up is an issue for nonprofits, too)	Public: Fuchs (2003) Nonprofit: NPO study
2. Proportions of different components of the total funding portfolio	Public: general social assistance (targets private households) in Vienna: 7 % recovery payments from beneficiaries or relatives Nonprofit: average organization: ¾ public funding, 11 % commercial income (incl. user fees); 13 % donations or membership fees (however, considerable heterogeneity within the third sector)	Public: Pratscher (2007) Nonprofit: NPO dataset (n=173, 31 % of total)
3. Proportions of nonprofits financed through performance-related payments and subsidies	Nonprofit: 84 % of organizations: subsidies: 75 % of organizations: performance-related payments; ~ 6 out of 10: both forms of finance	Nonprofit: NPO study and dataset (n=155 (28 %) – 169 (30 % of total))
4. Eligibility criteria applied	Public: many transfers targeted to specific groups, exception: (temporary) social assistance Nonprofit: a majority of nonprofits did not specialize on specific risk groups → rather universal approach	Public: Kammer für Arbeiter und Angestellte (2005) Nonprofit: NPO study (n=187, 33 % of total)

5. Composition of income poor groups served	Public: social assistance granted to private households in Vienna: 53 % women, 24 % < 15 years; 23 % 15 – 29 years; 11 % > 60 years (69 % of them females); 76 % held Austrian citizenship; 61 % had only elementary schooling; more one-person than multi-person households Nonprofit: 16 % < 19 years, 8 % > 65 years; more than half: only elementary schooling; ~60 % unemployed	Public: Pratscher (2007) Nonprofit: NPO study (n = 106 (19 %) – 150 (27 % of total))
6. Portfolio of products provided	Public: 48 % of all transfer expenditures in cash, 52 % in-kind Nonprofit: NA (however, one third of nonprofits delivered cash transfers)	Public: Σ means-tested transfers (Eurostat 2008) Nonprofit: NPO study (n=170, 30 % of total)

Source: own illustration; Note: NA = not available

Table 27: Privatization and marketization in the activity field of poverty relief in Austria

Privatization	Results	Data basis
1. Change in number of clients served	Public: 1995-2005: social assistance: + 63 %; unemployment assistance: + 35 %, compensation supplement: - 17 % Nonprofit: 2000-2005: 82 % of nonprofits noted that number of clients has increased (extent unknown)	Public: 3 (in terms of expenditures largest) means-tested transfers: BMAS (1996: 44ff); BMAGS (1997: 47, 1998: 37); Haydn (2006: 253ff); Pratscher (2007: 732ff) Nonprofit: NPO dataset (n=175, 31 % of total)
2. Change in total transfer expenditures	Public: 4 % of total social security expenditures in 1996 for means-tested transfers; 2005: 7 %; 1995-2005: social assistance: + 87 %; unemployment assistance: + 26 %, compensation supplement: - 0.3 % Nonprofit: 25 % increase of transfer expenditures between 2002 and 2004	Public: Σ means-tested transfers (Eurostat 2008); 3 (in terms of expenditures largest) means-tested transfers: BMAS (1996: 44ff); BMAGS (1997: 47, 1998: 37); Haydn (2006: 253ff); Pratscher (2007: 732ff) Nonprofit: 1 (large) nonprofit actor in Vienna (Till and Till-Tentschert 2003, Till 2005)
3. Change in the proportions of public and private funding sources	Public: no indication of an increase of private funding sources Nonprofit: no indication of an increase of private funding sources	Public: social assistance in Vienna (Stolitzka 1997, Pratscher 2007) Nonprofit: NPO study (n=173 (31 %) and n=137 (24 % of total))
4. Changes in the proportion of nonprofits engaged in joint provision	Nonprofit: 2000: 90 % held contracts with public actors; 2005: 91 % held contracts with public actors	Nonprofit: NPO dataset (n=187, 33 % of total)

5. Changes in the proportion of nonprofits that rely on subsidies and performance-related payments	Nonprofit: 2000: 84 % financed through subsidies; 2005: 84 %; 2000: 62 % financed through performance-related payments; 2005: 75 %; 2000: 43 % financed through subsidies and performance-related payments; 2005: 60 %	Nonprofit: NPO dataset (n=72 (13 %) and n=169 (30 % of total))
Marketization	**Results**	**Data basis**
1. Implementation of organizational reforms in public and nonprofit organizations	Public: The *AMS* (providing unemployment assistance) replaced *Arbeitsamt* and has been outsourced in 1994; MBO has been introduced since; two pension insurance institutions (one for blue-collar workers, one for white-collar workers) have been merged in 2003; social assistance in Vienna: various organizational reforms leading to one-stop shops and the foundation of the *FSW* (i.e. a new contracting partner for nonprofits providing social services in Vienna), which brought about more transparency and a formalization of contracts. Nonprofit: NA	Public: e.g. Arbeitsmarktservice Österreich (2004)
2. Reduction of non-take up rates of poverty relief transfers (if changes are motivated by market ethics)	Public: no comparable estimates Nonprofit: NA	Public: social assistance (Dimmel 1997, 2000, Fuchs 2003) Nonprofit: NPO study (n=173, 31 % of total)

3. Increase of paid staff in nonprofits (if changes are motivated by market ethics)	Nonprofit: 2000-2005: 57 % of nonprofits noted that number of paid staff has increased (extent unknown); 67 % noted that the amount of unpaid staff remained the same. However, no information on motivation for these changes.	Nonprofit: NPO dataset (n=132 (24 %) and n=173, 31 % of total)
4. Increase of user fees and/or commercial income	Public: no indication of an increase of user fees/commercial income Nonprofit: no increase of user fees/commercial income between 2000 and 2004	Public: social assistance in Vienna (Stolitzka 1997, Pratscher 2007) Nonprofit: NPO study (n=137 (24 %) -173, 31 % of total)
5. Substitution of subsidies through performance-related payments	Nonprofit: 2000: 84 % financed through subsidies; 2005: 84 %; 2000: 62 % financed through performance-related payments; 2005: 75 %; 2000: 43 % financed through subsidies and performance-related payments; 2005: 60 %	Nonprofit: NPO dataset (n=72 (13 %) and n=169, 30 % of total))
6. Changed eligibility criteria	Public: some transfers more closely linked to eligibility (e.g. unemployment assistance) Nonprofit: NA	Public: e.g. http://www.arbeiterkammer.at/bilder/d72/kurz studie_arbeitsmarktpolitik.pdf
7. Increase of transfer payments suspended due to inappropriate behaviour	Public: evidence for unemployment assistance Nonprofit: NA	Public: unemployment assistance (Arbeitsmarktservice Österreich 2002, 2006)

8. Shifts in the portfolio of products provided (if changes are motivated by market ethics)	Public: 1996: 20 % of transfer expenditures in-kind; 2005: 52 % (rather increase of service costs, e.g. social assistance, than deliberate shift away from cash transfers due to market motivations) Nonprofit: NA	Public: Σ means-tested transfers (Eurostat 2008)
9. Changes in the range of poverty relief products provided (if changes are motivated by market ethics)	Public: NA Nonprofit: NA (there is, however, anecdotal evidence that purposes for which support is granted have changed)	

Source: own illustration

Given the parallel expansion of public provision, moreover, the growth of nonprofit provision does not suffice to confirm hypotheses of a privatization of poverty relief concerning the element of production and/or delivery. In terms of finance, there has not been any change concerning the composition of funding sources for public poverty relief programmes. This also applies for nonprofit provision. Hence there is no evidence to support the hypothesis of increasing privatization concerning the element of finance. With regard to provider decisions, the increase of performance-related contracts does point to an enhanced role of public agencies in this respect (rather than a decreasing role, which would support the hypothesis of privatization). However, as the proportion of nonprofits relying on subsidies has not changed between 2000 and 2005, the former development does not suffice to suggest that the decision-making powers have been shifted from the producer/deliverer to the financier of poverty relief transfers.

Concerning marketization, evidence for organizational reforms implemented within the public sector has been presented, whereas relevant information for nonprofit poverty relief actors is missing. Whereas paid staff seems to have substituted voluntary workers between 2000 and 2005 in nonprofits, there is no information that would confirm that these changes were motivated by a drive to implement market principles. In terms of finance, a shift towards user fees and commercial income, which would support the hypothesis of an increased marketization concerning this element of provision, could not be confirmed for either public or nonprofit poverty relief actors. As mentioned earlier, performance-related payments have gained in importance, which suggests a more marketized relationship between public and nonprofit actors in joint provision. However, the proportion of nonprofits relying on subsidies remained stable between 2000 and 2005, which yet again contradicts this hypothesis. There is evidence that some public transfers have linked stronger benefit receipt to appropriate behaviour, which is again an indication for an enhanced orientation towards the 'market'. A considerable shift from cash towards in-kind transfers has been evidenced for the public sector (from 20 % in 1996 to 52 % in 2005). However, this change appears to be caused by increasing costs rather than being a deliberate decision for a more commercially oriented product portfolio. Unfortunately, no secondary information on changes concerning provider decisions is available for nonprofit actors.

Apart from collecting data to illustrate Type I and Type II welfare mix as well as specific changes this chapter has pursued the overall aim to evaluate the **effectiveness of the framework** in assisting this exercise. Two dimensions have been identified as particularly apt to examine this effectiveness. First, indicators that allow for a clear and comprehensive representation of the concepts elaborated in the first part of the book, and that allow for potential country-specifics and time-specifics, ought to be deducted from the framework. Second, information on the indicators selected ought to be available in the form of secondary data.

Regarding operationalization, the concepts of 'income poverty' and 'poverty relief' allowed for a precise deduction of indicators, which, in addition, are not least easy to measure. The detection of public and nonprofit actors turned out to be more difficult, given a variety of organizations that are perceived as 'public' or 'nonprofit' in Austria without meeting (all of) the criteria identified for these organizations in the first part of this study. As operationalization has to allow for country-specifics, therefore, the definitions were adapted to meet these particularities. Whereas the operationalization of public poverty relief actors was quite straightforward (covering all public actors that provide poverty relief transfers), problems of nonprofit provision (which consists of idiosyncratic support rather than standardized transfers) necessitated an alternative approach. The study relied on a selection of nonprofits that were – for a former study – identified by two large network organizations as 'primarily engaged to combat poverty'. Whereas this pragmatic approach might cover nonprofits that do not qualify as poverty relief actors (as they also support the nonpoor), it might fail to spot those organizations that, although being poverty relief actors, have not been identified by the network organizations.

Indicators that capture the characteristics of the current balance of the welfare mix and changes thereof have been deducted against the background of the three elements of provision identified in the first part of the book. Concerning both Type I welfare mix and privatization, selecting indicators representing the elements of production/delivery and finance has not been a problem. However, provider decisions have only been operationalized through a crude proxy, i.e. the financial agreement in case of joint provision. Whereas this allows for some conclusions concerning the distribution of decision-making powers, it does not enable capturing dual or joint decision-making.

Concerning Type II welfare mix and marketization, the identification of indicators to describe the elements of finance and provider decisions has not been a particular problem. Yet the element of production and/or delivery has been operationalized only insufficiently through non-take up rates. The process of production/delivery comprises a variety of different stages (from application procedures to the actual delivery and processes to control *ex post* compliance). While several indicators (e.g. waiting times, location of delivery etc.) may capture some of the characteristics of production/delivery, they only represent a part of the picture, whereas non-take up rates more generally reflect the acceptance of poverty relief transfers. However, non-take up is not only influenced by the production and/or delivery of transfers. It is also the result of specific behaviour of the demanders or users of transfers. Moreover, the indicator is inapt for nonprofit provision, as no estimate for non-take-up exists for these welfare actors. Regarding marketization, indicators to capture changes have been identified. However, as shifts might have been caused by a variety of reasons, the motivation for these changes become vital. Only shifts that have been implemented to copy market mechanisms qualify as marketization, therefore motivations had to be explored as well.

In terms of information sources, it has been possible to rely on some publications that contain data on all means-tested public transfers in Austria. Even though means-tested transfers are a broader category as compared with income-tested transfers (i.e. poverty relief transfers), the three largest public transfers do qualify as poverty relief transfers. Whenever aggregate information was missing, data on these transfers allowed closing some of the information gaps. One of the transfers examined, i.e. social assistance, is a legal competence of the nine Austrian *Länder* rather than the nation state, though – which leads to differences concerning the social assistance schemes. Whereas quantitative information on, for example, clients served or transfer expenditures relies on data from all social assistance schemes in Austria, further information concerning these important poverty relief transfers has been provided for the scheme of Vienna only – not least, because some data were available for this province only. Despite this limiting approach, however, it has not been possible to gather information on all of the indicators selected to operationalize Type I and Type II welfare mix, privatization and marketization. This mainly refers to the latter development and particularly to evidence on the motivations for shifts.

Concerning nonprofit provision, the NPO study and dataset contained information for up to a third of all nonprofit poverty relief actors in Austria, i.e. the largest sample for which secondary information is available. However, some of the data of this sample is not available in as much detail as would have been necessary (e.g. transfer expenditures). Moreover, while the NPO study includes information on recent changes (e.g. in terms of the number of clients served or products provided), this information is based on retrospective questions (i.e. interviewees were asked in 2005 to compare the current situation with the one in 2000). Thus, results might be biased due to inaccurate memories. Whenever it has been necessary to rely on other data than that derived from the NPO study and dataset, evidence derived either from a few nonprofits that are located in Vienna or from 'anecdotal evidence', i.e. experiences of professionals on specific issues. However, the latter type of data has not been collected systematically. Thus, most of the information presented on nonprofit provision is not representative for the sector. Moreover, it has not been possible to identify (secondary) information for each of the selected indicators (most notably concerning Type II welfare mix and marketization). This necessitates finding better indicators to operationalize these theoretical concepts, and it also suggests collecting primary data that would advance the quality of the empirical evidence. Proposals for a primary data collection therefore are included in the final chapter.

Conclusions

This study embarked on exploring the following research questions:

- How can we capture the concepts 'welfare mix', 'privatization' and 'marketization'? How are these concepts linked together?

- In how far does a conceptual framework that organizes and links the concepts 'welfare mix', 'privatization' and 'marketization' help to illustrate both (i) the characteristics of the current welfare mix in poverty relief as well as (ii) recent shifts thereof that might qualify as 'privatization' and/or 'marketization' in an empirical investigation?

In what follows, Section 1 summarizes the main findings of this research endeavour, thereby answering the research questions. Section 2 then discusses implications of the findings for public and private poverty relief actors as well as for public policy in Austria, i.e. the locus of the empirical investigation. Section 3 finally proposes some potential future research endeavours, which are partly derived from the results of this study.

1. Synthesis of the main findings

Chapter I set out to examine the concept of poverty alleviation, i.e. the activity field the empirical part of this study focuses on. Poverty has been defined rather narrowly as income poverty. Income is an important indicator that not only establishes the material well-being of people but also influences their possibilities to integrate in society and thus to experience social inclusion. The model applied to identify the meaning of 'relief' derives from the social risk management framework elaborated by the World Bank, which distinguishes between actions set before a disadvantaged situation has occurred and actions set afterwards. For the purpose of this study, poverty relief has been interpreted as covering *ex post* measures, which target the income poor only. Thus, income poverty is the critical event that differentiates poverty relief measures from other social security measures. Based on this conceptualization of 'poverty relief', instruments as well as providers of poverty alleviation have been presented. Regarding the former, transfers were divided into (bounded and unbounded) cash transfers as well as in-kind transfers, which were further distinguished into goods and social services. After having described these instruments as well as their likely welfare effects, the study turned to an analysis of potential providers of poverty relief. The introduction has made clear that only public and nonprofit actors are relevant organizational providers of poverty alleviation. For-profits only play a negligible role in poverty relief in most European countries, whereas assistance of the informal sector offers non-organized support. The study therefore limited itself to discussing the principal role of public and third-sector organizations in welfare provision. It could be seen that there is quite some scepticism as to both the efficiency and distributional implications of public and nonprofit provision.

The objective of Chapter II has been to answer the first research question. It has been argued that concepts such as 'welfare mix', 'plural economy of welfare' or 'mixed economy of welfare' are often used interchangeably, even though different interpretations are adopted in the literature. I proposed to differentiate two types of readings. 'Type I welfare mix' focuses on the mix of actors that provide welfare. A specific form of this type is joint provision, in which the responsibility of provision is shared between actors from different societal sectors. 'Type II welfare mix' focuses on the modes of provision and contracting applied by welfare actors. This alternative interpretation of 'welfare mix' derives from the norms, values and rationales that guide actors and thus help to explain how they provide welfare. The separation of the welfare mix into this dual model is – at least in part – artificial, as the two interpretations overlap. To capture the characteristics of Type I and Type II welfare mix, the concept of 'provision' becomes essential. For the purpose of this study, I differentiated between three components of provision. In addition to the conventional split between finance and production (the latter has been termed production and/or delivery), I adopted a third dimension, i.e. 'provider decisions'. Two types of provider decisions are relevant in the context of this study, i.e. who makes provider decisions (Type I welfare mix) and which decisions have been made in terms of clients targeted and products provided (Type II welfare mix).

Chapter II proceeded to examine changes of Type I and Type II welfare mix. Two developments have been at the core of this study: 'Privatization' refers to specific changes of Type I welfare mix (i.e. 'who provides welfare?') but does not necessarily imply complete shifts from public towards private provision – changes within only one or two elements of provision also qualify as (partial) privatization. 'Marketization' suggests that reforms implemented to introduce market ethics and principles in provision influence both (i) how welfare is provided and (ii) how contracting in case of joint provision is organized. Consequently, marketization refers to specific changes of Type II welfare mix. It has been argued further that privatization and marketization may be captured by examining shifts within the three elements of provision: production and/or delivery, finance and provider decisions.

Against the background of this conceptual framework, Chapter III elaborated on the empirical evidence collected, thereby illustrating the current balance in the provision of poverty relief in Austria and recent changes thereof that might qualify as privatization and/or marketization. The actual aim of the chapter, however, was to examine the framework's usefulness in assisting the empirical investigation thereby answering the second research question. The chapter therefore started by explaining the empirical research approach, identifying two criteria to evaluate the effectiveness of the framework. First, the concepts elaborated in Chapters I and II must allow for clear-cut operationalization. This required identifying indicators that clearly and comprehensively represent all of the relevant theoretical concepts (income poverty, poverty relief, public poverty relief actors, nonprofit poverty relief actors, Type I welfare mix, Type II welfare mix, privatization and marketization) and allow for their empirical measurement. As has been shown, operationalization proved to be difficult both in the case of the element of provider decisions with regard to Type I welfare mix and privatization, and the element of production and/or delivery as regards Type II welfare mix and marketization. The problems encountered suggest to further advance the framework with regard to these aspects of provision and/or revising the indicators chosen (see Section 3).

The second criterion for evaluating the framework's effectiveness in assisting the empirical assessment is that of availability of information. It has been argued that the framework is particularly apt if it permits to rely on secondary data only. However, several problems have been encountered. First, aggregate information on public poverty relief actors has been available only for means-tested transfers (i.e. an inaccurate proxy to poverty relief transfers). Moreover, information on a variety of indicators could not been derived from aggregate data, so it was necessary to rely on information from a few means-tested transfers. Given the differences of means-tested transfers across Austria, some of the information presented only refers to the situation in the capital city, Vienna. Second, it has not been possible to access any information on the aggregate of nonprofit poverty relief actors. Some data has been available for a subsample of nonprofits (covering up to a third of all nonprofit poverty relief actors). For a variety of indicators, however, secondary information derived from a few poverty relief programmes located in Vienna or from anecdotal evidence only. And although these results are not representative, it has not been possible to complete all data needs. This implies that the empirical investigation might be improved considerably by gathering primary data in addition to secondary data (see Section 3).

Following the explanation of the research approach, Chapter III presented evidence for the prevalent welfare mix in poverty relief in Austria and changes thereof. Concerning Type I welfare mix, data collected confirm the considerable role of both public actors (e.g. expenditures) and nonprofits (e.g. clients served) in the provision of poverty alleviation in Austria. There are, however, differences between them (e.g. concerning the relative importance of public and private funding sources). The proxy indicator chosen to capture provider decisions (i.e. the form of funding joint provision) proved as little helpful, given that most nonprofits are financed by a combination of subsidies and performance-related payments. The data collected does not allow to confirm privatization hypotheses: Whereas both public and nonprofit provision have increased (measured in terms of transfer expenditures and clients served), the size of this increase is known for public actors only. An increase of performance-related payment forms in contracting, last but not least points towards an increased (rather than a decreased) role of public actors in decision-making.

With regard to Type II welfare mix, information gathered suggests neither client differentiation nor product differentiation concerning the two types of providers examined. The proxy indicator chosen to capture production and/or delivery (i.e. non-take up rate) proved as problematic – also, because no estimates exist for nonprofit transfers and most public transfers. Some of the information gathered points towards an enhanced importance of market principles in the provision of both public and nonprofit actors (e.g. organizational reforms implemented, enhanced relevance of workfare benefits). However, the combination of both, inadequate indicators and a lack of data, does not allow confirming or rejecting hypotheses of marketization any further. This suggests that the effectiveness of the framework in assisting the empirical investigation ought to be enhanced. There is quite some scope (i) for making the conceptual framework better, (ii) for improving the operationalization of the concepts and (iii) for advancing data availability (by, for example, collecting primary in addition to secondary information). In what follows, some of the implications of the findings concerning public policy and the two actors examined are discussed, before the last section discusses potential future research endeavours based on the results of this study.

2. Implications of the findings

This section discusses potential implications of the findings of this research endeavour. They refer to (i) the two types of actors examined, i.e. public and nonprofit poverty relief organizations in Austria, and (ii) public policy.

Concerning implications for poverty relief actors, the data collected on the current **provision of nonprofits** in poverty relief impressively underlines the significant role of these organizations in Austria. Especially the number of clients that turned to third sector organizations for help is impressive. Moreover, the workload appears to have increased in recent years, as evidenced by a rising number of clients served and products provided. Nonprofits handle this rising workload in different ways. For example, most third sector organizations were employing more paid staff in recent years, while keeping the number of volunteers constant. This implies an increasing professionalization in terms of employees. However, there is also anecdotal evidence suggesting that excessive demand has led to a prolongation of waiting periods in some organizations: People in need of support have to wait for several weeks before getting an appointment. There is further evidence that potential clients perceive support delivered by nonprofits as stigmatizing – which might lead to non-take up of this kind of support (even though no estimate of non-take up rates exists). These pieces of evidence suggest that many of the changes in nonprofit provision refer to shifts of Type II welfare mix rather than Type I welfare mix. Even though these changes do not necessarily lead to a more marketized provision, they do affect the very characteristics of nonprofits; characteristics that, after all, have led to the foundation of these types of organizations (Steinberg 2006, Badelt 2007) – and thus challenge their very role in the welfare market. Despite these developments, findings also suggest that the provision by nonprofits remains more idiosyncratic as compared to public sector provision: The examination of a sample of Austrian nonprofits showed that these not only attracted a heterogeneous group of people in need of support but also provided a heterogeneous mix of measures to support their clients.

However, anecdotal evidence also suggests that the purposes for which poverty relief transfers are granted by nonprofits have changed. Whereas in the past many of the transfers produced and/or delivered enabled the inclusion of families (for example, by paying for their children's school holidays, etc.), transfers granted at present tend to cover expenditures for necessities. Some transfers delivered by nonprofits thus serve as a part of minimum income to meet basic needs, which used to be the primary task of public support. These welfare actors thus appear to substitute (the lack of) public provision.

However, evidence presented suggests that provision of poverty relief in recent years has increased not only on the part of nonprofits but also of **public actors**. This shows in both the size of transfer expenditures and the number of clients served. These increases in both societal sectors are astonishing, given that the extent of income poverty in Austria (and Vienna) remained relatively stable between 1995 and 2005 (see *Excursus* in the *Annex*). This also implies that alternative systems to acquire income might have weakened. Available evidence supports this hypothesis. In terms of social assistance, for example, information for Vienna suggests a considerable increase of temporary social assistance transfers paid to individuals in private households, which more than tripled between 1995 and 2005 (see also table 22). In contrast, the number of recipients of permanent support (which are, above all, old-aged people and people in need of housing benefit) increased only slightly (by 12 per cent) in the same time period. The number of recipients living in institutions, such as homes for the elderly, even remained stable between 1995 and 2005. Nowadays, temporary transfers of the social assistance scheme are mostly paid as supplements to the reference rate (*Richtsatzergänzung*). This implies that a household disposes over income other than social assistance transfers. This income usually derives from either paid employment, from insurance transfers (such as unemployment benefit, i.e. *Arbeitslosengeld*, or unemployment assistance) or from universal transfers (such as childcare allowance, i.e. *Kinderbetreuungsgeld*). However, the available income does not suffice to lift the household above the income poverty line (nor, for that matter, above the much lower reference rate for social assistance). Thus, the original purpose of social assistance – granting a minimum income to households without any other income – appears to have changed. In many instances, incomes from the employment system, the *ex ante* social security system and/or private transfers are available, but too small to allow for an economically independent living. This suggests that social assistance transfers are increasingly becoming relevant for the working poor, the unemployed or families with children.

Last but not least, this development makes a case for interventions of **public policy**, even though the results of this study do not support an outright shift of responsibilities for poverty relief from the public towards the nonprofit sector. Indeed, the welfare state has not changed much, if measured in terms of instruments provided (Tálos and Badelt 1999, Unger and Heitzmann 2003): The conservative welfare state model still relies primarily on social insurance and universal transfers, with means-tested transfers only obtaining a minor (yet somewhat increased) role in terms of total expenditures.

However, measured by outcomes, both the rise of recipients of means-tested transfers as well as the increase of clients turning to nonprofits for support point to a growing significance of the 'residual welfare state model' elaborated by Titmuss (1974). This puts considerable pressure on a particular part of the welfare state, and especially on the *Länder*, which are responsible for the provision of many means-tested benefits in Austria. Indeed, the systems that set out to prevent income poverty (i.e. social insurance and universal transfers) appear to have become more permeable. The social assistance schemes, and thus the budgets of the Austrian *Länder*, are struggling with taking on this burden – which does not reflect the purpose, for which social assistance originally had been established within the Austrian welfare state. This problem is set to be prolonged even after the implementation of the means-tested minimum income scheme in 2010 (Dimmel 2009, see also: Dimmel *et al.* 2009a).

3. Proposals for future research

In what follows, this last section first puts forward some proposals to improve the research approach adopted in this study. Second, it discusses further topics that could be explored to better understand the mixed economy (of poverty relief) and its shifts.

Adopting the research approach of this study

One aim of this study was to construct a conceptual framework to understand the links between the concepts welfare mix, privatization and marketization. A revision of the framework is particularly critical concerning the concept of marketization. It has been argued that the modes that actors apply in welfare provision (i.e. Type II welfare mix) derive from the norms, values and rationales by which they are governed. If the modes of provision change, however, the motivations that have brought about these changes become crucial, as only they might explain whether changes have been implemented to copy market mechanisms. This requires improving conceptually the link between the norms, values and rationales by which welfare actors are governed and the actual provision they adopted. Alternatively, and given the difficult concepts of both privatization and marketization, the framework could focus on all changes of Type I and Type II welfare mix, rather than on the specific changes towards privatization and marketization only. This would allow capturing the general dynamics of the welfare mix – without limiting the approach by including some (fashionable) changes and excluding others that are not discussed at length in the literature.

The second aim of this study was to examine the framework's effectiveness in assisting an empirical investigation that focuses on the activity field of poverty relief in Austria. In terms of operationalizing the concepts, i.e. one of two criteria adopted to scrutinize the effectiveness of the framework, two weaknesses have become apparent. Concerning the concepts of Type I welfare mix and privatization, it has been difficult to operationalize 'provider decisions'. It has not only been impossible to unambiguously detect who decides in case of joint provision. Against the background of a study relying on secondary information only, it has not been possible to identify indicators that allow for an identification of dual or joint decision-making. This requires revising the indicators chosen in order to capture the characteristics of provider decisions (or the type of data the study ought to rely on, see also below). In terms of Type II welfare mix and marketization, operationalization of the element of production and/or delivery proved difficult – given the complex process of production/delivery, which ranges from application procedures towards *ex post* control of compliance. This implies, again, to revise the indicators chosen to better illustrate this element. Two approaches might be applied to improve operationalization: Either, indicators are derived from the literature on the mixed economy and adopted for the activity field of poverty relief (an approach this study followed at least in part), or the discovery of indicators is defined as a separate research project. For example, interviews with experts from both societal sectors studied could be conducted to assist in determining indicators for this exercise.

In terms of available secondary data sources, i.e. the second criterion adopted to scrutinize the framework's effectiveness, the results of the study suggest that there are various problems in relying on this type of information only. Due to both considerable data problems and information gaps, a primary data collection accompanying or substituting secondary information is strongly proposed. This not only refers to information concerning nonprofit provision of poverty relief in Austria. Information gaps have also been detected with regard to public poverty relief actors, e.g. concerning shifts of public provision. For the collection of primary data, several methods could be applied (Atteslander 2008: 65ff): First, questionnaires could be sent to providers of poverty relief in Austria. With regard to changes of the welfare mix, moreover, the collection of panel data (e.g. on an annual basis) would be useful, as retrospective questions might prove problematic and subject to false or incomplete memories. Alternatively (or additionally) to information collected by questionnaires, more or less informal expert interviews could be conducted with experts from a selected number of public and nonprofit organizations (Bewley 2002, Gläser and Laudel 2004). Moreover, the assessment of a variety of case studies of public and nonprofit poverty relief programmes would help both to shed more light on the current balance of the welfare mix and recent changes thereof (Yin 2003) and to revise the conceptual framework (Eisenhardt 1989).

Proposals for potential future research

This study set out to examine the characteristics of and the links between concepts such as 'welfare mix', 'privatization' and 'marketization'. Moreover, and against the background of the conceptual framework elaborated, it attempted to illustrate the prevalent welfare mix in the activity field of poverty relief and recent shifts of the mix that led to the contemporary welfare mix in Austria. Despite the results gathered, there are many aspects of the mixed economy (of poverty relief) and its shifts which need to be understood much better for public policy reasons. For example, some actors have hardly been considered in the theoretical analysis and not all in the empirical assessment. Most notably, this refers to informal actors. A study on their contributions in poverty relief would considerably enhance the understanding of the mixed economy. This also applies to the (actual, but also potential) contributions of the for-profit sector in poverty alleviation.

One concept – hybridization – has been discussed in the conceptual part of the study as a potential outcome of marketization processes. However, the concept has not been explored further in the empirical part – not least due to a lack of data. Nonetheless, an assessment of the characteristics of hybridization would allow to better understand the likely effects of a changing welfare mix concerning the providers and their very role in welfare provision.

It would further be worthwhile to assess the implications of the welfare mix and changes thereof for the income poor, as this would also facilitate examining the effectiveness of a changing mixed economy from the perspective of the 'users', 'clients' or 'consumers' of poverty relief.

Further possibilities to first examine and second to advance the conceptual framework would arise, if alternative activity fields of social policy, such as care for the elderly or unemployment, were examined empirically – and guided by the framework elaborated. Similarly, a comparative analysis – in which empirical evidence on the welfare mix and changes thereof concerning the activity field of poverty relief is collected for and compared across a variety of different welfare states – would be useful (and not least allow examining in how far the empirical findings gathered for Austria are country-specific).

Annex

Excursus: Development of income poverty in Austria and Vienna

This *Excursus* examines the development of income poverty in Austria and Vienna, covering the period from 1995 to 2005. It aims to assess whether and to what extent the level of income poverty and its composition have changed. For this overview, data from the EU-SILC and the ECHP have been utilized. Both samples are not particularly large. The first wave of the EU-SILC, which contains data for 2003, holds information on 4,623 households in Austria (927 are located in Vienna). In the third wave of the EU-SILC, which refers to the year 2005, 875 households, or 17 per cent of all households questioned, derived from Vienna. The ECHP contains seven waves of data. For the following assessment, the last six waves have been utilized, covering the period from 1995 to 2000. Sample sizes in the ECHP are even lower than in the EU-SILC. In the working file constructed for this analysis, the unweighted base amounted from 8,552 Austrian individuals covered in Wave 2 to 6,586 in Wave 7. The respective sample sizes for Vienna ranged from 1,350 to 883. Given these small sample sizes from Viennese households, the results tend to be volatile (see figure A.1).

To take account of this volatility, which appears to be particularly problematic regarding the situation in Vienna, the data forwarded in this section represent three-year averages[56] (i.e. averages of the years 1995 to 1997; 1998 to 2000; and 2003 to 2005). This is a common method applied in case of small sample sizes (Betti *et al.* 2003: 81ff). For example, a three-year average has been used for calculating regional income poverty rates in the Household Below Average Income (HBAI) statistics in Great Britain (Department for Work and Pensions 2006).

In what follows, I examine the relevance of individual and household characteristics to explain income poverty in Austria and Vienna. The characteristics selected for this exercise are commonly used in poverty statistics (e.g. Statistik Austria 2006b). Table A.1 includes descriptive

---

56 For comparative reasons, the data on Austria is based on three-year averages as well.

statistics of the variables selected using the most recent wave of the EU-SILC utilized in this study. The selected variables are described in more detail below.

Figure A.1: Income poverty rates, Austria and Vienna, 1995 – 2005

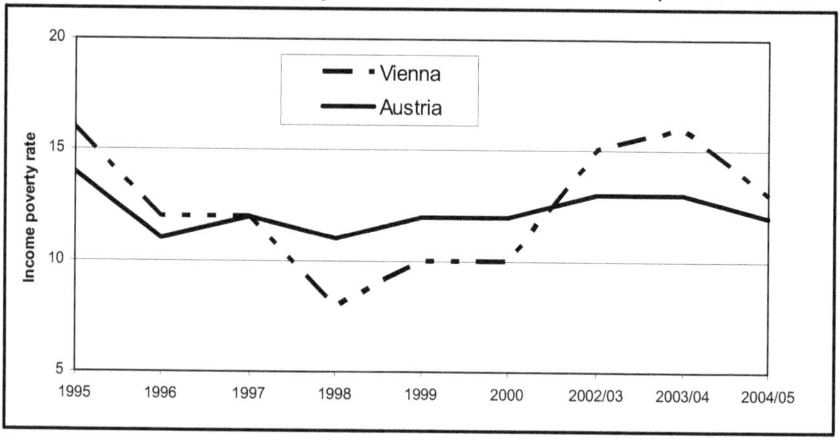

Sources: data for 1995 – 2000: ICCR-IFS: ECHP Dataset, Waves 2 to 7; data for 2003 – 2005: Statistik Austria: EU-SILC Dataset, Waves 1 to 3; own analysis

As discussed in Section III.1.1.1, the income poverty rate, which corresponds to the Laeken indicator 'at-risk-of-poverty', is the indicator chosen to define income poverty in this study. The income poverty threshold for a single household in Austria amounted to € 900 per month in 2005. 12 % of all citizens in the country had equivalized disposable incomes below this line. The median income poverty gap, which indicates how far off poor individuals are from the poverty line, amounted to 15 %. This implies that half of the income poor in Austria obtained an equivalized disposable income of less than € 762 per month (threshold for a single person household).

If the reference society is limited and income poverty is calculated on the basis of the income distribution within Austria's capital city only, the income poverty threshold in 2005 amounts to € 959. This is by almost € 60 per month higher as compared to the national level. However, preliminary analysis suggests that income poverty rates calculated for Vienna and based on a regional poverty line do not differ much from data derived from the national threshold. Therefore, both data for Austria and Vienna presented in this section are calculated on the basis of the Austrian income distribution and the Austrian poverty line.

In what follows, I first present results on income poverty in Austria and Vienna based on a cross-sectional analysis and covering the period from 1995 to 2005 (Section 1). Then, I add results from a dynamic analysis, covering the period from 1995 to 2000 (Section 2).

Table A.1: Descriptive statistics of independent variables, Austria and Vienna, 2005

			Mean / Mode*		Sample size (n)	
Variables	**Min.**	**Max.**	Austria	Vienna	Austria	Vienna
Sex (1=male)	1	2	2	2	13,044	1,834
Age cohorts (1=<20; 2=20-39; 3=40-64; 4=>64)	1	4	2.4	2.4	13,044	1,834
Citizenship (1=Austria, EU-15, EFTA; 2=other)	1	2	1	1	12,939	1,812
Educational level (1=max. primary; 3=above secondary)	1	3	2.0	2.2	10,419	1,520
Main activity last year (1=employment; 2=pension; 3=unemployment; 4=other)	1	4	1	1	10,348	1,505
Health status (1=poor or very poor; 2=better than poor)	1	2	1.9	1.9	10,413	1,518
Household type (1=one-person household; 2=MAH without children; 3=lone parent household; 4=MAH with 1 or 2 children; 5=MAH with 3 or more children)	1	5	4	2	13,044	1,834
Employment intensity (1=no employment in household; 3=full employment in household)	1	3	2.4	2.4	11,889	1,631
Main income source of household (1=employment income; 2=social transfers; 3=pensions)	1	3	1	1	12,914	1,816

*Source: Statistik Austria: EU-SILC Dataset, Wave 3; own analysis. Notes: data are unweighted; * for nominal variables, the mode instead of the mean is listed.*

1. Cross-sectional analysis of income poverty

Income poverty remained relatively stable in Austria during the 11-year period analyzed, ranging from 12 to 13 per cent. Variations that are more considerable are evidenced for Vienna, which started in 1995/97 with a higher than the country average income poverty rate. The rate then decreased considerably to 10 per cent – only to achieve a new peak in 2003/05 at 15 per cent. As noted earlier, part of the explanation for this development in Vienna are small sample sizes. One problem with the ECHP was panel attrition, which negatively affected the reliability of results for specific sub-groups, including the income poor population in Vienna. However, another part of explaining the cyclical development of income poverty rates in Vienna derives from the general socio-economic development. Key variables such as unemployment, net migration or GDP-growth affected the capital city to a different extent than the rest of the country – and these indicators changed considerably within the period examined (table A.2).

Table A.2: Socio-economic development in Austria and Vienna, 1995 – 2005

	Austria			Vienna		
	1995	2000	2005	1995	2000	2005
Unemployment rate (in %)	4.1*	3.5	5.2	5.9*	5.7	9.1
Net migration	+ 2,080	+ 17,272	+ 49,172	- 143	+ 7,460	+ 20,463
GDP: regional accounts (€ per capita; current prices)	22,100	26,300	28,800**	31,800	37,000	40,300**

*Source: Statistik Austria (2009b). Notes: * data for 1996; ** data for 2004*

1.1 Individual characteristics of income poverty

Table A.3 contains information on the relevance of individual characteristics of income poverty in Austria and Vienna. The data suggest that **income poverty is female**. With one exception (Vienna in 2003/05), female income poverty rates were higher than those of males. The traditional female life pattern (with females largely carrying out unpaid household and care work) prevalent in Austria thus contains a considerable income poverty risk (Heitzmann and Schmidt 2002, Heitzmann 2004a).

Table A.3: Income poverty rates (three-year averages) by individual characteristics, Austria and Vienna, 1995 – 2005

	Income poverty rates: Austria			Income poverty rates: Vienna		
	∅ 95-97	∅ 98-00	∅ 03-05	∅ 95-97	∅ 98-00	∅ 03-05
Total population	13	12	13	13	10	15
Sex						
Men	11 *	10 *	12	12	9	15
Women	14 *	13 *	14	14	10	14
Age cohorts						
< 20 yrs.	15	14	15 *	16	(12)	20
20-39	11 *	9 *	12	15	12	17
40-64	10 *	9 *	10 *	(10)	(7)	12
65+	18 *	19 *	16	X	X	(8) *
Citizenship						
Austria, EU-15, EFTA	12	11	12 *	11	9	12 *
Migrants	32 *	20 *	28 *	(27) *	(15)	31 *
Educational level[1)]						
Primary or less	16 *	17 *	19 *	(16)	(13)	22 *
Below 2nd degree	9 *	8 *	9 *	(8)	(6)	10
Above 2nd degree	10	8 *	9 *	14	9	12
Main activity last year[1)]						
Employment	6 *	6 *	7 *	(5) *	(5) *	9 *
Pension	13	12	13	X	X	(7) *
Unemployment	34 *	26 *	37 *	(45) *	X	(43) *
Other	19 *	19 *	22 *	24 *	19 *	29 *
Health status[1)]						
Poor or very poor	19 *	19 *	22 *	X	X	(18)
Better	11	10	11	11	8	13
Unweighted base	*758 < n > 1,521*			*81 < n > 325*		

*Sources: data for 1995 – 2000: ICCR-IFS: ECHP Dataset, Waves 2 to 7; data for 2003/05: Statistik Austria: EU-SILC Dataset, Waves 1 to 3; own analysis. Notes: data are weighted; (.) indicates a cell size of less than 30 unweighted observations in at least one wave; X indicates a cell size of less than 10 unweighted observations in at least one wave; * significant at a 5 per cent level in all waves examined to calculate the average; 1) data include only individuals aged 16+*

In terms of **age cohorts**, the results for Austria suggest that young persons (aged below 20 years), but even more so the elderly (aged 65+) are particularly threatened by income poverty. Their rates were above the country average throughout the period studied. In 2003/05, child poverty (< 20 years) and income poverty of the elderly in Austria amounted to 15 percent and to 18 per cent, respectively. In contrast to young and elderly people, working age adults in Austria had lower than average income poverty rates throughout the 11-year period analyzed. The results for Vienna differ somewhat: Whereas child poverty rates have been above the average rate in 1995/97 and 2003/05, and achieved a maximum of 20 per cent in 2003/05, the elderly are less likely to be income poor. In 2003/05, they even had the lowest income poverty rate of all age cohorts analyzed, i.e. 8 per cent. Even though this result is statistically significant, low sample sizes suggest interpreting this figure with care (however, see Heitzmann and Eiffe 2008). A further difference between Austria and Vienna concerns the population in working age. Income poverty rates in Austria's capital city were consistently below average only for the cohort aged between 40 and 64 years. The younger cohort obtained a higher than average income poverty rate in Vienna throughout the decade analyzed – in contrast to the situation in Austria. One explanation for this comparatively high rate is the fact that many young adults in Vienna are still in education and training, and most of the country's universities are located in the capital city.

Citizenship considerably influences the likelihood of experiencing income poverty (Heitzmann and Förster 2007, Gächter 2009). Within the decade examined, members of the EU-15 or EFTA states (including Austrian citizens) had a mean income poverty rate of between 11 and 12 per cent in Austria and 9 to 15 per cent in Vienna. The corresponding rates for citizens from other countries (which are defined as 'migrants' here) were up to almost three times higher. The decreasing proportion of migrant poverty in Austria and Vienna between 1995/97 and 1998/2000 may be explained by panel attrition and a deterioration of the representativeness of this population group in later waves of the ECHP, rather than by an actual decrease of income poverty risk. In 2003/05, 28 per cent of all migrants in Austria and even 31 per cent in the country's capital city, qualified as income poor.

Many studies point to a close link between income poverty and **educational attainment** (e.g. Bacher 2003, Schlögl 2009). The significance of this correlation has been confirmed for both Vienna and Austria. An educational level above primary schooling significantly reduces income poverty in both Austria and Vienna. In 2003/05, 9 per cent of individuals in Austria (12 per cent in Vienna) with an educational attainment above secondary degree (i.e. they have at least *Matura*) experienced income poverty. This compares to 19 per cent of individuals (22 per cent in Vienna) with only primary education or less. However, available data for Vienna suggest that people with an educational level above secondary degree had above average income poverty rates in 1995/97. This result is not statistically significant, though.

The variable '**main activity**' only covers individuals aged 16+ in the ECHP and the EU-SILC. These were asked to identify their main activity status for each of the twelve months preceding the year before the interview. The most frequently cited activity was then defined as 'main activity last year'. The results impressively underline the importance of paid work to prevent income poverty. Both in Austria and in Vienna, income poverty rates of people whose main activity was employment were significantly lower than average rates. This finding holds for the whole decade analyzed. In Austria, income poverty rates were up to seven percentage points below the average rate. In Vienna, the difference amounted to 8 percentage points. However, both in Austria and, especially, in Vienna, the significance of paid employment as a protective shield against income poverty appears to have become more permeable with the highest – as compared to earlier years – income poverty rates for this population group being recorded in 2003/05.

While the income poverty rate for people who qualified themselves as pensioners corresponded to the Austrian average, it was significantly below average in Vienna. In 2003/05, it achieved a value of 7 per cent, while adults whose main activity was unemployment had rates amounting to 43 per cent in Vienna and 37 per cent in Austria. These high rates were characteristic not only of the period 2003/05 but also of the past, which is evidenced by high income poverty risks for the unemployed in the period from 1995 to 2000. Further analysis suggests that income poverty risks rise with the length of unemployment. Data for 2005 suggest that in Austria, the short-term unemployed (i.e. less than six months) had an income poverty rate of 16 per cent. When the unemployment spell lasted longer, the rate amounted to 30 per cent. One explanation for these high rates is an insufficient level of social security transfers. Indeed, in Austria, the levels of unemployment benefit and unemployment assistance depend on previous employment income. They are thus especially low for individuals with low employment incomes. Average unemployment benefit in 2005 amounted to € 24.10 per day, average unemployment assistance to € 18.70 (Arbeitsmarktservice Österreich 2006: 34). These average transfers are lower than the income poverty threshold calculated for a single person in Austria for the year 2005.

An above-average income poverty risk – albeit a lower one than for that of the unemployed – is evidenced for the last group assessed, the 'other'. This group mainly includes people in education or those primarily engaged with household activities. Their income poverty rates were above-average both in Austria and in Vienna. In 2003/05, these rates amounted to 22 per cent in Austria and even 29 per cent in Vienna. These results proved to be statistically significant at a 5 per cent level.

A final variable included in the analysis of individual characteristics of the income poor was that of the **health status** of people aged 16+, based on their self-evaluation. There is evidence of a close correlation between income poverty and health status (e.g. Pochobradsky *et al.* 2002, Habl 2009). Data for Vienna suggest that in 2003/05, 18 per cent of all adults who indicated to have a poor or very poor health status were income poor, as opposed to 13 per cent with a better health status. In Austria, the difference has even been more pronounced (22 versus 11 per cent). The dispersion of income poverty rates between these two groups even increased between 1995/97 and 2003/05 in Austria.

1.2 Household characteristics of income poverty

In addition to individual characteristics, the composition of the household people live in determines their likelihood of experiencing income poverty. For example, an unemployed person living alone has a different probability of actually experiencing income poverty than would be the case if this person lived together with another adult who is in paid employment. In multi-person households, resources may be pooled and distributed (more or less equally, see Footnote 29) between the household members. Thus, household characteristics both influence and explain the probability of individuals to experience income poverty.

Table A.4: Income poverty rates by household characteristics (three-year averages), Austria and Vienna, 1995 – 2005

	Income poverty rates: Austria			Income poverty rates: Vienna		
	∅ 95-97	∅ 98-00	∅ 03-05	∅ 95-97	∅ 98-00	∅ 03-05
Total population	13	12	13	13	10	15
Household type						
One-person household	24 *	21 *	21 *	(22) *	(17) *	17
MAH without children	9 *	9 *	9 *	(6) *	X	9 *
Lone parent household	23 *	17	28 *	(24) *	X	(31) *
MAH with 1 or 2 children	9 *	8 *	10 *	10	(9)	12
MAH with 3 or more children	16	17 *	21 *	X	X	(31) *
Employment intensity[1)]						
No employment in hh	32 *	25 *	27 *	(33) *	(23) *	33 *
Partial employment	15 *	13 *	17 *	21	15	21 *
Full employment	6 *	6 *	6 *	(5) *	(4) *	8 *
Main income source in hh						
Employment income	8 *	7 *	8 *	7 *	6 *	10 *
Social transfers	39 *	31 *	47 *	(50) *	(38) *	55 *
Pensions	20 *	20 *	15	(11)	(10)	8 *
Unweighted base	*758 < n > 1,521*			*81 < n > 325*		

*Sources: data for 1995 – 2000: ICCR-IFS: ECHP Dataset, Waves 2 to 7; data for 2002/03 to 2004/05: Statistik Austria: EU-SILC Dataset, Waves 1 to 3; own analysis. Notes: data are weighted; (.) indicates a cell size of less than 30 unweighted observations in at least one wave; X indicates a cell size of less than 10 unweighted observations in at least one wave; * significant at a 5 per cent level in all waves examined to calculate the average; MAH=multi-adult household; hh=household; 1) includes only households with at least one member in working age (20-64 years)*

Table A.4 summarizes results of a bivariate analysis of the EU-SILC and the ECHP on household characteristics and income poverty. The variable '**household type**' differentiates between different compositions of households. Households without children are separated according to the number of household members (one-person versus multi-adult households). Households with children[57] are differentiated into lone parent and

[57] Household members below the age of 16 are defined as dependent children. Addi-

multi-adult households[58]. The latter category is further divided into households with up to two children and households with three or more children. The results suggest that – even though income poverty rates varied from year to year – three of the household types analyzed are particularly affected by income poverty, i.e. one-person households, lone parent households and multi-adult households with three or more children. In the periods between 1995/97 and 2003/05, they invariably obtained above-average income poverty rates both in Austria and Vienna. In 2003/05, the highest income poverty rate in Austria was obtained by members of lone parent households (28 per cent). In Vienna, the rate for this group amounted to even 31 per cent, which corresponds to the rate shown for members of multi-adult households with three or more children. An explanation for the high income poverty risks of these two household types is once more related to the employment behaviour of parents: the poverty risk increases if one parent, usually the mother, reduces her/his employment participation.

A second variable included in the analysis reflects the '**employment intensity**' of households. This variable is constructed from the 'main activity status' of individuals (see above), assuming an individual employment potential of twelve months for each working-age adult (i.e. adults between 20 and 64 years)[59]. Multiplication of the number of working-age adults in the household with 12 produces the household's annual employment potential. A comparison with the actual months in which paid work was indicated as the main activity leads to the construction of three categories of employment intensity. If the number of months of actual employment within the household amounts to zero, there is 'no employment'. 'Full employment' is achieved if the actual employment months amount to at least 75 per cent of the household's employment potential. Employment intensity between 'no employment' and 'full employment' is defined as 'partial employment'. For the analysis of the data, only house-

---

tionally, young adults below the age of 27, who live with at least one parent and whose main activity is neither employment nor unemployment, are defined as children. This definition follows stipulations of Statistik Austria (2006b).

[58] In lone parent households, there is only one adult with her/his child or children, in multi-adult households there are at least two household members who are not defined as children – independent of whether there are two parents in the household. This definition follows stipulations of Statistik Austria (2006b).

[59] Owing to missing data in the ECHP sample, is has not been possible to distinguish between part-time and full-time employment.

holds with at least one working-age adult were considered (above all to exclude households of pensioners with no employment intensity).

As expected, employment intensity significantly influences the income poverty rates of all household members. Throughout the period analyzed, income poverty rates in households with full employment were below average in both Austria and Vienna. In households with only partial employment, income poverty rates were already above average, amounting to 17 per cent in Austria and 21 per cent in Vienna in 2003/05. The income poverty risk increases further in households, in which none of the working age adults were in employment. In Austria, income poverty rates for members of these households amounted to between 25 and 32 per cent in the period analyzed. In Vienna, the corresponding rates amounted from 23 per cent to 33 per cent. Even though the variations of the income poverty rate for this group – and the other groups – thus vary considerably within the decade analyzed, the principal pattern remains robust. If working age adults are in (full) employment, income poverty risks appear to be lower than if they are not.

A third variable included in the analysis reflects the **main income source** within the household. I present data for three categories: (i) households in which employment income forms the main income source, (ii) households, which rely primarily on pensions and (III) households that live on social transfers other than pensions. The results confirm the pattern of income poverty risks already discussed. Members of households of the first category had below average rates in both Vienna and Austria throughout the period analyzed. While the rates for Austria remained stable at 7 and 8 per cent, the income poverty rates for Vienna amounted to 7 per cent in 1995/97, 6 per cent in 1998/00 and then increased to 10 per cent (2003/05). This implies that the potential of employment to prevent income poverty in Vienna has decreased.

A below average income poverty rate has also been ascertained for members of households in which pensions formed the main income source. However, only for 'pensioners' living in Vienna (and only if they were males; indeed, there is a statistically significant difference between male and female poverty rates in Vienna with regard to this group). In Austria, income poverty rates of households with pension income as main source amounted to 15 per cent in 2003/05 and to 20 per cent in

1995/97, suggesting a decrease of the poverty risk for this group over time. Members of households in which social transfers (excluding pensions) form the main income source were most likely to experience income poverty both in Austria and in Vienna. Between a third and half of all members of such households experienced income poverty in the years between 1995/97 to 2003/05.

The results of the bivariate analysis presented so far suggest an above-average risk to experience income poverty for young people (and outside of Vienna, also for the elderly), migrants, for people with a low educational attainment, for working-age adults out of paid employment and for individuals with a poor or very poor health status. In terms of household composition, it is one-person households without children and lone parent as well as multi-adult households with three or more children that are particularly affected by income poverty in both Austria and Vienna. The relevance of paid employment, both as main activity and in terms of main income source within a household, as a shield against income poverty is confirmed by an analysis of household characteristics. Income poverty risks, moreover, correlate with the extent of employment intensity within a household.

There are some differences between Austria and Vienna in terms of the characteristics examined. However, small sample sizes suggest interpreting these differences with some caution. Overall, the assessment provided evidence that not only the *extent* of income poverty has remained relatively robust within the period examined both in Austria and in Vienna, but also the *composition* of income poor groups.

2. Dynamic analysis of income poverty

In addition to the cross-sectional analysis, the results of which are reproduced above, this section includes results of a bivariate analysis on income poverty in Austria and Vienna, utilizing the panel character of the ECHP. This involves that the following information is based only on those members of the ECHP sample that participated in the survey throughout the period from 1995 to 2000. The sample size in the combined file, which serves as a basis for the dynamic analyses, amounted to 5,281 (Austria) and 634 (Vienna) individuals. Two indicators have been chosen for the illustration of the dynamics of income poverty. 'Temporary income poverty' includes all individuals who were income poor at least once during the period between 1995 and 2000. 'Persistent income poverty' refers to people who experienced income poverty in the year 2000, and in at least two of the previous years (and thus for at least half of the six years analyzed within the ECHP dataset).

Table A.5: Temporary and persistent income poverty rates by individual characteristics, Vienna and Austria, 1995-2000

	Temporary income poverty		Persistent income poverty	
	Austria	**Vienna**	**Austria**	**Vienna**
Total population	29	25	7	(7)
Sex				
Males	25 *	22	6 *	(6)
Females	33 *	27	8 *	(7)
Age cohorts				
< 20 yrs.	36 *	(28)	8	X
20-39	28	35 *	4 *	X
40-64	24 *	18 *	5 *	(6)
65+	34 *	(20)	14 *	X
Citizenship				
Austria, EU-15 and EFTA	28	24	6	(6)
Other	50 *	(35) *	(18) *	X
Educational level1)				
Primary or less	30 *	32 *	11 *	(8)
Below 2nd degree	23 *	17 *	4 *	X
Above 2nd degree	24 *	26	(4) *	(8)
Main activity status1)				
Employed	23 *	20 *	3 *	X
Pension	27	(17) *	9 *	X
Unemployed	52 *	X	X	X
Other	38 *	38 *	12 *	(15) *
Health status1)				
Poor or very poor	36 *	(32)	16 *	X
Better	27	23	6 *	(6)

*Source: ICCR-IFS, ECHP Dataset, Waves 2 to 7, own analysis; Notes: data are weighted by panel weights; X indicates a cell size of less than 10 observations (temporary income poverty: in at least one wave); (.) indicates a cell size of between 10 and 30 observations (temporary income poverty: in at least one wave); * significant at a 5 per cent level; 1) includes only individuals aged 16+*

29 per cent of all citizens in Austria and 25 per cent in Vienna experienced temporary income poverty at least once in the six year period examined (table A.5). Thus, in Austria relatively low incomes are a problem

that affects much more people than suggested by cross-sectional analysis. Evidence suggests that 7 per cent of the population in both Austria and its capital city experienced income poverty for at least three years. Unfortunately, small sample sizes hampered the analysis of persistent income poverty in Vienna.

It is not surprising that characteristics that led to an above-average rate of income poverty in a cross-sectional analysis also turned out to be particularly relevant in a dynamic analysis. In terms of **individual characteristics**, temporary income poverty of females in Austria was by 8 percentage points higher than that of males (in Vienna: by 5 percentage points). Moreover, females in Austria and Vienna were more likely than their male counterparts to remain income poor also in the period between 1995 and 2000. In terms of age groups, both the youngest and the oldest age cohorts examined had above average rates of temporary income poverty in Austria. In Vienna, this pattern was different: the two youngest age cohorts were most likely to be threatened by temporary income poverty – again a result that already showed in the cross-sectional analysis. Data on persistent income poverty suggests that the elderly in Austria were most likely to remain poor, with a persistent income poverty rate amounting to 14 per cent. They are no longer able to increase their income through employment. Thus, their disposable income level (which mainly consists of pensions) remains stable over time. If pension income is low, it tends to remain low.

Every second individual with a migrant background experienced income poverty between 1995 and 2000 in Austria. The proportion in Vienna was with 35 per cent much lower. However, small sample sizes suggest interpreting this figure with caution. This also applies to the information on persistent income poverty. While sample sizes are too low to reproduce results for Vienna, data on Austria suggest a particularly high rate of persistent income poverty among migrants, amounting to 18 per cent, i.e. three times higher than that of the non-migrant population.

The relevance of a high educational level as a protection against income poverty is confirmed by the results of the dynamic analysis. Similar to cross-sectional data presented earlier, an education above primary degree appears to make a difference in terms of poverty risks, while educational attainment above secondary degree even enhances income poverty rates as opposed to educational attainment below secondary and above primary schooling.

In terms of main activities, data for Austria suggest that every second unemployed person in 2000 was income poor at least once between 1995 and 2000. The lowest temporary rates of income poverty were obtained by the employed (Austria) and pensioners (Vienna). Moreover, individuals who perceived their health as poor or very poor had considerably higher temporary and persistent poverty rates than their counterparts, confirming a correlation between material deprivation and (subjective perceptions of) one's own health.

Table A.6: Temporary and persistent income poverty rates by household characteristics in Vienna and Austria, 1995-2000

	Temporary income poverty		Persistent income poverty	
	Austria	**Vienna**	**Austria**	**Vienna**
Household type				
One-person household	40 *	40 *	14 *	(12) *
MAH without children	21 *	11 *	6	X
Single parent household	55 *	(33)	(7)	X
MAH with 1 or 2 children	24 *	23	4 *	X
MAH with 3 or more children	39 *	(42) *	11 *	X
Employment intensity[1)]				
No employment in hh	42 *	(38) *	15 *	X
Partial employment in hh	32 *	37 *	7 *	(10) *
Full employment in hh	24 *	18 *	3 *	(4) *
Main income source				
Employment income	25 *	22 *	4 *	(5)
Social transfers	62 *	(63) *	16 *	X
Pensions	33 *	(22)	14 *	X
Unweighted base	*n = 1,523*	*n = 135*	*n = 414*	*n = 33*

*Source: ICCR-IFS, ECHP Dataset, Waves 2 to 7, own analysis; Notes: data are weighted by panel weights; MAH=multi-adult households; hh=household; X indicates a cell size of less than 10 observations (temporary income poverty: in at least one wave); (.) indicates a cell size of between 10 and 30 observations (temporary income poverty: in at least one wave); * significant at a 5 per cent level; 1) includes only households with at least one member in working age (20-64 years)*

In addition to individual characteristics, **household characteristics** also influence the likelihood of experiencing temporary or persistent income poverty in Austria and Vienna (see table A.6). In terms of household types, the over-proportional high risks of income poverty of one-person households, lone parent households and multi-adult households with three or more children are reflected in large proportions of temporary income poor and (with the exception of lone-parent households, the result of which is based on small sample sizes, though) persistent income poor. In terms of employment intensity, both temporary and persistent income poverty rates decrease with the employment intensity in Austria. The difference between no employment intensity and partial employment intensity is not very large in Vienna, though. Again, however, small sample sizes suggest considering the reliability of this result with care. The final variable examined is the main income source of households. Again, the findings of the cross-sectional analysis are confirmed by the dynamic analysis. Members of households in which the majority of income derived from employment were least likely to experience temporary or persistent income poverty in Austria and Vienna. In contrast, members of households who relied on social transfers (other than pensions) had the highest income poverty risks. 62 per cent of these individuals in Austria (and 63 per cent in Vienna) experienced income poverty at least once between 1995 to 2000. 16 per cent of these household members were in persistent poverty in Austria (no data is available for Vienna). As expected, there appears to be a difference between Austria and Vienna, if pensions are the main income source. While a third of all members of households in which pensions were the major income source were income poor at least once between 1995 and 2000 in Austria, this only applies to 22 per cent in Vienna (which is a lower rate as compared to the average rate of the Viennese population). Data for Austria suggest once more that households living on pension income had a particularly high persistent income poverty risk, amounting to 14 per cent (due to small sample sizes no data is available for Vienna). The dynamic analysis thus confirms the relevance of certain individual and household characteristics to explain income poverty both in Austria and in Vienna.

References

Ahonen, P., Hyyryläinen, E. and Saminen, A. (2006). Looking for governance configurations of European welfare states. *Journal of European Social Policy*, 16/1, 173-184.

Alcock, P. (1997). *Understanding poverty*, 2nd edition. Basingstoke: Palgrave.

Anheier, H. K. (2005). *Nonprofit organizations: Theory, management, policy*. London / New York: Routledge.

Anheier, H. K. and Salamon, L. M. (1992). *In search of the nonprofit sector I: The question of definitions*. Baltimore: The Johns Hopkins Institute for Policy Studies.

Anheier, H. K. and Seibel, W. (eds.). (1990). *The third sector: Comparative studies of nonprofit organizations*. Berlin / New York: de Gruyter.

Anheier, H. K. and Seibel, W. (1998). The nonprofit sector and the transformation of societies: A comparative analysis of East Germany, Hungary and Poland. In: Powell, W. W. and Clemens, E. S. (eds.). *Private action and the public good*, pp. 177-192. New Haven: Yale University Press.

Arbeitsmarktservice Österreich (2002). *Geschäftsbericht 2001*. http://www.ams.at/-_docs/gb01.pdf (last accession date: September 2009).

Arbeitsmarktservice Österreich (2004). *10 Jahre AMS: 1994 - 2004*. Wien: Arbeitsmarktservice Österreich.

Arbeitsmarktservice Österreich (2006). *Geschäftsbericht 2005*. http://www.ams.at/-_docs/001_GB_2005.pdf (last accession date: September 2009).

Ascoli, U. and Ranci, C. (2002a). Changes in the welfare mix: The European path. In: Ascoli, U. and Ranci, C. (eds.). *Dilemmas of the welfare mix: The new structure of welfare in an era of privatization*, pp. 225-243. New York: Kluwer.

Ascoli, U. and Ranci, C. (2002b). The context of new social policies in Europe. In: Ascoli, U. and Ranci, C. (eds.). *Dilemmas of the welfare mix: The new structure of welfare in an era of privatization*, pp. 1-24. New York: Kluwer.

Ascoli, U. and Ranci, C. (eds.). (2002c). *Dilemmas of the welfare mix: The new structure of welfare in an era of privatization*. New York: Kluwer.

Atkinson, A. B. (1993). The institution of an official poverty line and economic policy. *WSP Discussion Paper*, 98.

Atkinson, A. B. (1998). *Poverty in Europe*. Oxford: Blackwell.

Atkinson, A. B. (2000). Reform of the welfare state and economic performance. In: Hauser, R. (ed.) *Die Zukunft des Sozialstaates. Jahrestagung 1998 des Vereins für Socialpolitik*, pp. 53-72. Berlin: Duncker + Humblot.

Atkinson, A. B., Cantillon, B., Marlier, E. and Nolan, B. (2002). *Social indicators: The EU and social inclusion*. Oxford: Oxford University Press.

Atteslander, P. (2008). *Methoden der empirischen Sozialforschung*, 12th edition. Berlin: Erich Schmidt Verlag.

Bacher, J. (2003). Soziale Ungleichheit und Bildungspartizipation im weiterführenden Schulsystem Österreichs. *Österreichische Zeitschrift für Soziologie*, 28/3, 3-32.

Bachstein, W. (1997). *Nonprofit Organisationen im Bereich sozialer Dienste: Beschäftigung und sozialpolitische Implikationen*. Dissertation an der Wirtschaftsuniversität Wien: Wirtschaftsuniversität Wien.

Badelt, C. (ed.) (1996). *Handbuch der Nonprofit Organisation: Strukturen und Management*, 1st edition. Stuttgart: Schäffer-Poeschel.

Badelt, C. (2001). Soziale Dienste als neue Herausforderung für den Sozialstaat. In: Theurl, E. (ed.) *Der Sozialstaat an der Jahrtausendwende: Analysen und Perspektiven*, pp. 115-134. Heidelberg: Physika-Verlag.

Badelt, C. (2003). Entrepreneurship in nonprofit organizations: Its role in theory and in the real world nonprofit sector. In: Anheier, H. K. and Ben-Ner, A. (eds.). *The study of the nonprofit enterprise: Theories and approaches*, pp. 139-159. New York et al.: Kluwer.

Badelt, C. (2007). Zwischen Marktversagen und Staatsversagen? Nonprofit Organisationen aus sozioökonomischer Sicht. In: Badelt, C., Meyer, M. and Simsa, R. (eds.). *Handbuch der Nonprofit Organisation: Strukturen und Management*, 4th edition, pp. 98-119. Stuttgart: Schäffer-Poeschel.

Badelt, C., Meyer, M. and Simsa, R. (2007a). Ausblick: Entwicklungsperspektiven des Nonprofit Sektors. In: Badelt, C., Meyer, M. and Simsa, R. (eds.). *Handbuch der Nonprofit Organisation: Strukturen und Management*, 4th edition, pp. 620-642. Stuttgart: Schäffer-Poeschel.

Badelt, C., Meyer, M. and Simsa, R. (2007b). Die Wiener Schule der NPO-Forschung. In: Badelt, C., Meyer, M. and Simsa, R. (eds.). *Handbuch der Nonprofit Organisation: Strukturen und Management*, 4th edition, pp. 3-16. Stuttgart: Schäffer-Poeschel.

Badelt, C. and Österle, A. (2001a). *Grundzüge der Sozialpolitik: Sozialökonomische Grundlagen - Allgemeiner Teil*, 2nd edition. Wien: Manz.

Badelt, C. and Österle, A. (2001b). *Grundzüge der Sozialpolitik: Sozialpolitik in Österreich - Spezieller Teil*, 2nd edition. Wien: Manz.

Barr, N. (2004). *Economics of the welfare state*, 4th edition. Oxford: Oxford University Press.

Bartlett, W., Propper, C., Wilson, D. and Le Grand, J. (eds.). (1994). *Quasi-markets in the welfare state*. Bristol: SAUS.

Bauer, R. (ed.) (1993). *Intermediäre Nonprofit-Organistionen in einem Neuen Europa*. Rheinfelden / Berlin: Schäuble.

Becker, S. (1997). *Responding to poverty: The politics of cash and care*. London / New York: Longman.

Belfield, C., R. (2002). The privatization and marketization of US schooling. *Zeitschrift für Erziehungswissenschaft*, 5/2, 222-240.

Ben-Ner, A. and Van Hoomissen, T. (1993). Nonprofit organizations in the mixed economy: A demand and supply analysis. In: Ben-Ner, A. and Gui, B. (eds.). *The nonprofit sector in the mixed economy*, pp. 27-58. Ann Arbor: The University of Michigan Press.

Bendick, M. (1989). Privatizing the delivery of social welfare services: An idea to be taken seriously. In: Kamerman, S. B. and Kahn, A. J. (eds.). *Privatization and the welfare state*, pp. 97-120. Princeton: Princeton University Press.

Berghman, J. (1995). Social exclusion in Europe: Policy context and analytical framework. In: Room, G. J. (ed.) *Beyond the threshold: The measurement and analysis of social exclusion*, pp. 10-28. Bristol: The Policy Press.

Betti, G., Lemmi, A., Mulas, A., Natilli, M., Neri, L., Salvati, N. and Verma, V. (2003). *Regional indicators to reflect social exclusion and poverty*. Brussels: European Commission.

Bevir, M., Rhodes, R. A. W. and Weller, P. (2003). Traditions of governance: Interpreting the changing role of the public sector. *Public Administration*, 81/1, 1-17.

Bewley, T. (2002). Interviews as a valid empirical tool in economics. *Journal of Socio-Economics*, 2002/31, 343-353.

Bifulco, L. and Vitale, T. (2006). Contracting for welfare services in Italy. *Journal of Social Policy*, 35/3, 495-513.

Biricz, J. and Kniesz, J. (2005). Lohnsteuerstatistik 2003. *Statistische Nachrichten*, 60/1, 68-79.

Blank, R. (2000). When can public policy makers rely on private markets? The effective provision of social service. *The Economic Journal*, 110, C34-C49.

BMAGS (1997). *Bericht über die soziale Lage 1996*. Wien: BMAGS.

BMAGS (1998). *Bericht über die soziale Lage 1997*. Wien: BMAGS.

BMAS (1996). *Bericht über die soziale Lage 1995*. Wien: BMAS.

Bode, I. (2006). Disorganized welfare mixes: Voluntary agencies and new governance regimes in Western Europe. *Journal of European Social Policy*, 16/4, 346-359.

Boeßenecker, K.-H., Trube, A. and Wohlfahrt, N. (eds.). (2000). *Privatisierung im Sozialsektor: Rahmenbedingungen, Verlaufsformen und Probleme der Ausgliederung sozialer Dienste*. Münster: Votum.

Bonoli, G., George, V. and Taylor-Gooby, P. (2000). *European welfare futures: Towards a theory of retrenchment*. Cambridge: Polity Press.

Borzaga, C. and Santuari, A. (2003). New trends in the non-profit sector in Europe: The emergence of a social entrepreneurship. In: OECD (ed.) *The non-profit sector in a changing economy*, pp. 31-59. Paris: OECD.

Bosanquet, N. (1984). Is privatisation inevitable? In: Le Grand, J. and Robinson, R. (eds.). *Privatisation and the welfare state*, pp. 58-69. London et al.: George Allen & Unwin.

Brodkin, E. Z. and Young, D. R. (1989). Making sense of privatization: What can we learn from economic and political analysis. In: Kamerman, S. B. and Kahn, A. J. (eds.). *Privatization and the welfare state*, pp. 121-154. Princeton: Princeton University Press.

Brown, E. and Slivinski, A. (2006). Nonprofit organizations and the market. In: Powell, W. W. and Steinberg, R. (eds.). *The nonprofit sector: A research handbook*, 2nd edition, pp. 140-158. New Haven / London: Yale University Press.

Brudney, J. L. and Gazley, B. (2002). Testing the conventional wisdom regarding volunteer programs: A longitudinal analysis of the Service Corps of Retired Executives and the U.S. Small Business Administration *Nonprofit and Voluntary Sector Quarterly*, 31/4, 525-548.

Budäus, D. and Grüning, G. (1997). Public Private Partnership: Konzeption und Probleme eines Instruments zur Verwaltungsreform aus Sicht der Public-Choice Theorie. In: Budäus, D. and Eichhorn, P. (eds.). *Public Private Partnership: Neue Formen der öffentlichen Aufgabenerfüllung*, pp. 25-66. Baden-Baden: Nomos.

Bundeskanzleramt Österreich (2007). *Regierungsprogramm 2007-2010*. http://www.austria.gv.at/DocView.axd?CobId=19542 (last accession date: September 2009).

Burchardt, T. (1997). *Boundaries between public and private welfare: A typology and map of services*, No. CASEpaper 2. London: Centre for the Analysis of Social Exclusion / London School of Economics.

Burtless, G. and Smeeding, T. M. (2001). The level, trend, and composition of poverty. In: Danziger, S. H. and Haveman, R. H. (eds.). *Understanding poverty*, pp. 27-68. Cambridge / London: Harvard University Press.

Burton, J. (1987). Privatization: The Thatcher case. *Managerial and Decision Economics*, 8/1, 21-29.

Caritas Erzdiözese Wien (2006). *Von Mensch zu Mensch: Jahresbericht 2005 der Caritas der Erzdiözese Wien*. http://www.caritas-wien.at/fileadmin/user/noeost/PDFs/-Caritas_Jahresbericht_2005.pdf (last accession date: September 2009).

Castles, F. G. (2004). *The future of the welfare state: Crisis myths and crisis realities*. Oxford: Oxford University Press.

Cécora, J. (1991). *The role of 'informal' activity in household economic behaviour*. Berlin: Duncker & Humblot.

Coudouel, A., Hentschel, J. S. and Wodon, Q. T. (2002). Poverty measurement and analysis. In: The World Bank (ed.) *PRSP Sourcebook, Volume 1: Core techniques and cross cutting Issues*, pp. 27-74. Washington D.C.: The World Bank.

Cullis, J. and Jones, P. (1998). *Public finance and public choice*, 2nd edition. Oxford: Oxford University Press.

Dahl, R. A. and Lindblom, C. (1953). *Politics, economics, and welfare: Planning and politic-economic systems resolved into basic social processes*. New York: Harper & Row.

Dawid, E. and Heitzmann, K. (2006a). *Endbericht: Forschungsprojekt "Leistungen der NROs in der Armutsbekämpfung Studie zur Bestandsaufnahme der Leistungen sozialer Dienste in der Vermeidung und Bekämpfung von Armut in Österreich"*. Wien: Forschungsbericht 03/2006 des Instituts für Sozialpolitik.

Dawid, E. and Heitzmann, K. (2006b). *Zwischenbericht: Forschungsprojekt "Leistungen der NROs in der Armutsbekämpfung Studie zur Bestandsaufnahme der Leistungen sozialer Dienste in der Vermeidung und Bekämpfung von Armut in Österreich"*. Wien: mimeo.

de Andrés-Alonso, P., Cruz, N. M. and Romero-Merino, M. E. (2006). The governance of nonprofit organizations: Empirical evidence form nongovernmental development organizations in Spain. *Nonprofit and Voluntary Sector Quarterly*, 35/4, 588-604.

Deakin, N. (1996). The devils in the detail: Some reflections on contracting for social care by voluntary organizations. *Social Policy & Administration*, 30/1, 20-38.

Dennis, I. and Guio, A.-C. (2003). Monetary poverty in EU acceding and candidate countries. *Statistics in Focus - Population and social conditions*, 2003/21.

Department for Work and Pensions (2006). *Households Below Average Income (HBAI) 1994/95 - 2004/05*. http://research.dwp.gov.uk/asd/hbai/hbai2008/pdf_files/-full_hbai09.pdf (last accession date: September 2009).

Dimmel, N. (1997). *Sozialmanagement oder Wohlfahrtsverwaltung? Überlegungen zum Umbau des Wohlfahrtsstaates*. Frankfurt: Peter Lang.

Dimmel, N. (2000). *Drohen - Betteln - Verhandeln*. Frankfurt: Peter-Lang.

Dimmel, N. (2009). Konsequenzen und Perspektiven der Armutsbekämpfung im Kontext der Bedarfsorientierten Mindestsicherung (BMS). In: Dimmel, N., Heitzmann, K. and Schenk, M. (eds.). *Handbuch Armut in Österreich*, pp. 718-731. Innsbruck: Studienverlag.

Dimmel, N., Heitzmann, K. and Schenk, M. (2009a). Ausblick: Entwicklungen und Herausforderungen in der Bekämpfung der Armut. In: Dimmel, N., Heitzmann, K. and Schenk, M. (eds.). *Handbuch Armut in Österreich*, pp. 742-761. Innsbruck: Studienverlag.

Dimmel, N., Heitzmann, K. and Schenk, M. (eds.). (2009b). *Handbuch Armut in Österreich*. Innsbruck: Studienverlag.

Dimmel, N. and Pfeil, W. J. (2009). Armutsbekämpfung durch Transferleistungen. In: Dimmel, N., Heitzmann, K. and Schenk, M. (eds.). *Handbuch Armut in Österreich*, pp. 464-511. Innsbruck: Studienverlag.

Dowling, M. (1999). Social exclusion, inequality and social work. *Social Policy & Administration*, 33/3, 245-261.

Drechsler, W. (2008). Aufstieg und Untergang des New Public Management. *Kurswechsel*, 2008/2, 17-26.

Eiffe, F. F. (2009). Konzepte der Armut im europäischen Kontext: Ein geschichtlicher Überblick. In: Dimmel, N., Heitzmann, K. and Schenk, M. (eds.). *Handbuch Armut in Österreich*, pp. 67-90. Innsbruck: Studienverlag.

Eiffe, F. F. and Heitzmann, K. (2006). Armut im Kontext reicher Staaten: Zur wissenschaftlichen Operationalisierung eines normativen Begriffs. *Vierteljahreshefte zur Wirtschaftsforschung*, 75/1, 43-57.

Eikenberry, A. M. and Kluver, J. D. (2004). The marketization of the nonprofit sector: Civil society at risk? *Public Administration Review*, 64/2, 132-140.

Eisenhardt, K. M. (1989). Building theories from case study research. *Academy of Management Review*, 14/4, 532-550.

Esping-Andersen, G. (1990). *The three worlds of welfare capitalism*. Cambridge: Polity Press.

Esping-Andersen, G. (1999). *Social foundations of postindustrial economies*. Oxford: Oxford University Press.

Esping-Andersen, G., with Gallie, D., Hemerijck, A. and Myles, J. (2002). *Why we need a new welfare state*. Oxford: Oxford University Press.

European Commission (2002). *Joint report on social inclusion*. Luxemburg: Office for Official Publications of the European Communities.

Eurostat (2007). *European social statistics: Social protection expenditure and receipts: Data 1996-2004*. Luxembourg: Office for Official Publications of the European Communities.

Eurostat (2008). *European Social Statistics: Social protection expenditure and receipts, Data 1997-2005*. Luxembourg: Office for Official Publications of the European Communities.

Evers, A. (1993). The welfare mix approach. Understanding the pluralism of welfare systems. In: Evers, A. and Svetlik, I. (eds.). *Balancing pluralism: New welfare mixes in care for the elderly*, pp. 3-31. Aldershot et al.: Avebury.

Evers, A. (2003). Öffentliche Einrichtungen als soziale Unternehmen: Potenziale hybrider Organisationsformen im Bereich sozialer Dienstleistungen. In: Allmendinger, J. (ed.) *Entstaatlichung und soziale Sicherheit: Verhandlungen des 31. Kongresses der Deutschen Gesellschaft für Soziologie in Leipzig 2002*, pp. 975-990. Opladen: Leske + Budrich.

Evers, A. (2005). Mixed welfare systems and hybrid organizations: Changes in the governance and provision of social services. *International Journal of Public Administration*, 28, 737-748.

Evers, A. and Laville, J.-L. (2004). Defining the third sector in Europe. In: Evers, A. and Laville, J.-L. (eds.). *The Third Sector in Europe*, pp. 11-42. Cheltenham / Northampton: Edward Elgar.

Evers, A. and Olk, T. (eds.). (1996). *Wohlfahrtspluralismus*. Opladen: Westdeutscher Verlag.

Evers, A. and Svetlik, I. (eds.). (1993). *Balancing pluralism*. Aldershot et al.: Avebury.

Evers, A. and Wintersberger, H. (eds.). (1988). *Shifts in the welfare mix: Their impact on work, social services and welfare policies*. Wien: Europäisches Zentrum für Ausbildung und Forschung auf dem Gebiet der sozialen Wohlfahrt.

Feldstein, M. (ed.) (1998). *Privatizing social security*. Chicago: University of Chicago Press.

Fershtman, C. (1990). The interdependence between ownership status and market structure: The case of privatization. *Economica*, 57/227, 319-328.

Foldvary, F. (1994). *Public goods and private communities: The market provision of social services*. Aldershot / Brookfield: Edward Elgar.

Förster, M. and d'Ecole, M. M. (2005). Income distribution and poverty in OCED countries in the second half of the 1990s. *OECD Social, Employment and Migration Working Papers*, No. 29.

Förster, M. and Heitzmann, K. (2002). Einkommensarmut und akute Armut in Österreich. In: Bundesministerium für Soziale Sicherheit und Generationen (ed.) *Bericht über die soziale Lage 2001-2002: Analysen und Ressortaktivitäten*, pp. 187-209. Wien: BMSG.

Fuchs, M. (2003). *Social assistance – no, thanks? Empirical analysis of non-take-up in Austria 2003.* Wien: European Centre for Social Welfare Policy and Research.

Fuchs, M. (2009). Nicht-Inanspruchnahme von Sozialleistungen am Beispiel der Sozialhilfe. In: Dimmel, N., Heitzmann, K. and Schenk, M. (eds.). *Handbuch Armut in Österreich*, pp. 317-331. Innsbruck: Studienverlag.

Fullerton, D. and Geruso, M. (2006). The many definitions of social security privatization. *Economists' voice*, 3/4 (http://www.bepress.com/ev/vol3/iss4/art3/), 1-5.

Gächter, A. (2009). Die Armut der Eingewanderten. In: Dimmel, N., Heitzmann, K. and Schenk, M. (eds.). *Handbuch Armut in Österreich*, pp. 184-197. Innsbruck: Studienverlag.

Galaskiewicz, J. and Sinclair Colman, M. (2006). Collaboration between corporations and nonprofit organizations. In: Powell, W. W. and Steinberg, R. (eds.). *The nonprofit sector: A research handbook*, pp. 180-204. New Haven / London: Yale University Press.

Genser, B. and Holzmann, R. (2001). Öffentlicher Sektor: Finanz- und Sozialpolitik. In: Neck, R., Nowotny, E. and Winckler, G. (eds.). *Grundzüge der Wirtschaftspolitik Österreichs*, 3rd edition, pp. 214-265. Wien: Manz.

Gidron, B., Kramer, R. M. and Salamon, L. M. (1992). Government and the third sector in comparative perspective: Allies or adversaries? In: Gidron, B., Kramer, R. M. and Salamon, L. M. (eds.). *Government and the third sector: Emerging relationships in welfare states*, pp. 1-30. San Francisco: Jossey-Bass Publishers.

Gilbert, N. (2001). Renegotiating social allocations: Choices and issues. In: Gilbert, N. (ed.) *Targeting social benefits: International perspectives & trends*, pp. 211-225. New Brunswick / London: Transaction Publishers.

Gilbert, N. (2004). *Transformation of the welfare state: The silent surrender of public responsibility.* Oxford: Oxford University Press.

Gillie, A. (1996). The origin of the poverty line. *The Economic History Review*, 49/4, 715-730.

Gläser, J. and Laudel, G. (2004). *Experteninterviews und qualitative Inhaltsanalyse.* Wiesbaden: VS Verlag für Sozialwissenschaften.

Gurin, A. (1989). Social welfare and privatization: The British experience. In: Kamerman, S. B. and Kahn, A. J. (eds.). *Privatization and the welfare state*, pp. 179-205. Princeton: Princeton University Press.

Habl, C. (2009). Gesundheit und soziale Ungleichheit. In: Dimmel, N., Heitzmann, K. and Schenk, M. (eds.). *Handbuch Armut in Österreich*, pp. 172-183. Innsbruck: Studienverlag.

Hagenaars, A. J. M. and Van Praag, B. M. S. (1985). A synthesis of poverty line definitions. *Review of Income and Wealth*, 31/2, 139-154.

Haider, A., Schneider, U., Leisch, R. and Stöger, K. (2008). Neue Datengrundlage für den Non-Profit-Bereich. *Statistische Nachrichten*, 63/8, 754-761.

Handy, F., Mook, L. and Quarter, J. (2008). The Interchangeability of Paid Staff and Volunteers in Nonprofit Organizations. *Nonprofit and Voluntary Sector Quarterly*, 37/1, 76-92.

Hansmann, H. (1980). *The role of non-profit enterprise*. PONPO Working Paper No. 1: Yale University.

Hansmann, H. (1987a). Economic theories of nonprofit organizations. In: Powell, W. W. (ed.) *The nonprofit sector: A research handbook*, pp. 27-42. New Haven / London: Yale University Press.

Hansmann, H. (1987b). The effect of tax exemption and other factors on nonprofit versus for-profit firms. *National Tax Journal*, 40, 71-82.

Harris, B. (2000). Seebohm Rowntree and the measurement of poverty, 1899 - 1951. In: Bradshaw, J. and Sainsbury, R. (eds.). *Getting the measure of poverty: The early legacy of Seebohm Rowntree*, pp. 60-84. Aldershot et al.: Ashgate.

Haydn, R. (2006). Die österreichische Sozialversicherung im Jahr 2005. *Soziale Sicherheit*, 59/6, 250-276.

Heitzmann, K. (2001). *Dimensionen, Bedeutung und Strukturen des Nonprofit Sektors: Eine theoretisch-konzeptionelle und empirische Analyse für Österreich*. Wien: Service Fachverlag.

Heitzmann, K. (2002). Armut ist weiblich! --- Ist Armut weiblich? In: Heitzmann, K. and Schmidt, A. (eds.). *Frauenarmut: Hintergründe, Facetten, Perspektiven*, 2nd edition, pp. 121-136. Frankfurt am Main *et al.*: Peter Lang.

Heitzmann, K. (2003). Characteristics and dynamics of income poverty and multidimensional deprivation in Austria. In: Apospori, E. and Millar, J. (eds.). *The dynamics of social exclusion in Europe: Comparing Austria, Germany, Greece, Portugal and the UK*, pp. 41-62. Cheltenham / Northampton: Edward Elgar.

Heitzmann, K. (2004a). Frauenarmut in Österreich: Geschlechtsspezifische Ungleichheiten in der Armutspopulation. In: Heitzmann, K. and Schmidt, A. (eds.). *Wege aus der Frauenarmut*, pp. 59-74. Frankfurt am Main et al.: Peter Lang.

Heitzmann, K. (2004b). Funktionen und Leistungen von NPOs im Wandel: Illustriert anhand der Entwicklung der institutionellen Armenfürsorge in Österreich. In: Witt, D., Purtschert, R. and Schauer, R. (eds.). *Funktionen und Leistungen von Nonprofit-Organisationen. 6. Internationales Colloquium der NPO-Forscher. Technische Universität München, 25. - 26. März 2004*, pp. 213-225. Wiesbaden: Gabler.

Heitzmann, K. (2004c). NPOs und der öffentliche Sektor in Österreich: In einer veritablen Beziehungskrise? In: Berger, J. (ed.) *Zerreißt das soziale Band? Beiträge zu einer aktuellen gesellschaftspolitischen Debatte*, pp. 201-220. Frankfurt / New York: Campus.

Heitzmann, K., Canagarajah, S. R. and Siegel, P. B. (2002). *Guidelines for assessing the sources of risk and vulnerability*. Washington D. C.: Social Protection Discussion Paper 0218. The World Bank.

Heitzmann, K. and Eiffe, F. F. (2008). *Gibt es einen Großstadtfaktor in der Armutsgefährdung und Deprivation älterer Menschen? Eine empirische Ananlyse für Österreich*. Wien: Forschungsbericht des Forschungsinstituts für Altersökonomie No. 3/2008.

Heitzmann, K. and Förster, M. (2007). Armutsgefährdung, manifeste Armut und Einkommenschancen von MigrantInnen in Österreich. In: Fassmann, H. (ed.) *2. Österreichischer Migrations- und Einkommensbericht*, pp. 291-302. Wien: Drava.

Heitzmann, K. and Österle, A. (2008). Lange Traditionen und neue Herausforderungen: Das österreichische Wohlfahrtssystem. In: Schubert, K., Hegelich, S. and Bazant, U. (eds.). *Europäische Wohlfahrtssysteme: Ein Handbuch*, pp. 47-69. Wiesbaden: VS Verlag für Sozialwissenschaften.

Heitzmann, K. and Schmidt, A. (eds.). (2002). *Frauenarmut: Hintergründe, Facetten, Perspektiven*, 2nd edition. Frankfurt am Main et al.: Peter Lang.

Heitzmann, K. and Wallner-Ewald, S. (1999). Social exclusion statistics in the European Union: Availability, plans and action in Austria. In: *Social exclusion statistics: Conference papers*, pp. 42-47. London.

Hills, J., Le Grand, J. and Piachaud, D. (eds.). (2002). *Understanding social exclusion*. Oxford: Oxford University Press.

Höck, C. (1996). Wohlfahrtsverbände und Staat in der lokalen Armutspolitik - Tendenzen der Pluralisierung und Politisierung im Netzwerk zur Erstellung des Hamburger Armutsberichtes. *Zeitschrift für Sozialreform*, 42/7, 448-476.

Holoubek, M., Damjanovic, D. and Holzinger, K. (2007). Die Vergabe öffentlicher Aufträge als sozialpolitisches Instrument: Zu den rechtlichen Rahmenbedingungen. In: Schneider, U. and Trukeschitz, B. (eds.). *Quasi-Märkte und Qualität: Die Qualität arbeitsmarktpolitischer und sozialer Dienstleistungen im Kontext öffentlicher Beschaffungspolitik*, pp. 33-56. Baden-Baden: Nomos.

Holzmann, R. and Heitzmann, K. (2002). Die Reform der Alterssicherung in Österreich. In: Theurl, E., Winner, H. and Sausgruber, R. (eds.). *Kompendium der österreichischen Finanzpolitik*, pp. 507-542. Wien / New York: Springer.

Holzmann, R. and Jørgensen, S. L. (1999). *Social protection as social risk management: Conceptual underpinnings for the Social Protection Sector Strategy Paper.* Washington D.C.: Social Protection Discussion Paper 9904. The World Bank.

Holzmann, R. and Jørgensen, S. L. (2000). *Social risk management: A new conceptual framework for social protection and beyond.* Washington D.C.: Social Protection Discussion Paper 0006. The World Bank.

Holzmann, R., Sherburne-Benz, L. and Tesliuc, E. (2003). *Social risk management: The World Bank's approach to social protection in a globalizing world.* Washington, D.C.: The World Bank.

Horak, C., Matul, C. and Scheuch, F. (2007). Ziele und Strategien von NPOs. In: Badelt, C., Meyer, M. and Simsa, R. (eds.). *Handbuch der Nonprofit Organisation: Strukturen und Management*, 4th edition, pp. 178-201. Stuttgart: Schäffer-Poeschel.

Huque, A. S. (2005). Contracting out and trust in the public sector: Cases of management from Hong Kong. *Public Organization Review*, 5/1, 69-84.

Jacobs, H. (1995). Armut. Zum Verhältnis von gesellschaftlicher Konstituierung und wissenschaftlicher Verwendung eines Begriffs. *Soziale Welt*, 46/4, 403-420.

Jahn, E. J. and Ochel, W. (2007). Contracting-out employment services: Temporary agency work in Germany. *Journal of European Social Policy*, 17/2, 125-138.

James, E. (1986). Comments. In: Rose-Ackerman, S. (ed.) *The economics of nonprofit institutions: Studies in structure and policy*, pp. 154-158. Oxford / New York: Oxford University Press.

James, E. (1990). Economic theory of the nonprofit sector: A comparative perspective. In: Anheier, H. K. and Seibel, W. (eds.). *The third sector: Comparative studies of nonprofit organizations*, pp. 21-29. Berlin / New York: de Gruyter.

James, E. and Rose-Ackerman, S. (1986). *The nonprofit enterprise in market economics*. Chur: Harwood Academic Publishers.

Jenkins, S. P. (1991). Poverty measurement and the within-household distribution: Agenda for action. *Journal of Social Policy*, 20/4, 457-483.

Jenkins, S. P. (2000). Dynamics of household incomes. In: Berthoud, R. and Gershuny, J. (eds.). *Seven years in the lives of British families: Evidence on the dynamics of social change from the British Household Panel Survey*, pp. 107-131. Bristol: Polity Press.

Johne, G. (1993). Soziale Dienste als Forschungsgegenstand: Konzepte und Perspektiven. In: Braun, H. and Johne, G. (eds.). *Die Rolle sozialer Dienste in der Sozialpolitik*, pp. 117-134. Frankfurt / New York: Campus.

Johnson, N. (1990). *Reconstructing the welfare state: A decade of change 1980-1990*. New York et al.: Harvester Wheatsheaf.

Johnson, N. (1999). *Mixed economies of welfare*. London et al.: Prentice Hall Europe.

Jordan, B. (1996). *A theory of poverty and social exclusion*. Cambridge: Polity Press.

Jordan, B. (2001). Tough love: Social work, social exclusion and the Third Way. *British Journal of Social Work*, 31/4, 527-546.

Jordan, B. (2005). Public services and the service economy: Individualism and the choice agenda. *Journal of Social Policy*, 35/1, 143-162.

Kamerman, S. B. and Kahn, A. J. (eds.). (1989). *Privatization and the welfare state*. Princeton: Princeton University Press.

Kammer für Arbeiter und Angestellte (2005). *Sozialstaat Österreich: Sozialleistungen im Überblick. Ausgabe 2005*, 7th edition. Wien: ÖGB Verlag.

Kammer für Arbeiter und Angestellte (2006). *Sozialstaat Österreich: Sozialleistungen im Überblick. Ausgabe 2006*, 8th edition. Wien: ÖGB-Verlag.

Kammer für Arbeiter und Angestellte (2008). *Sozialstaat Österreich: Sozialleistungen im Überblick. Ausgabe 2008*. Wien: ÖGB-Verlag.

Katz, M. B. and Sachße, C. (1996). Introduction. In: Katz, M. B. and Sachße, C. (eds.). *The mixed economy of social welfare*, pp. 9-22. Baden-Baden: Nomos.

Kingma, B. R. (2003). Public good theories of the nonprofit sector: Weisbrod revisited. In: Anheier, H. K. and Ben-Ner, A. (eds.). *The study of the nonprofit enterprise: Theories and approaches*, pp. 53-65. New York et al.: Kluwer.

Klimont, J., Kytir, J. and Leitner, B. (2007). *Österreichische Gesundheitsbefragung 2006/2007: Hauptergebnisse und methodische Dokumentation*. Wien: Statistik Austria.

Knieps, G. (2001). *Wettbewerbsökonomie*. Berlin: Springer et al.

Kniesz, J. (2005). Integrierte Lohn- und Einkommenssteuerstatistik 2001. *Statistische Nachrichten*, 60/1, 80-89.

Koch, S., Stephan, G. and Walwei, U. (2005). Workfare: Möglichkeiten und Grenzen. *Zeitschrift für Arbeitsmarktforschung*, 38/2-3, 419-440.

Kolderie, T. (1986). The two different concepts of privatization. *Public Administration Review*, 46/4, 285-291.

Kotlikoff, L. J. (2000). Privatizing social security the right way. *The Independent Review*, 5/1, 55-63.

Kotlikoff, L. J., Smetters, K. A. and Walliser, J. (1998). Social security: Privatization and progressivity. *The American Economic Review*, 88/2, 137-141.

Kräkel, M. (1999). *Organisation und Management*. Tübingen: Mohr Siebeck.

Kramer, R. M. (1981). *Voluntary agencies in the welfare state*. Berkeley et al.: University of California Press.

Kramer, R. M. (2004). Alternative paradigms for the mixed economy: Will sector matter? In: Evers, A. and Laville, J.-L. (eds.). *The third sector in Europe*, pp. 219-236. Cheltenham / Northampton: Edward Elgar.

Krejci, H. (1996). Privatisierung ohne Dogma! *Zeitschrift für Gemeinwirtschaft*, 96/1, 7-10.

Lamei, N. and Till-Tentschert, U. (2005). Messung von Armutsgefährdung und Deprivation. *Statistische Nachrichten*, 60/4, 349-359.

Le Grand, J. and Bartlett, W. (eds.). (1993). *Quasi-markets and social policy*. Basingstoke: Macmillan.

Le Grand, J. and Robinson, R. (1984). Privatisation and the welfare state: An introduction. In: Le Grand, J. and Robinson, R. (eds.). *Privatisation and the welfare state*, pp. 1-14. London et al.: George Allen & Unwin.

Leibfried, S. (2003). Sozialpolitikforschung und Wohlfahrtsdemokratie: Entwicklungen und Perspektiven. *ZeS report*, 8/2, 3-9.

Lewis, J. (1992). Gender and the development of welfare regimes. *Journal of European Social Policy*, 2/3, 159-175.

Lewis, J. (1994). Voluntary organizations in "new partnership" with local authorities: The anatomy of a contract. *Social Policy & Administration*, 28/3, 206-220.

Lewis, J. (2004). The state and the third sector in modern welfare states: Independence, instrumentality, partnership. In: Evers, A. and Laville, J.-L. (eds.). *The third sector in Europe*, pp. 169-187. Cheltenham / Northampton: Edward Elgar.

Lister, R. (2004). *Poverty*. Cambridge: Policy Press.

Litschel, V. and Wetzel, P. (2004). Sozialwirtschaft ist ... Diskussion mit Nikolaus Dimmel, Andreas Riesenfelder und Ruth Simsa. *Kurswechsel*, 2004/4, 7-16.

Lloyd, P. (2004). The European Union and its programmes related to the third sector. In: Evers, A. and Laville, J.-L. (eds.). *The third sector in Europe*, pp. 188-215. Cheltenham: Edward Elgar.

Lødemel, I. and Trickey, H. (eds.). (2001). *An offer you can't refuse: Workfare in international perspective*. Bristol: Policy Press.

Lutz, H., Wagner, M. and Wolf, W. (1993). *Von Ausgrenzung bedroht: Struktur und Umfang der materiellen Armutsgefährdung im österreichischen Wohlfahrtsstaat der achtziger Jahre. Forschungsberichte aus Sozial- und Arbeitsmarktpolitik Nr. 50.* Wien: Bundesministerium für Arbeit und Soziales.

Mansfield, E. and Yohe, G. (2000). *Microeconomics*, 10th edition. New York / London: W. W. Norton & Company.

Martens, K. (2002). Mission Impossible? Defining nongovernmental organizations. *Voluntas*, 13/3, 271-285.

Marwell, N. P. and McInerney, P.-B. (2005). The nonprofit / for-profit continuum: Theorizing the dynamics of mixed-form markets. *Nonprofit and Voluntary Sector Quarterly*, 34/1, 7-28.

McNutt, P. (2002). *The economics of public choice*, 2nd edition. Cheltenham / Northampton: Edward Elgar.

Megginson, W. L. and Netter, J. M. (2001). From state to market: A survey of empirical studies on privatization. *Journal of Economic Literature*, XXXIX/2, 321-389.

Meyer, M. (2007). Von der öffentlichen Bürokratie zur technokratischen NPO? Über die Effekte leistungsvertraglicher Finanzierungsformen auf die Organisationsstrukturen von NPO. In: Schneider, U. and Trukeschitz, B. (eds.). *Quasi-Märkte und Qualität: Die Qualität arbeitsmarktpolitischer und sozialer Dienstleistungen im Kontext öffentlicher Beschaffungspolitik*, pp. 85-100. Baden-Baden: Nomos.

Middleton, S., Ashworth, K. and Braithwaite, I. (1997). *Small fortunes: Spending on children, childhood poverty and parental sacrifice*. York: Joseph Rowntree Foundation.

Millar, J. and Glendinning, C. (1989). Gender and poverty. *Journal of Social Policy*, 18/3, 363-381.

Minkoff, D. C. and Powell, W. W. (2006). Nonprofit mission: Constancy, responsiveness, or deflection? In: Powell, W. W. and Steinberg, R. (eds.). *The nonprofit sector: A research handbook*, pp. 591-611. New Haven / London: Yale University Press.

Mitchell, O. S. and Zeldes, S. P. (1996). Social security privatization: A structure for analysis. *The American Economic Review*, 86/2, 363-367.

Mok, K. H. (1997). Privatization or marketization: Educational development in post-Mao China. *International Review of Education*, 43/5-6, 547-567.

Morris, S. (2000). Defining the nonprofit sector: Some lessons from history. *Voluntas*, 11/1, 25-43.

Musgrave, R. A., Musgrave, P., B. and Kullmer, L. (1990). *Die öffentlichen Finanzen in Theorie und Praxis*, 5th edition. Tübingen: J. C. B. Mohr (Paul Siebeck).

Neumayr, M. and Schneider, U. (2008). Nonprofit Organisationen – mehr als nur Dienstleister. Empirische Befunde zu den Funktionen von Nonprofit Organisationen in Österreich und der Tschechischen Republik. In: Schauer, R., Helmig, B., Purtschert, R. and Witt, D. (eds.). Wiesbaden: DUV-Gabler (forthcoming).

Neumayr, M., Schneider, U., Meyer, M. and Haider, A. (2007). *The non-profit sector in Austria: An economic, legal and political appraisal*. Wien: Working Paper des Instituts für Sozialpolitik, 01/2007.

Newman, J. (2004). Modernizing the state: A new style of governance? In: Lewis, J. and Surender, R. (eds.). *Welfare state change: Towards a Third Way?*, pp. 69-88. Oxford: Oxford University Press.

Newman, J. and Kuhlmann, E. (2007). Consumers enter the political stage? The modernization of health care in Britain and Germany. *Journal of European Social Policy*, 17/2, 99-111.

Nisar, T. M. (2007). Risk management in public-private partnership contracts. *Public Organization Review*, 7/1, 1-19.

Noordhoek, P. and Saner, R. (2005). Beyond new public management: Answering the claims of both politics and society. *Public Organization Review*, 5/1, 35-53.

Nowotny, E. (1996). Zur Privatisierungsdebatte. *Zeitschrift für Gemeinwirtschaft*, 96/1, 11-25.

Nowotny, E. (1999). *Der öffentliche Sektor*, 4th edition. Berlin / Heidelberg: Springer.

Nullmeier, F. (2003a). Wohlfahrtsdemokratie. *ZeS report*, 8/2, 9-13.

Nullmeier, F. (2003b). Wohlfahrtsmärkte und Bürgerengagement in der Marktgesellschaft. In: Allmendinger, J. (ed.) *Entstaatlichung und soziale Sicherheit: Verhandlungen des 31. Kongresses der Deutschen Gesellschaft für Soziologie in Leipzig 2002*, pp. 961-974. Opladen: Leske + Budrich.

O'Higgins, M. (1989). Social welfare and privatization: The British experience. In: Kamerman, S. B. and Kahn, A. J. (eds.). *Privatization and the welfare state*, pp. 157-177. Princeton: Princeton University Press.

Orshansky, M. (1963). Children of the poor. *Social Security Bulletin*, 26/July, 3-13.

Orshansky, M. (1965). Counting the poor: Another look at the poverty profile. *Social Security Bulletin*, 28/1, 3-29.

Orshansky, M. (1969). How poverty is measured. *Monthly Labour Review*, 92/2, 37-41.

Österle, A. (2001). *Equity choices and long-term care policies in Europe: Allocating resources, and burdens in Austria, Italy, the Netherlands and the United Kingdom.* Aldershot et al.: Ashgate.

Pearson, M. and Martin, J. P. (2005). Should we extend the role of private social expenditure? *OECD Social, Employment and Migration Working Papers*, No. 23.

Pfeil, W. J. (2001). *Sozialhilfe: Rechtswissenschaftliche Studie - Vergleich der Sozialhilfesysteme der österreichischen Bundesländer.* Wien: BMSG.

Pinker, R. (1992). Making sense of the mixed economy of welfare. *Social Policy & Administration*, 26/4, 273-284.

Pochobradsky, E., Habl, C. and Schleicher, B. (2002). *Soziale Ungleichheit und Gesundheit: Studie im Auftrag des BMSG.* Wien: ÖBIG.

Pomper, M. F. (2007). *Corporate citizenship in Österreich.* Wien: Dissertation an der Wirtschaftsuniversität Wien.

Powell, M. (ed.) (2007). *Understanding the mixed economy of welfare.* Bristol: The Policy Press.

Powell, M. and Hewitt, M. (2002). *Welfare state and welfare change.* Buckingham / Philadelphia: Open University Press.

Pratscher, K. (2007). Sozialhilfe, Behindertenhilfe und Pflegegeld der Bundesländer im Jahr 2005 und in der Entwicklung seit 1995. *Statistische Nachrichten*, 62/8, 730-743.

Pratscher, K. (2008). Sozialhilfe, Behindertenhilfe und Pflegegeld der Bundesländer im Jahr 2006 und in der Entwicklung seit 1996. *Statistische Nachrichten*, 63/7, 598-611.

Ringen, S. (1988). Direct and indirect measures of poverty. *Journal of Social Policy*, 17/3, 351-365.

Riphahn, R. T. (2001). Rational poverty or poor rationality? The take-up of social assistance benefits. *Review of Income and Wealth*, 47/3, 379-398.

Rodgers, G. (1995). What is special about a social exclusion approach? In: Rodgers, G., Gore, C. and Figueiredo, J. B. (eds.). *Social exclusion: Rhetoric, reality, responses*, pp. 43-55. Genf: ILO.

Room, G. J. (1995). Poverty and social exclusion: The new European agenda for policy and research. In: Room, G. J. (ed.) *Beyond the threshold: The measurement and analysis of social exclusion*, pp. 1-9. Bristol: The Policy Press.

Room, G. J. (1998). Armut und soziale Ausgrenzung. *Zeitschrift für Sozialreform*, 44/4-5, 268-277.

Room, G. J. (1999). Social exclusion, solidarity and the challenge of globalization. *International Journal of Social Welfare*, 8/3, 166-174.

Rose-Ackerman, S. (ed.) (1986). *The economics of nonprofit institutions: Studies in structure and policy*. Oxford / New York: Oxford University Press.

Rose-Ackerman, S. (1996). Altruism, nonprofits, and economic theory. *Journal of Economic Literature*, XXXIV/June, 701-728.

Rose-Ackerman, S. (1997). Altruism, ideological entrepreneurs and the non-profit firm. *Voluntas*, 8/2, 120-134.

Rosner, P. G. (2003). *The economics of social policy*. Cheltenham / Northampton: Edward Elgar.

Rowntree, B. S. (1901/1971/2001). Poverty: A study of town life. In: Smith, G. D., Dorling, D. and Shaw, M. (eds.). *Poverty, inequality and health in Britain: 1800-2000. A reader*, pp. 98-105. Bristol: Polity Press.

Salamon, L. M. (1993). The marketization of welfare: Changing nonprofit and for-profit roles in the American welfare state. *Social Service Review*, 1993/March, 16-39.

Salamon, L. M. (1995). *Partners in public service: Government-nonprofit relations in the modern welfare state*. Baltimore / London: The Johns Hopkins University Press.

Salamon, L. M. and Anheier, H., K. (1996). *The international classification of nonprofit organizations: ICNPO-Revision 1, 1996. The Johns Hopkins Comparative Nonprofit Sector Project: Working Paper Nummer 19.* Baltimore: The Johns Hopkins Institute for Policy Studies.

Salamon, L. M. and Anheier, H. K. (1998). Social origins of civil society: Explaining the nonprofit sector cross-nationally. *Voluntas*, 9/3, 213-249.

Salamon, L. M., Anheier, H. K., List, R., Toepler, S. and Sokolowski, W. S. (eds.). (1999). *Global civil society: Dimensions of the nonprofit sector*. Baltimore: The Johns Hopkins Centre for Civil Society Studies.

Salamon, L. M., Anheier, H. K., Sokolowski, W. and Associates (1995). *The emerging sector: A statistical supplement*. Baltimore: The Johns Hopkins University.

Salamon, L. M., Sokolowski, W. S. and List, R. (2003). *Global civil society: An overview*. Baltimore: Johns Hopkins University.

Samuelson, P. A. and Nordhaus, W. D. (2001). *Economics*, 17th edition. Boston et al.: McGraw-Hill.

Sarker, A. E. (2005). New public management, service provision and non-governmental organizations in Bangladesh. *Public Organization Review*, 5/3, 249-281.

Schaden, M. (1995). *Nonprofit-Organisationen in der ökonomischen Theorie: Eine Analyse der Entwicklung und der Handlungsmotivation der Freien Wohlfahrtspflege*. Wiesbaden: Gabler.

Scheil-Adlung, X. (ed.) (2001). *Gestaltung der sozialen Sicherheit: Die Rolle der Privatisierung*. Bern et al.: Peter Lang.

Schiller, B. R. (2001). *The economics of poverty and discrimination*, 8th edition. Upper Saddle River: Prentice-Hall.

Schlögl, P. (2009). Bildungsarmut und -benachteiligung: Befunde und Herausforderungen für Österreich. In: Dimmel, N., Heitzmann, K. and Schenk, M. (eds.). *Handbuch Armut in Österreich*, pp. 157-171. Innsbruck: Studienverlag.

Schneider, U., Badelt, C. and Hagleitner, J. (2007). Der Nonprofit Sektor in Österreich. In: Badelt, C., Meyer, M. and Simsa, R. (eds.). *Handbuch der Nonprofit Organisation: Strukturen und Management*, 4th edition, pp. 55-80. Stuttgart: Schäffer-Poeschel.

Schneider, U. and Hagleitner, J. (2005). *Knowledge discovery in databases am Beispiel des österreichischen Nonprofit Sektors*. Wien: Institut für Sozialpolitik.

Schneider, U. and Trukeschitz, B. (2007a). Öffentliche Beschaffungspolitik im Bereich sozialer und arbeitsmarktpolitischer Dienstleistungen. In: Schneider, U. and Trukeschitz, B. (eds.). *Quasi-Märkte und Qualität: Die Qualität arbeitsmarktpolitischer und sozialer Dienstleistungen im Kontext öffentlicher Beschaffungspolitik*, pp. 9-30. Baden-Baden: Nomos.

Schneider, U. and Trukeschitz, B. (eds.). (2007b). *Quasi-Märkte und Qualität: Die Qualität arbeitsmarktpolitischer und sozialer Dienstleistungen im Kontext öffentlicher Beschaffungspolitik*. Baden-Baden: Nomos.

Schuster, M. J. (1997). Deconstructing a Tower of Babel: Privatisation, decentralisation and devolution as ideas in good currency in cultural policy. *Voluntas*, 8/3, 261-282.

Seibel, W. (1992). *Funktionaler Dilettantismus: Erfolgreich scheiternde Organisationen im 'Dritten Sektor' zwischen Markt und Staat*. Baden-Baden: Nomos.

Seibel, W. (1997). Erfolgreich gescheiterter Institutionentransfer: Eine politische Analyse des Dritten Sektors in den Neuen Bundesländern. In: Anheier, H. K., Priller, E., Seibel, W. and Zimmer, A. (eds.). *Der Dritte Sektor in Deutschland: Organisationen zwischen Staat und Markt im gesellschaftlichen Wandel*, pp. 127-149. Berlin: Sigma.

Sen, A. K. (1981). *Poverty and famines*. Oxford: Clarendon Press.

Sen, A. K. (1992). *Inequality reexamined*. Oxford: Oxford University Press.

Sen, A. K. (1999). *Development as freedom*. Oxford: Oxford University Press.

Shleifer, A. (1998). State versus private ownership. *Journal of Economic Perspectives*, 12/4, 133-150.

Smeeding, T. M., Saunders, P., Coder, J., Jenkins, S., Fritzell, J., Hagenaars, A. M., Hauser, R. and Wolfson, M. (1993). Poverty, inequality, and family living standards. Impacts across seven nations: The effect of noncash subsidies for health, education and housing. *Review of Income and Wealth*, 39/3, 229-256.

Smith, S. R. and Lipsky, M. (1993). *Nonprofits for hire: The welfare state in the age of contracting*. Cambridge / London: Harvard University Press.

Smithies, R. (2005). Public and private welfare activity in the United Kingdom, 1979 to 1999. CASEpaper No. 2.

Snower, D. J. (1996). The modern welfare state: Problems and suggested reforms. *Empirica*, 23/3, 207-223.

Starr, P. (1989). The meaning of privatization. In: Kamerman, S. B. and Kahn, A. J. (eds.). *Privatization and the welfare state*, pp. 15-48. Princeton: Princeton University Press.

Statistik Austria (2002). *Statistisches Jahrbuch Österreichs 2003*. Wien: Statistik Austria.

Statistik Austria (2005). *Einkommen, Armut und Lebensbedingungen: Ergebnisse aus EU-SILC 2003 in Österreich*. Wien: Statistik Austria.

Statistik Austria (2006a). *Arbeitsmarktstatistik. Jahresergebnisse 2006. Mikrozensus-Arbeitskräfteerhebung*. Schnellbericht 5.8.

Statistik Austria (2006b). *Einkommen, Armut und Lebensbedingungen: Ergebnisse aus EU-SILC 2004*. Wien: Statistik Austria.

Statistik Austria (2007a). *Einkommen, Armut und Lebensbedingungen: Ergebnisse aus EU-SILC 2005*. Wien: Statistik Austria.

Statistik Austria (2007b). *Statistisches Jahrbuch Österreichs 2008*. Wien: Statistik Austria.

Statistik Austria (2008). *Einkommen, Armut und Lebensbedingungen: Ergebnisse aus EU-SILC 2006*. Wien: Statistik Austria.

Statistik Austria (2009a). *Einkommen, Armut und Lebensbedingungen: Ergebnisse aus EU-SILC 2007*. Wien: Statistik Austria.

Statistik Austria (2009b). *Statistik Austria Database*. http://www.statistik-austria.at/-web_de/statistiken/index.html (last accession date: September 2009).

Steinberg, R. (2006). Economic theories of nonprofit organizations. In: Powell, W. W. and Steinberg, R. (eds.). *The nonprofit sector: A research handbook*, 2nd edition, pp. 117-139. New Haven / London: Yale University Press.

Steiner, H. (2009). Sozialausgaben. In: BMSK (ed.) *Sozialbericht 2007-2008: Ressortaktivitäten und sozialpolitische Analysen*, pp. 159-179. Wien: BMSK.

Steiner, H. and Wolf, W. (1996). *Armutsgefährdung in Österreich*. Wien: Bundesministerium für Arbeit und Soziales.

Steinwald, B. and Neuhauser, D. (1970). The role of the proprietary hospital. *Law and Contemporary Problems*, 35, 817-838.

Stiglitz, J. E. (2000). *Economics of the public sector*, 3rd edition. New York / London: W.W. Norton & Company.

Stitt, S. (1994). *Poverty and poor relief: Concepts and reality*. Aldershot et al.: Avebury.

Stolitzka, B. (1997). Sozialhilfe 1995. *Statistische Nachrichten*, 52/8, 650-654.

Sugden, R. (1984). Voluntary organisations and the welfare state. In: Le Grand, J. and Robinson, R. (eds.). *Privatisation and the welfare state*, pp. 70-89. London et al.: George Allen & Unwin.

Svetlik, I. (1993). Regulation of the plural and mixed welfare system. In: Evers, A. and Svetlik, I. (eds.). *Balancing pluralism: New welfare mixes in care for the elderly*, pp. 33-50. Aldershot et al.: Avebury.

Tálos, E. and Badelt, C. (1999). The welfare state between new stimuli and new pressures: Austrian social policy and the EU. *Journal of European Social Policy*, 9/4, 351-361.

Taylor, M. (2002). Government, the third sector and the contract culture: The UK experience so far. In: Ascoli, U. and Ranci, C. (eds.). *Dilemmas of the welfare mix: The new structure of welfare in an era of privatization*, pp. 77-108. New York: Kluwer.

Taylor, M. (2004). The welfare mix in the United Kingdom. In: Evers, A. and Laville, J.-L. (eds.). *The third sector in Europe*, pp. 122-143. Cheltenham / Northampton: Edward Elgar.

Thomas, J. J. (1992). *Informal economic activity*. New York et al.: Harvester Wheatsheaf.

Till-Tentschert, U., Lamei, N. and Bauer, M. (2004). Armut und Armutsgefährdung in Österreich. In: BMSG (ed.) *Bericht über die soziale Lage 2003-2004*, pp. 207-232. Wien: BMSG.

Till, M. (2005). *Leistung mit Profil 2004: Die CARITAS-Sozialberatung und ihre KlientInnen*. Unpublished report.

Till, M., Datler, G., Glaser, T., Heuberger, R., Kafka, E., Lamei, N. and Skina, M. (2009). Armutsgefährdung. In: BMSK (ed.) *Sozialbericht 2007-2008: Ressortaktivitäten und sozialpolitische Analysen*, pp. 237-258. Wien: BMSK.

Till, M. and Till-Tentschert, U. (2003). *Bericht über die Leistungsdaten der CARITAS-Sozialberatungsstellen in Österreich 2002*. Unpublished report.

Titmuss, R. (1974). *Social policy*. London: Allen and Unwin.

Toepler, S. (2006). Caveat venditor? Museum merchandising, nonprofit commercialization, and the case of Metropolitan Museum in New York. *Voluntas*, 17/2, 99-113.

Trube, A. and Wohlfahrt, N. (2000). Zur theoretischen Einordnung: Von der Bürokratie zur Merkatokratie? System- und Steuerungsprobleme eines ökonomisierten Sozialsektors. In: Boeßenecker, K.-H., Trube, A. and Wohlfahrt, N. (eds.). *Privatisierung im Sozialsektor: Rahmenbedingungen, Verlaufsformen und Probleme der Ausgliederung sozialer Dienste*, pp. 18-38. Münster: Votum.

Trukeschitz, B. (2006). *Im Dienst sozialer Dienste. Ökonomische Analyse der Beschäftigung in sozialen Dienstleistungseinrichtungen des Nonprofit Sektors*. Frankfurt et al.: Peter Lang.

Unger, B. and Heitzmann, K. (2003). The Adjustment Path of the Austrian Welfare State - Back to Bismarck? *Journal of European Social Policy*, 13/4, 371-387.

van Berkel, R. and van der Aa, P. (2005). The marketization of activation services: A modern panacea? Some lessons from the Dutch experience. *Journal of European Social Policy*, 15/4, 329-343.

van Oorschot, W. (1991). Non-take-up of social security benefits in Europe. *Journal of European Social Policy*, 1/1, 15-30.

Varian, H. R. (2003). *Intermediate microeconomics: A modern approach*, 6th edition. New York / London: W. W. Norton & Company.

Vickers, J. and Yarrow, G. (1991). Economic perspectives on privatization. *The Journal of Economic Perspectives*, 5/2, 111-132.

Vogel, J. (1999). The European "welfare mix": Institutional configuration and distributive outcome in Sweden and the European Union. A longitudinal and comparative perspective. *Social Indicators Research*, 48, 245-297.

Volkshilfe Wien (2007). *60 Jahre soziale Hilfe für die Schwächsten. 60 Jahre Volkshilfe Wien*. http://www2.volkshilfe-wien.at/archiv/zeitung/Ausgabe_1-07.pdf (last accession date: September 2009).

Walker, A. (1984). The political economy of privatisation. In: Le Grand, J. and Robinson, R. (eds.). *Privatisation and the welfare state*, pp. 19-44. London et al.: George Allen & Unwin.

Weisbrod, B. (1977). *The voluntary nonprofit sector*. Lexington / Toronto: Lexington.

Weisbrod, B. (1986). Toward a theory of the voluntary sector in a three-sector economy. In: Rose-Ackerman, S. (ed.) *The economics of nonprofit institutions: Studies in structure and policy*, pp. 21-44. Oxford / New York: Oxford University Press.

Weisbrod, B. (1988). *The nonprofit economy*. Cambridge / London: Harvard University Press.

Weller, C. E. (2006). Gambling with retirement: Market risk implications for social security privatization. *Review of Radical Political Economics*, 38/3, 334-344.

Wiener Hilfswerk (2005). 25 Jahre Nachbarschaftszentren des Wiener Hilfswerkes. *Hand in Hand*, 2005/special issue.

Wiener Hilfswerk (2006). *Jahresbericht 2005*. Wien: Wiener Hilfswerk.

Williamson, O. E. (1998). The institutions of governance. *The American Economic Review*, 88/2 (Papers and Proceedings of the Hundred and Tenth Annual Meeting of the American Economic Association), 75-79.

Wistow, G., Knapp, M., Hardy, B. and Allen, C. (1994). *Social care in a mixed economy*. Buckingham: Open University Press.

Wolfenden Committee (1978). *The future of voluntary organisations: Report of the Wolfenden Committee*. London: Croom Helm.

Yin, R. K. (2003). *Case Study Research: Design and Methods*, 3rd edition. Thousand Oaks et al.: Sage.

Young, D. R. (1999). Complementary, supplementary, or adversarial? A theoretical and historical examination of nonprofit-government relations in the United States. In: Boris, E. T. and Steuerle, C. E. (eds.). *Nonprofits and government: Collaboration and conflict*, pp. 31-67. Washington, D.C.: The Urban Institute Press.

Young, D. R. (2000). Alternative models of government-nonprofit sector relations: Theoretical and international perspectives. *Nonprofit and Voluntary Sector Quarterly*, 29/1, 149-172.

Young, D. R. (2003). Entrepreneurs, managers, and the nonprofit enterprise. In: Anheier, H. K. and Ben-Ner, A. (eds.). *The study of the nonprofit enterprise: Theories and approaches*, pp. 161-168. New York et al.: Kluwer.

Zauner, A. (2007). Über Solidarität zu Wissen. Ein systemtheoretischer Zugang zu Nonprofit Organisationen. In: Badelt, C., Meyer, M. and Simsa, R. (eds.). *Handbuch der Nonprofit Organisation: Strukturen und Management*, 4th edition, pp. 141-164. Stuttgart: Schäffer-Poeschel.

Zauner, A., Heimerl, P., Mayrhofer, W., Meyer, M., Nachbagauer, A. and Praschak, S. (2006). *Von der Subvention zum Leistungsvertrag: Neue Koordinations- und Steuerungsformen und ihre Konsequenzen für Nonprofit-Organisationen: Eine systemtheoretische Analyse*. Wien.

Zimmer, A. (1997). Public-Private Partnerships: Staat und Dritter Sektor in Deutschland. In: Anheier, H. K., Priller, E., Seibel, W. and Zimmer, A. (eds.). *Der Nonprofit Sektor in Deutschland*, pp. 75-98. Berlin: Sigma.

Zimmer, A. and Nährlich, S. (1997). Krise des Wohlfahrtsstaates und New Public Management. *Zeitschrift für Sozialreform*, 43/9, 661-685.

Peter Lang · Internationaler Verlag der Wissenschaften

Johannes Gräb

Econometric Analysis in Poverty Research

With Case Studies from Developing Countries

Frankfurt am Main, Berlin, Bern, Bruxelles, New York, Oxford, Wien, 2009.
XVIII, 129 pp., num. fig. and tab.
Göttingen Studies in Development Economics.
Edited by Hermann Sautter and Stephan Klasen. Vol. 26
ISBN 978-3-631-59710-1 · hardback € 34,80*

Poverty and inequality persist in many regions of the developing world. This may be due mainly to an ineffective targeting of policies to address the root causes of poverty. Sustainable policy interventions are in need of reliable concepts of poverty and of a thorough understanding of the underlying mechanism that lead to such deprivation. The three essays of this book add to the debate concerning appropriate statistical tools in empirical development economics. The work proposes specific methodologies to analyze the extent of poverty and its underlying factors based on recent household surveys. The first chapter deals with a concept of poverty comparisons when panel data is at hand. The second chapter studies the determinants of spatial inequality using multilevel modelling. The third chapter analyzes the relation between a child's nutritional status and its survival probability.

Content: Robust Multiperiod Poverty Comparisons · Explaining Spatial Inequality: Evidence from Burkina Faso · Low Malnutrition but High Mortality: Explaining the Paradox of the Lake Victoria Region

www.ingramcontent.com/pod-product-compliance
Ingram Content Group UK Ltd.
Pitfield, Milton Keynes, MK11 3LW, UK
UKHW021842100926
8556IPUK00019B/1004

9 783631 559161